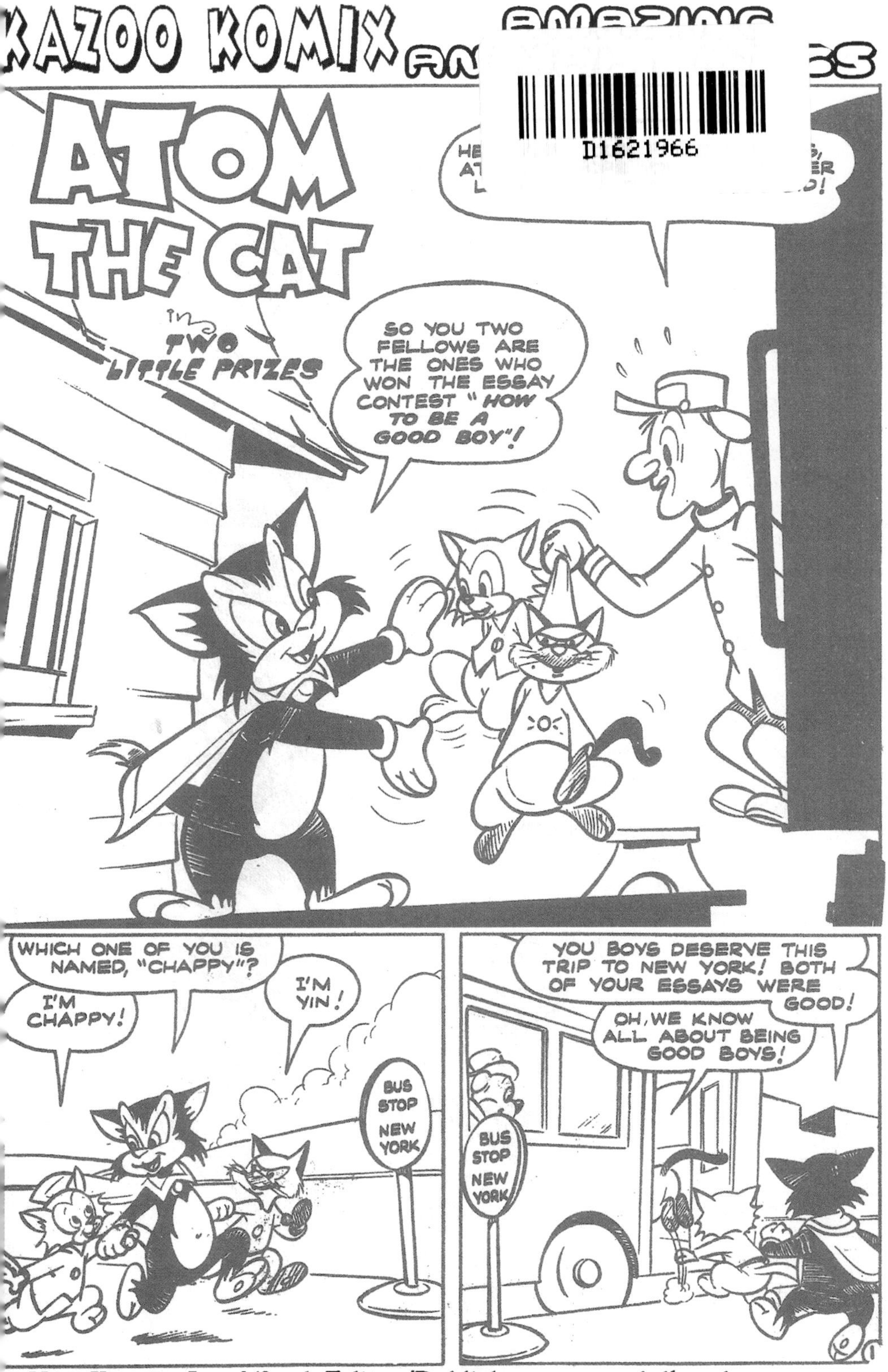
KAZOO KOMIX
ATOM THE CAT
in TWO LITTLE PRIZES
SO YOU TWO FELLOWS ARE THE ONES WHO WON THE ESSAY CONTEST "HOW TO BE A GOOD BOY"!
WHICH ONE OF YOU IS NAMED, "CHAPPY"?
I'M CHAPPY!
I'M YIN!
BUS STOP NEW YORK
YOU BOYS DESERVE THIS TRIP TO NEW YORK! BOTH OF YOUR ESSAYS WERE GOOD!
OH, WE KNOW ALL ABOUT BEING GOOD BOYS!
BUS STOP NEW YORK

Mini-Komix: Jer Alford, Editor/Publisher, www.minikomix.com
Additional material by Peter Cutler: peterlc.deviantart.com

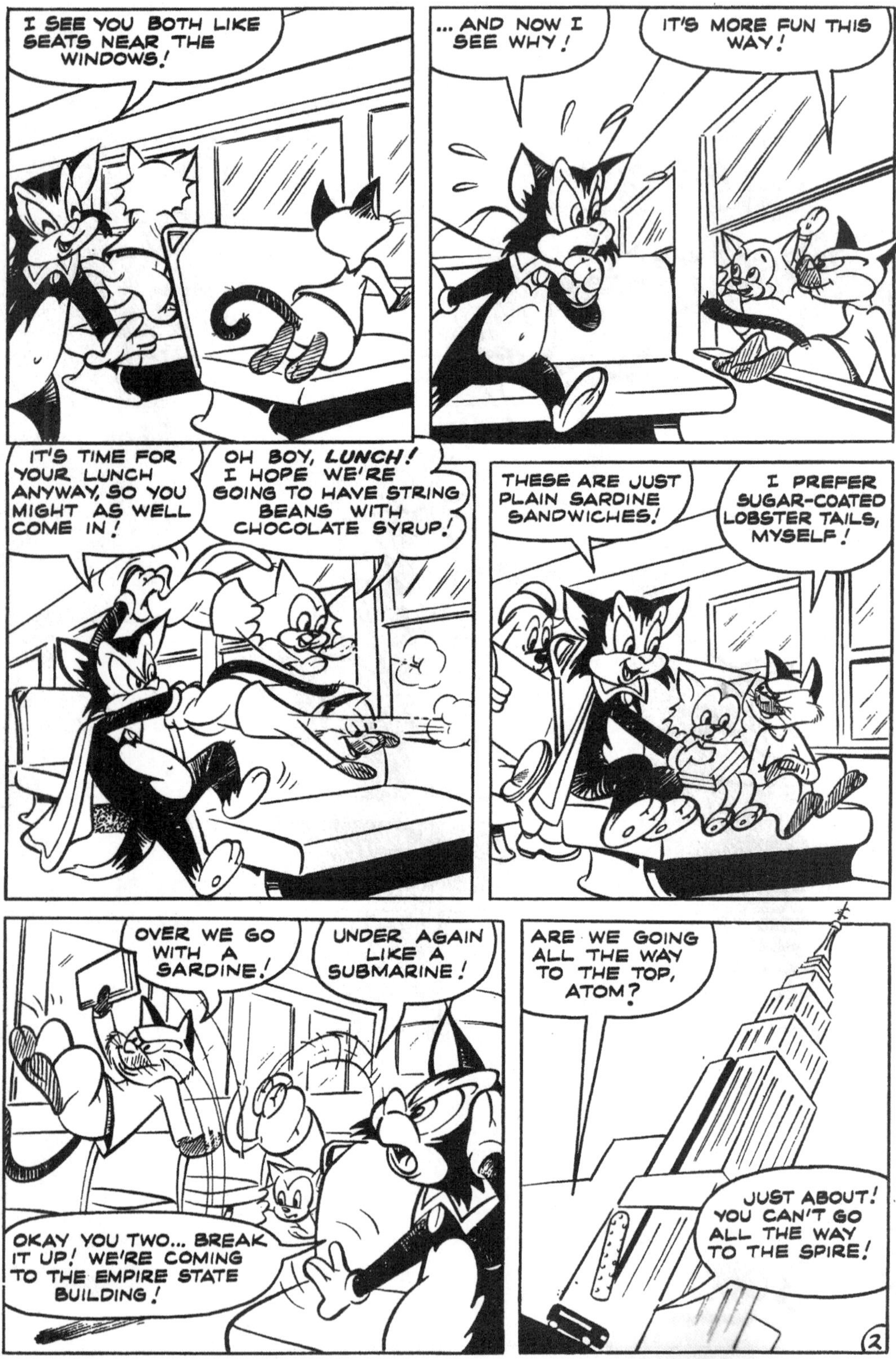
I SEE YOU BOTH LIKE SEATS NEAR THE WINDOWS!
... AND NOW I SEE WHY!
IT'S MORE FUN THIS WAY!
IT'S TIME FOR YOUR LUNCH ANYWAY, SO YOU MIGHT AS WELL COME IN!
OH BOY, LUNCH! I HOPE WE'RE GOING TO HAVE STRING BEANS WITH CHOCOLATE SYRUP!
THESE ARE JUST PLAIN SARDINE SANDWICHES!
I PREFER SUGAR-COATED LOBSTER TAILS, MYSELF!
OVER WE GO WITH A SARDINE!
UNDER AGAIN LIKE A SUBMARINE!
OKAY YOU TWO... BREAK IT UP! WE'RE COMING TO THE EMPIRE STATE BUILDING!
ARE WE GOING ALL THE WAY TO THE TOP, ATOM?
JUST ABOUT! YOU CAN'T GO ALL THE WAY TO THE SPIRE!
2

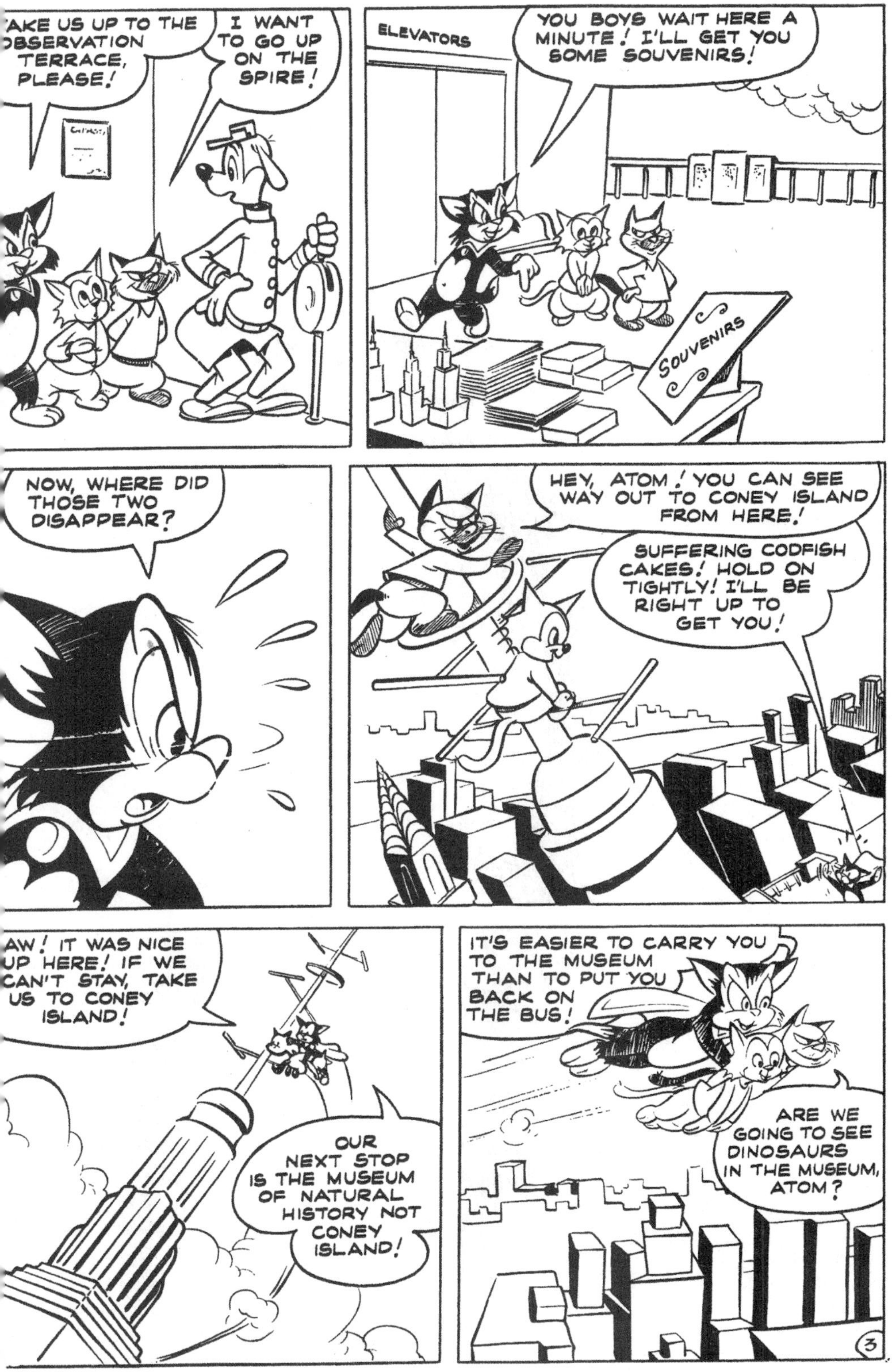
TAKE US UP TO THE OBSERVATION TERRACE, PLEASE!
I WANT TO GO UP ON THE SPIRE!
ELEVATORS
YOU BOYS WAIT HERE A MINUTE! I'LL GET YOU SOME SOUVENIRS!
SOUVENIRS
NOW, WHERE DID THOSE TWO DISAPPEAR?
HEY, ATOM! YOU CAN SEE WAY OUT TO CONEY ISLAND FROM HERE!
SUFFERING CODFISH CAKES! HOLD ON TIGHTLY! I'LL BE RIGHT UP TO GET YOU!
AW! IT WAS NICE UP HERE! IF WE CAN'T STAY, TAKE US TO CONEY ISLAND!
OUR NEXT STOP IS THE MUSEUM OF NATURAL HISTORY NOT CONEY ISLAND!
IT'S EASIER TO CARRY YOU TO THE MUSEUM THAN TO PUT YOU BACK ON THE BUS!
ARE WE GOING TO SEE DINOSAURS IN THE MUSEUM, ATOM?
3

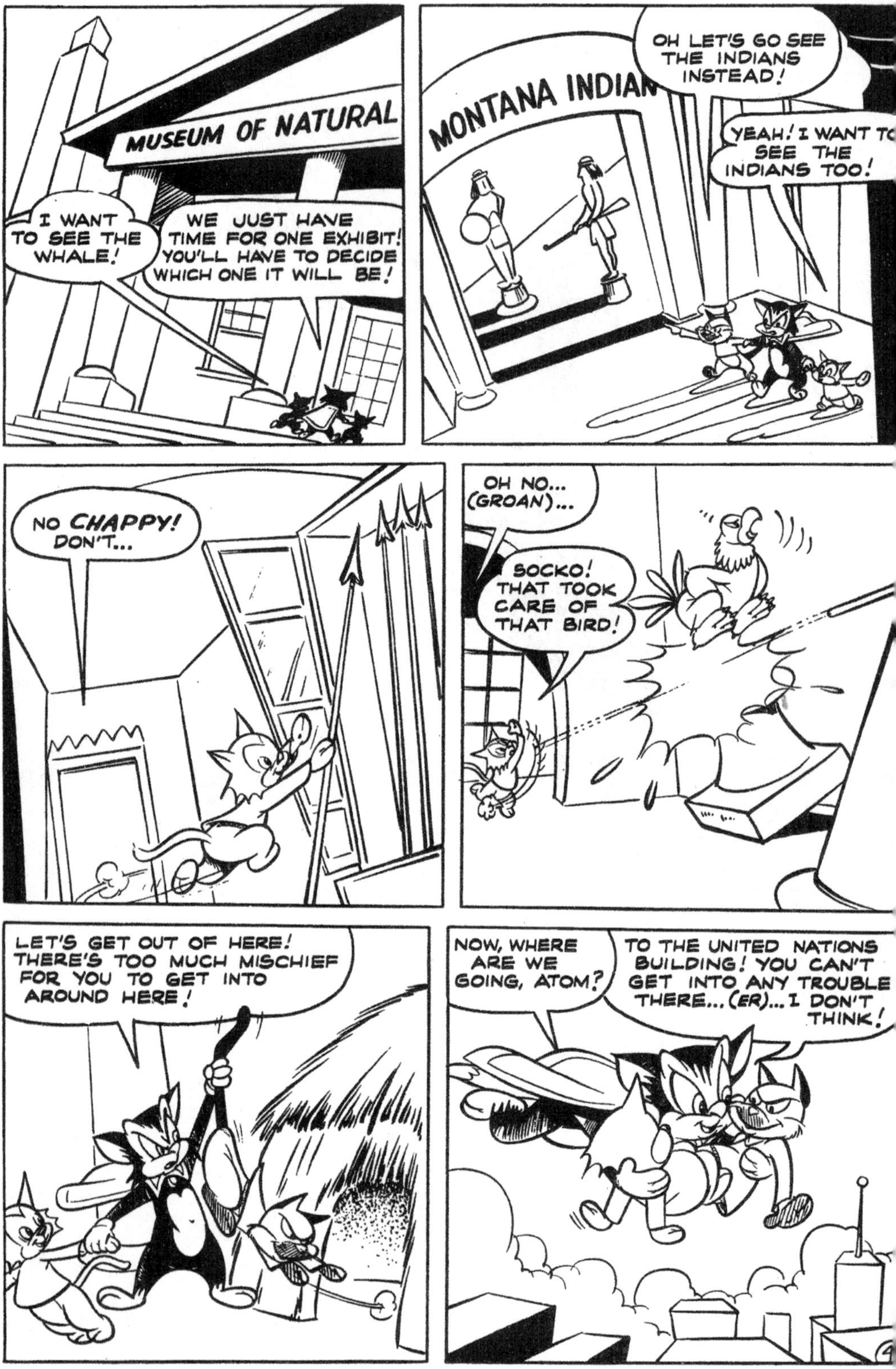
MUSEUM OF NATURAL
I WANT TO SEE THE WHALE!
WE JUST HAVE TIME FOR ONE EXHIBIT! YOU'LL HAVE TO DECIDE WHICH ONE IT WILL BE!
MONTANA INDIAN
OH LET'S GO SEE THE INDIANS INSTEAD!
YEAH! I WANT TO SEE THE INDIANS TOO!
NO CHAPPY! DON'T...
OH NO... (GROAN)...
SOCKO! THAT TOOK CARE OF THAT BIRD!
LET'S GET OUT OF HERE! THERE'S TOO MUCH MISCHIEF FOR YOU TO GET INTO AROUND HERE!
NOW, WHERE ARE WE GOING, ATOM?
TO THE UNITED NATIONS BUILDING! YOU CAN'T GET INTO ANY TROUBLE THERE... (ER)... I DON'T THINK!
4

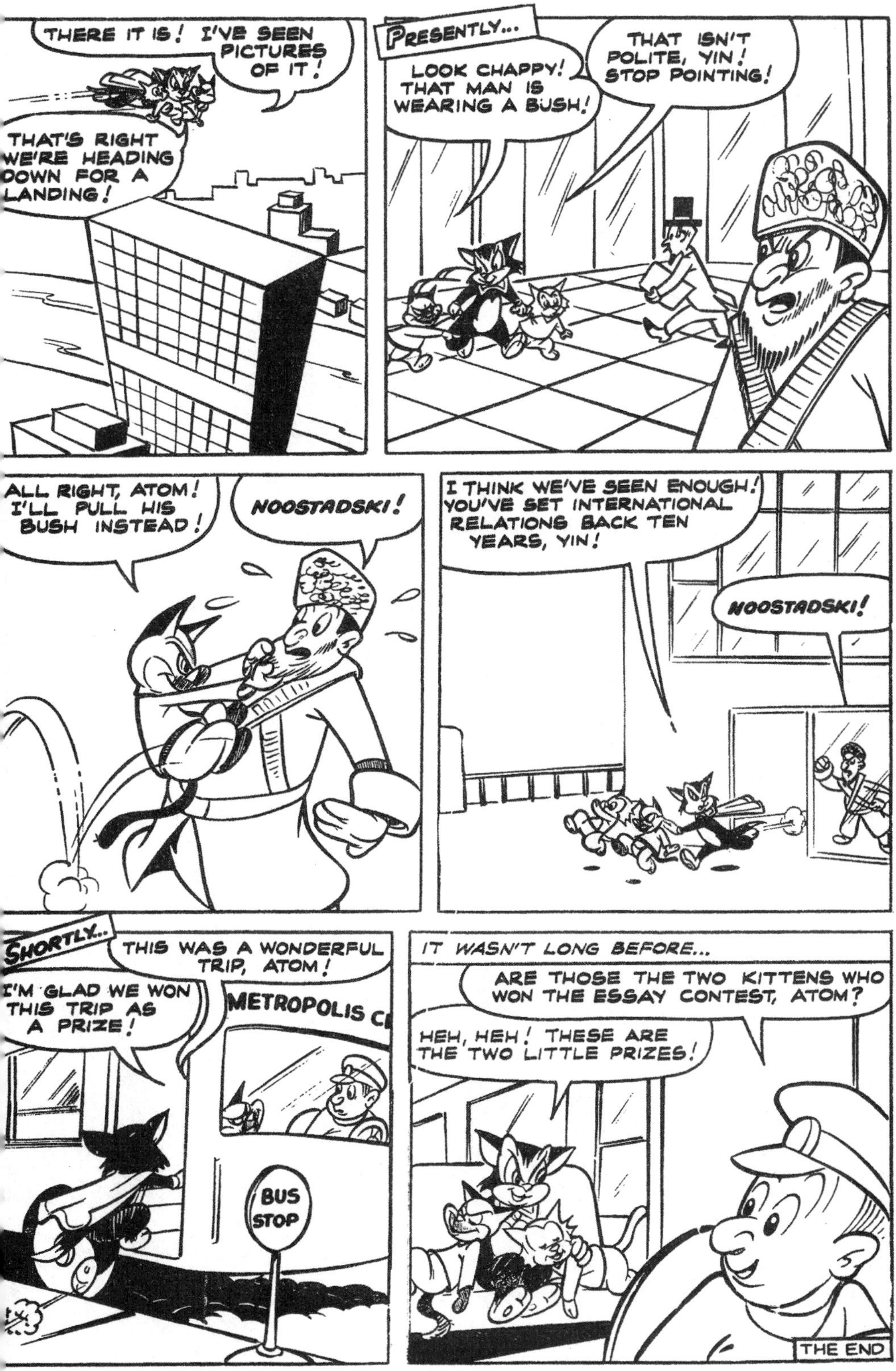
THERE IT IS! I'VE SEEN PICTURES OF IT!
THAT'S RIGHT WE'RE HEADING DOWN FOR A LANDING!
PRESENTLY...
LOOK CHAPPY! THAT MAN IS WEARING A BUSH!
THAT ISN'T POLITE, YIN! STOP POINTING!
ALL RIGHT, ATOM! I'LL PULL HIS BUSH INSTEAD!
NOOSTADSKI!
I THINK WE'VE SEEN ENOUGH! YOU'VE SET INTERNATIONAL RELATIONS BACK TEN YEARS, YIN!
NOOSTADSKI!
SHORTLY...
THIS WAS A WONDERFUL TRIP, ATOM!
I'M GLAD WE WON THIS TRIP AS A PRIZE!
METROPOLIS C
BUS STOP
IT WASN'T LONG BEFORE...
ARE THOSE THE TWO KITTENS WHO WON THE ESSAY CONTEST, ATOM?
HEH, HEH! THESE ARE THE TWO LITTLE PRIZES!
THE END

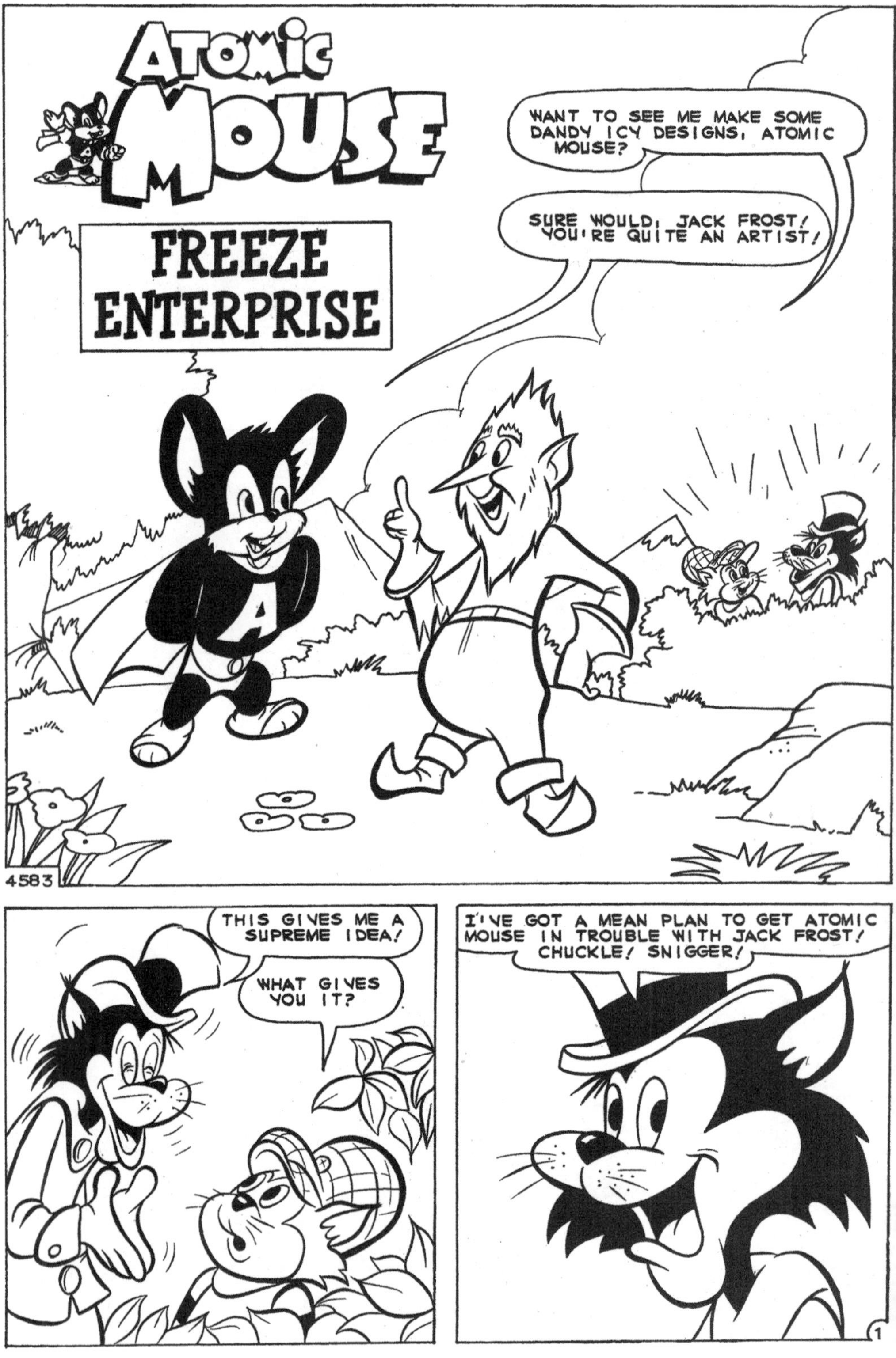
ATOMIC MOUSE
FREEZE ENTERPRISE
WANT TO SEE ME MAKE SOME DANDY ICY DESIGNS, ATOMIC MOUSE?
SURE WOULD, JACK FROST! YOU'RE QUITE AN ARTIST!
4583
THIS GIVES ME A SUPREME IDEA!
WHAT GIVES YOU IT?
I'VE GOT A MEAN PLAN TO GET ATOMIC MOUSE IN TROUBLE WITH JACK FROST! CHUCKLE! SNIGGER!
1

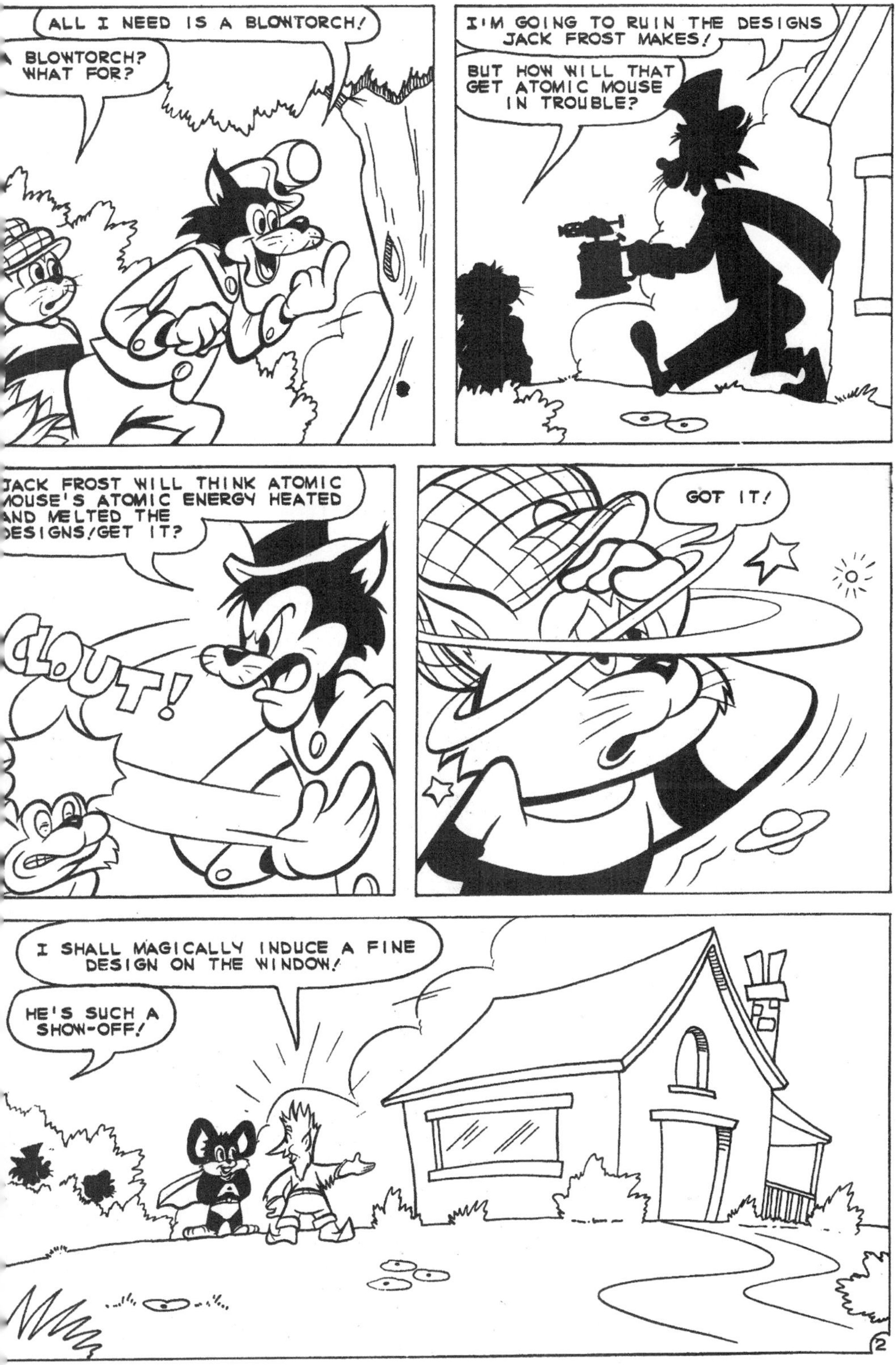
ALL I NEED IS A BLOWTORCH!
BLOWTORCH? WHAT FOR?
I'M GOING TO RUIN THE DESIGNS JACK FROST MAKES!
BUT HOW WILL THAT GET ATOMIC MOUSE IN TROUBLE?
JACK FROST WILL THINK ATOMIC MOUSE'S ATOMIC ENERGY HEATED AND MELTED THE DESIGNS! GET IT?
CLOUT!
GOT IT!
I SHALL MAGICALLY INDUCE A FINE DESIGN ON THE WINDOW!
HE'S SUCH A SHOW-OFF!
2

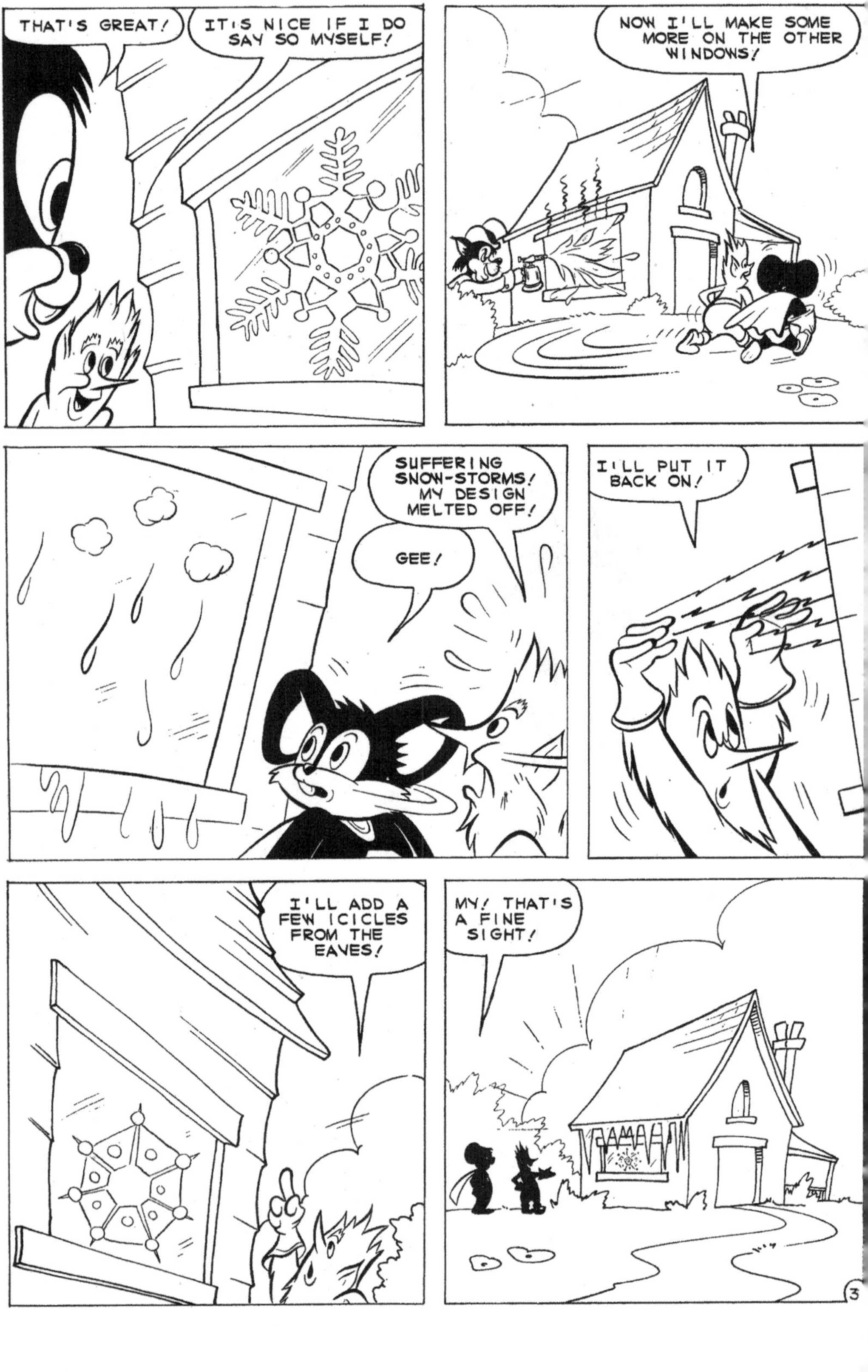
THAT'S GREAT!
IT'S NICE IF I DO SAY SO MYSELF!
NOW I'LL MAKE SOME MORE ON THE OTHER WINDOWS!
SUFFERING SNOW-STORMS! MY DESIGN MELTED OFF!
GEE!
I'LL PUT IT BACK ON!
I'LL ADD A FEW ICICLES FROM THE EAVES!
MY! THAT'S A FINE SIGHT!
3

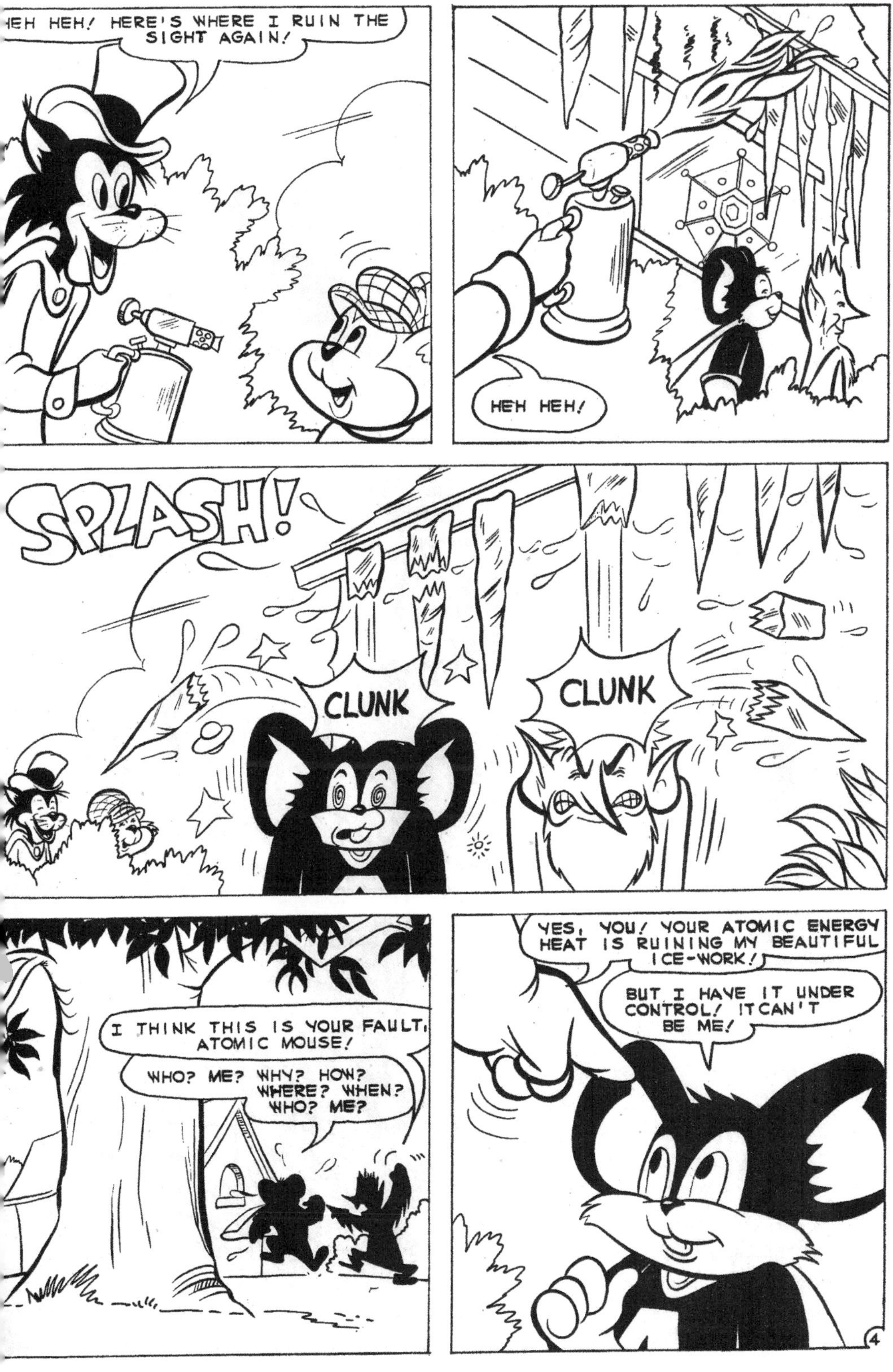
HEH HEH! HERE'S WHERE I RUIN THE SIGHT AGAIN!
HEH HEH!
SPLASH!
CLUNK
CLUNK
I THINK THIS IS YOUR FAULT, ATOMIC MOUSE!
WHO? ME? WHY? HOW? WHERE? WHEN? WHO? ME?
YES, YOU! YOUR ATOMIC ENERGY HEAT IS RUINING MY BEAUTIFUL ICE-WORK!
BUT I HAVE IT UNDER CONTROL! IT CAN'T BE ME!

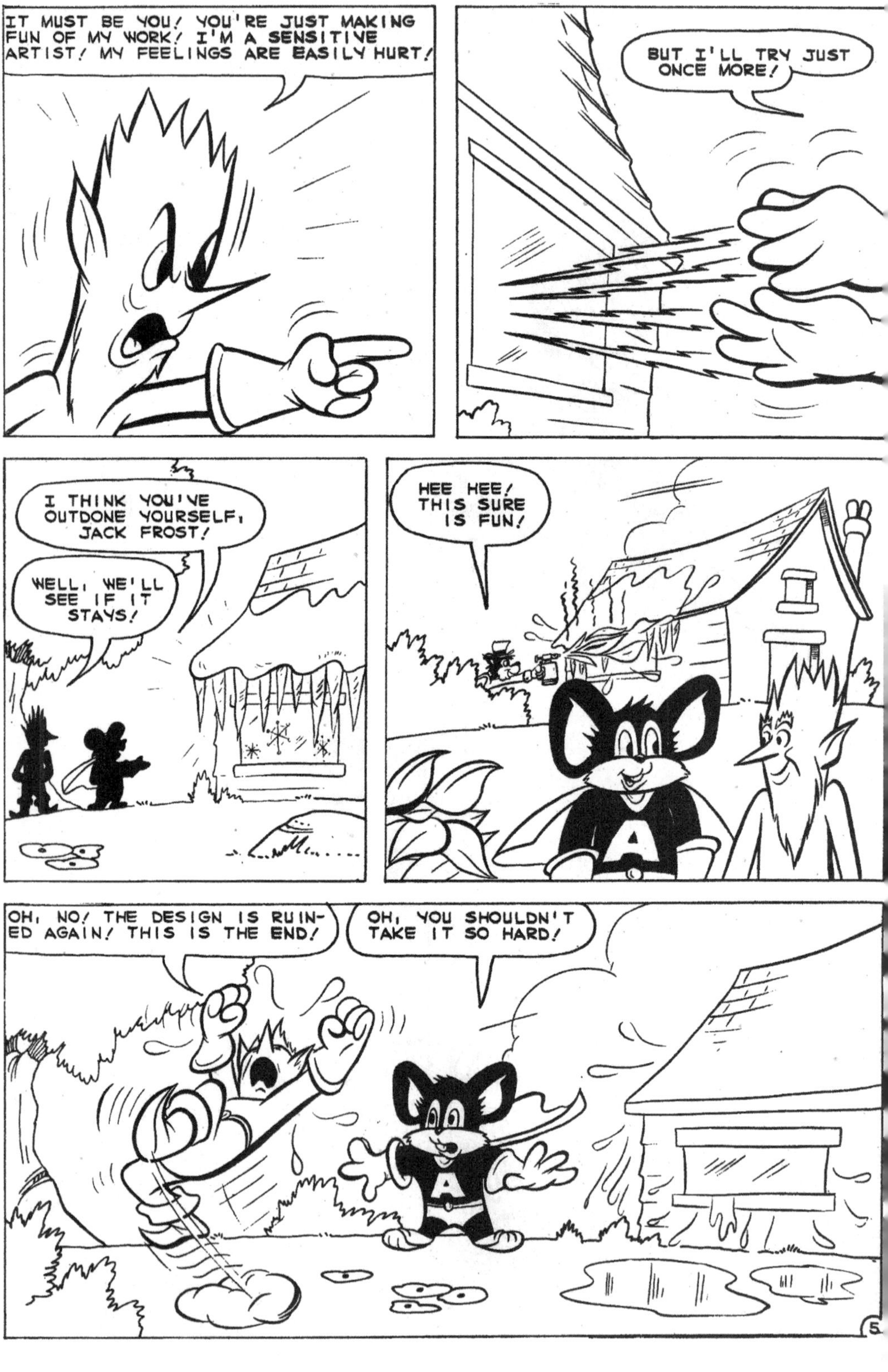
IT MUST BE YOU! YOU'RE JUST MAKING FUN OF MY WORK! I'M A SENSITIVE ARTIST! MY FEELINGS ARE EASILY HURT!
BUT I'LL TRY JUST ONCE MORE!
I THINK YOU'VE OUTDONE YOURSELF, JACK FROST!
WELL, WE'LL SEE IF IT STAYS!
HEE HEE! THIS SURE IS FUN!
OH, NO! THE DESIGN IS RUIN-ED AGAIN! THIS IS THE END!
OH, YOU SHOULDN'T TAKE IT SO HARD!
5

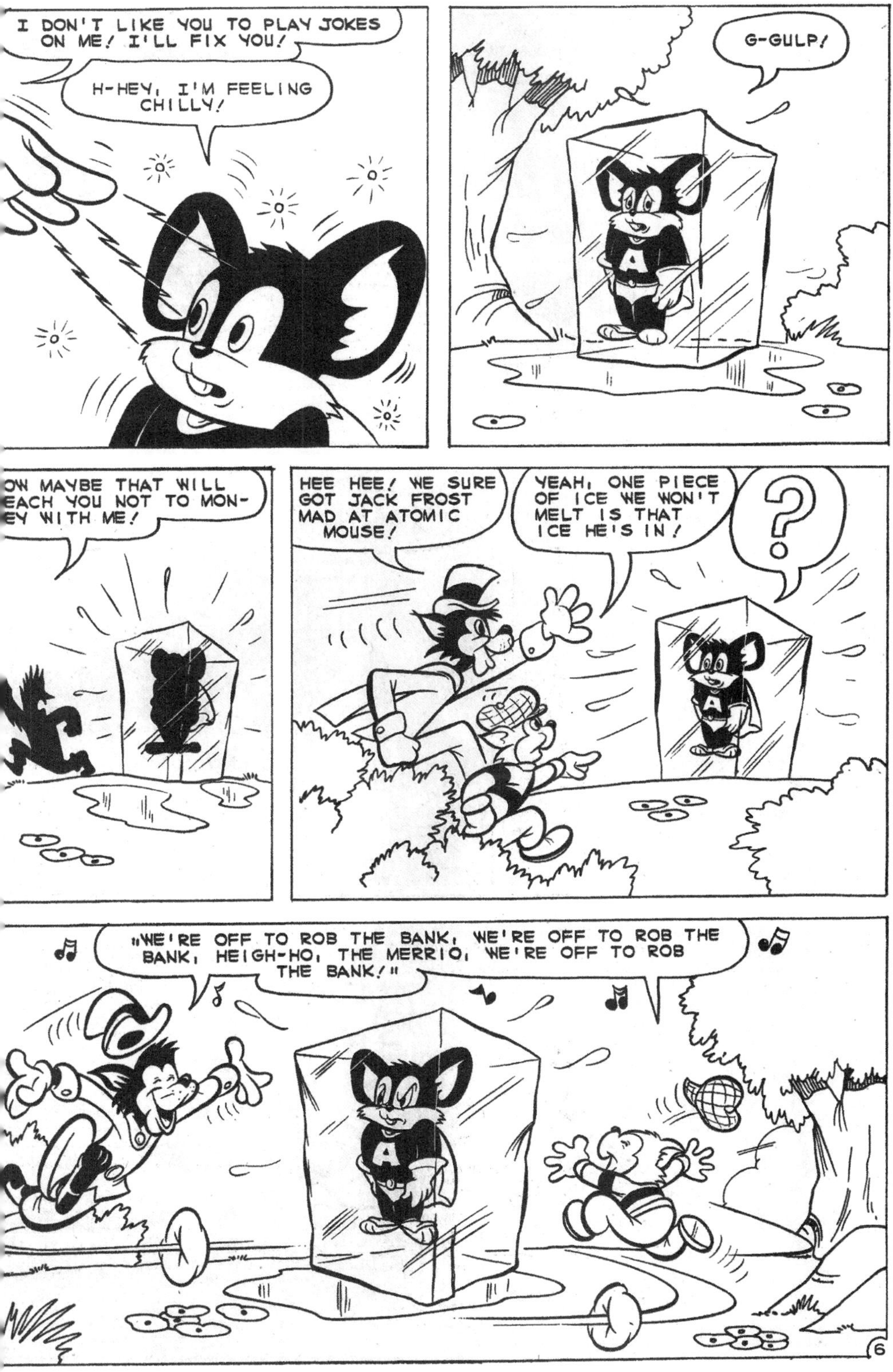
I DON'T LIKE YOU TO PLAY JOKES ON ME! I'LL FIX YOU!
H-HEY, I'M FEELING CHILLY!
G-GULP!
OW MAYBE THAT WILL EACH YOU NOT TO MON-EY WITH ME!
HEE HEE! WE SURE GOT JACK FROST MAD AT ATOMIC MOUSE!
YEAH, ONE PIECE OF ICE WE WON'T MELT IS THAT ICE HE'S IN!
?
"WE'RE OFF TO ROB THE BANK, WE'RE OFF TO ROB THE BANK, HEIGH-HO, THE MERRIO, WE'RE OFF TO ROB THE BANK!"
A
6

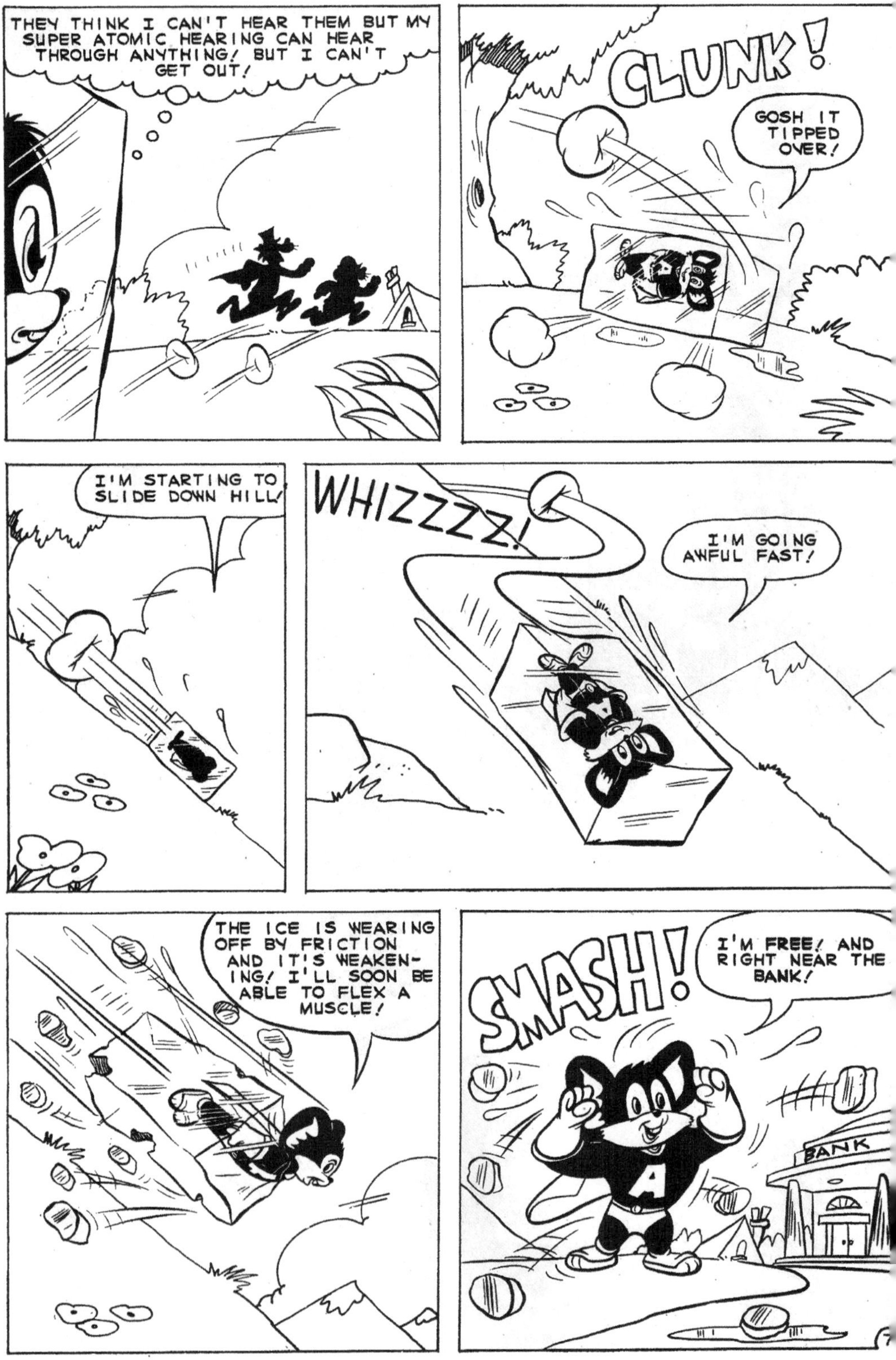
THEY THINK I CAN'T HEAR THEM BUT MY SUPER ATOMIC HEARING CAN HEAR THROUGH ANYTHING! BUT I CAN'T GET OUT!
CLUNK!
GOSH IT TIPPED OVER!
I'M STARTING TO SLIDE DOWN HILL!
WHIZZZZZ!
I'M GOING AWFUL FAST!
THE ICE IS WEARING OFF BY FRICTION AND IT'S WEAKENING! I'LL SOON BE ABLE TO FLEX A MUSCLE!
SMASH!
I'M FREE! AND RIGHT NEAR THE BANK!
BANK

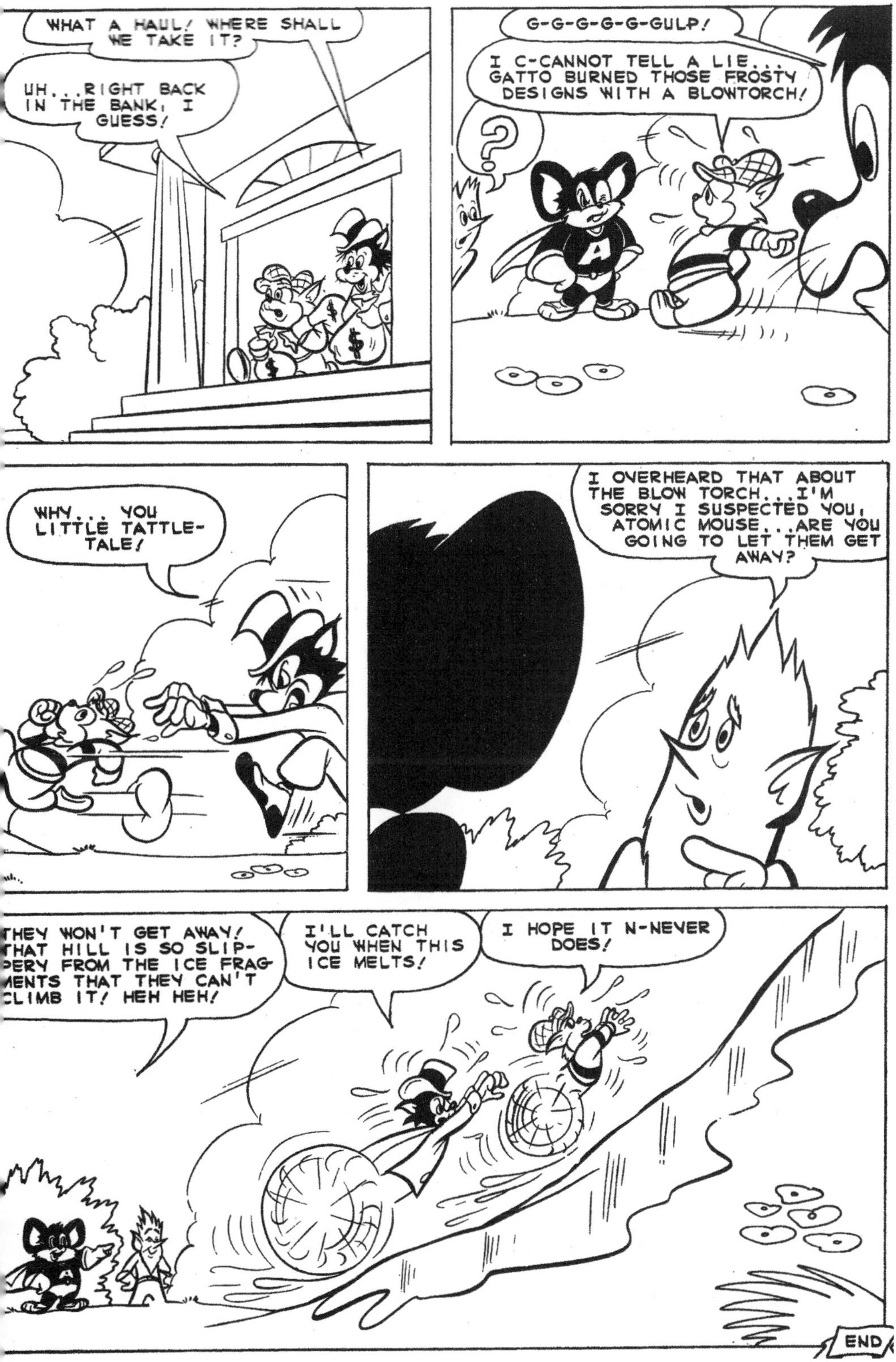
WHAT A HAUL! WHERE SHALL WE TAKE IT?
UH...RIGHT BACK IN THE BANK, I GUESS!
G-G-G-G-G-GULP!
I C-CANNOT TELL A LIE... GATTO BURNED THOSE FROSTY DESIGNS WITH A BLOWTORCH!
?
WHY... YOU LITTLE TATTLE-TALE!
I OVERHEARD THAT ABOUT THE BLOW TORCH...I'M SORRY I SUSPECTED YOU, ATOMIC MOUSE...ARE YOU GOING TO LET THEM GET AWAY?
THEY WON'T GET AWAY! THAT HILL IS SO SLIP-PERY FROM THE ICE FRAG-MENTS THAT THEY CAN'T CLIMB IT! HEH HEH!
I'LL CATCH YOU WHEN THIS ICE MELTS!
I HOPE IT N-NEVER DOES!
END

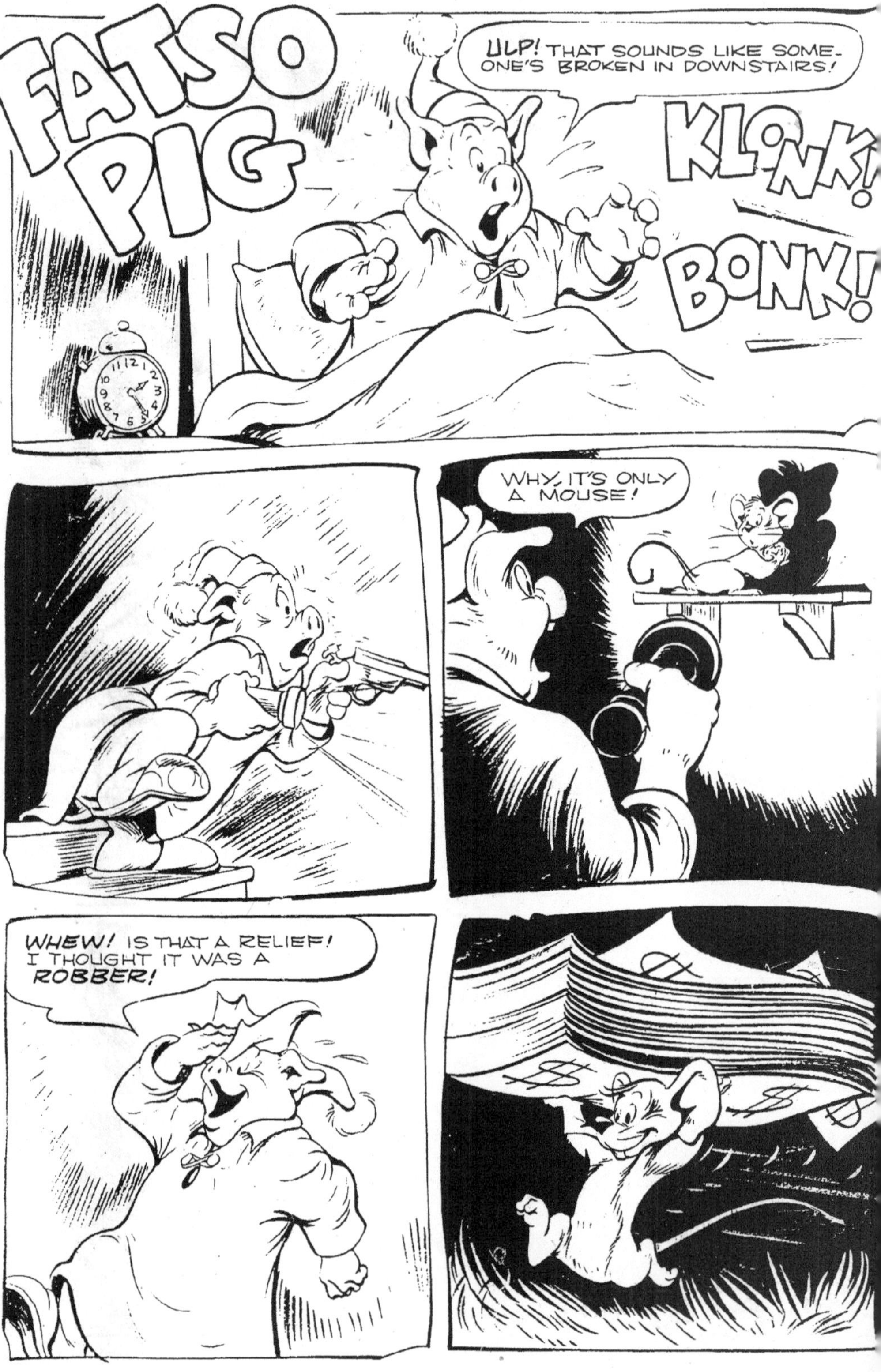
FATSO PIG
ULP! THAT SOUNDS LIKE SOME-ONE'S BROKEN IN DOWNSTAIRS!
KLONK!
BONK!
WHY, IT'S ONLY A MOUSE!
WHEW! IS THAT A RELIEF! I THOUGHT IT WAS A ROBBER!

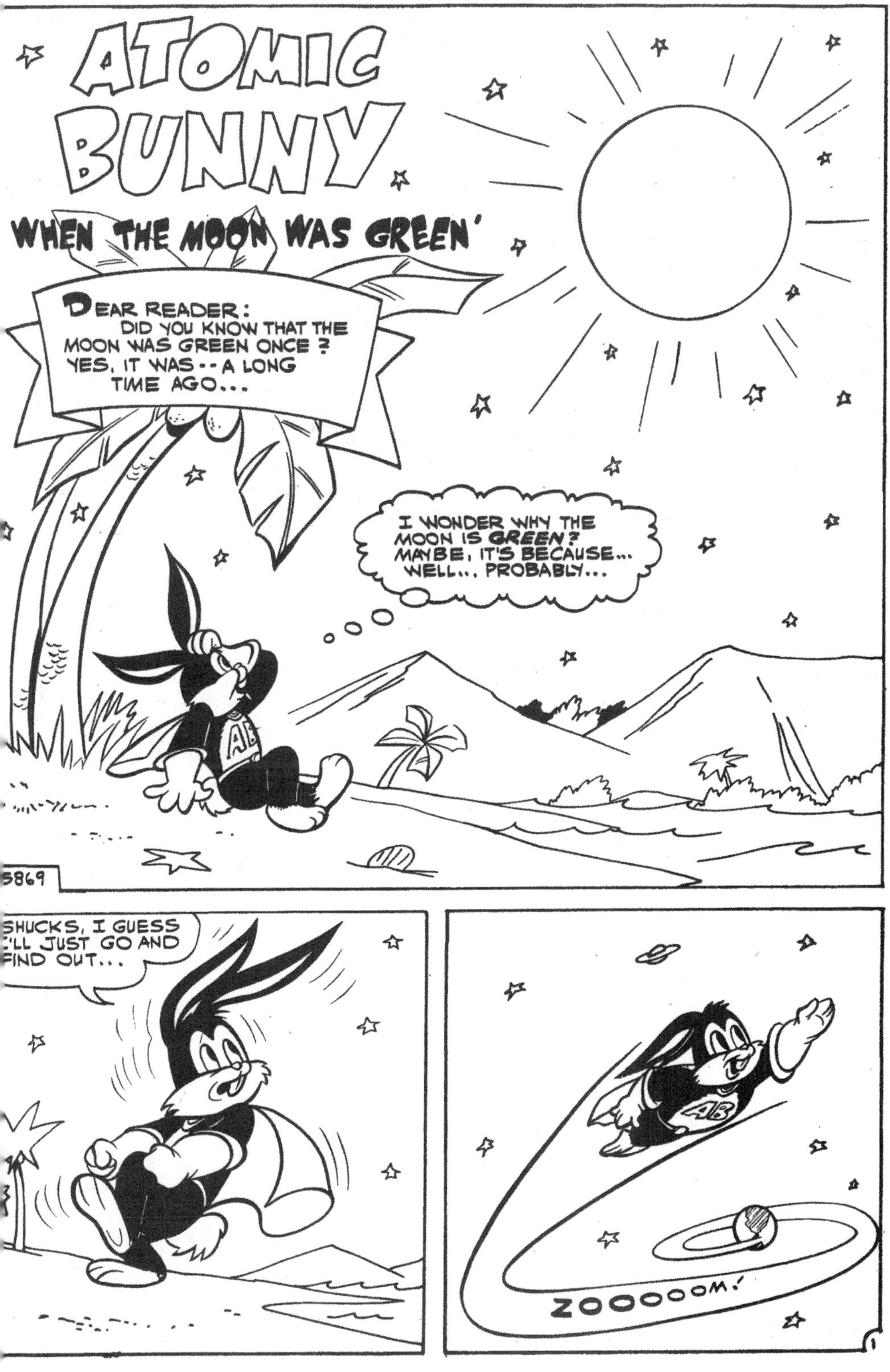
ATOMIC BUNNY
'WHEN THE MOON WAS GREEN'
DEAR READER: DID YOU KNOW THAT THE MOON WAS GREEN ONCE? YES, IT WAS--A LONG TIME AGO...
I WONDER WHY THE MOON IS GREEN? MAYBE, IT'S BECAUSE... WELL... PROBABLY...
5869
SHUCKS, I GUESS I'LL JUST GO AND FIND OUT...
ZOOOOOOM!
1

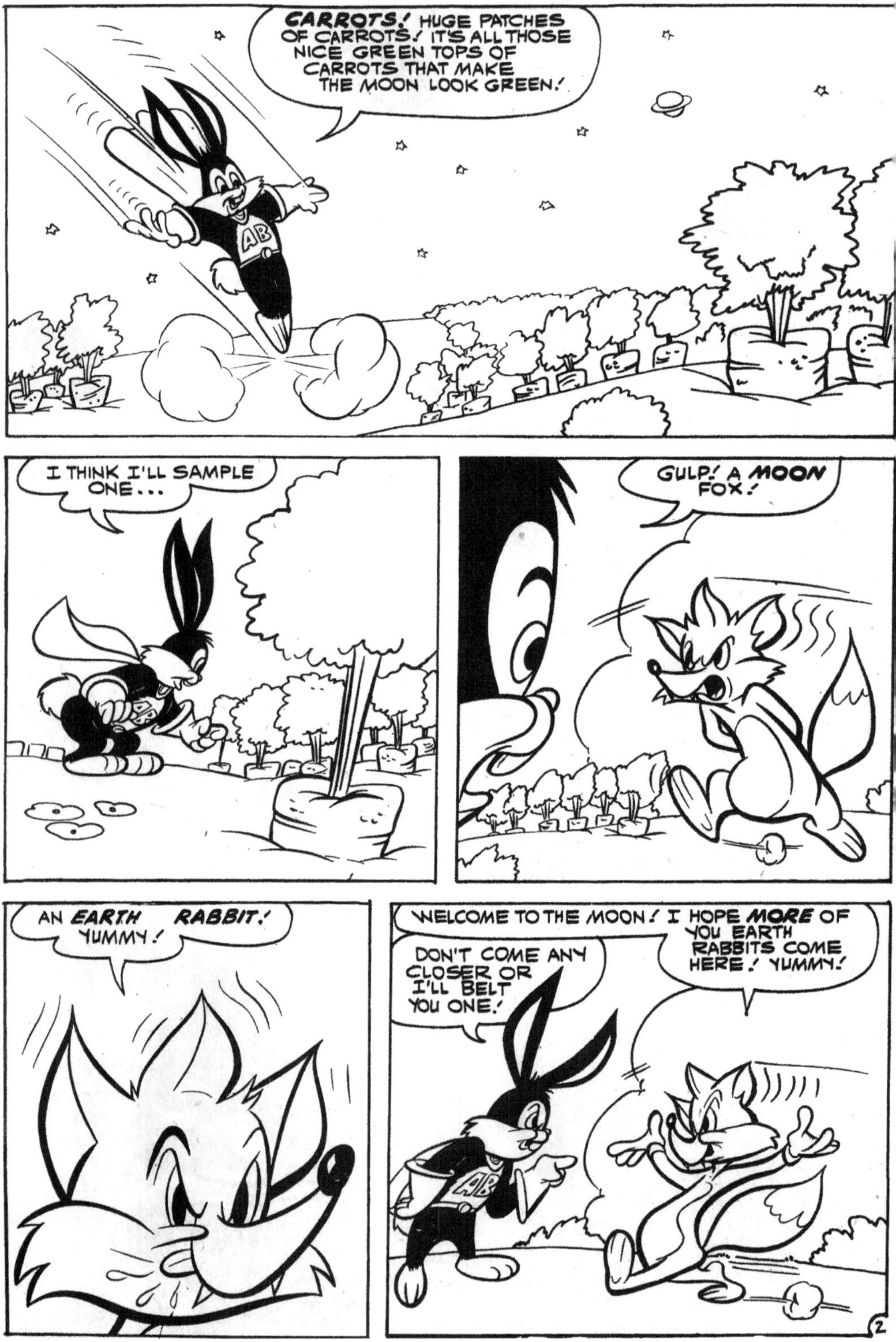
CARROTS! HUGE PATCHES OF CARROTS! IT'S ALL THOSE NICE GREEN TOPS OF CARROTS THAT MAKE THE MOON LOOK GREEN!
I THINK I'LL SAMPLE ONE...
GULP! A MOON FOX!
AN EARTH RABBIT! YUMMY!
WELCOME TO THE MOON! I HOPE MORE OF YOU EARTH RABBITS COME HERE! YUMMY!
DON'T COME ANY CLOSER OR I'LL BELT YOU ONE!
2

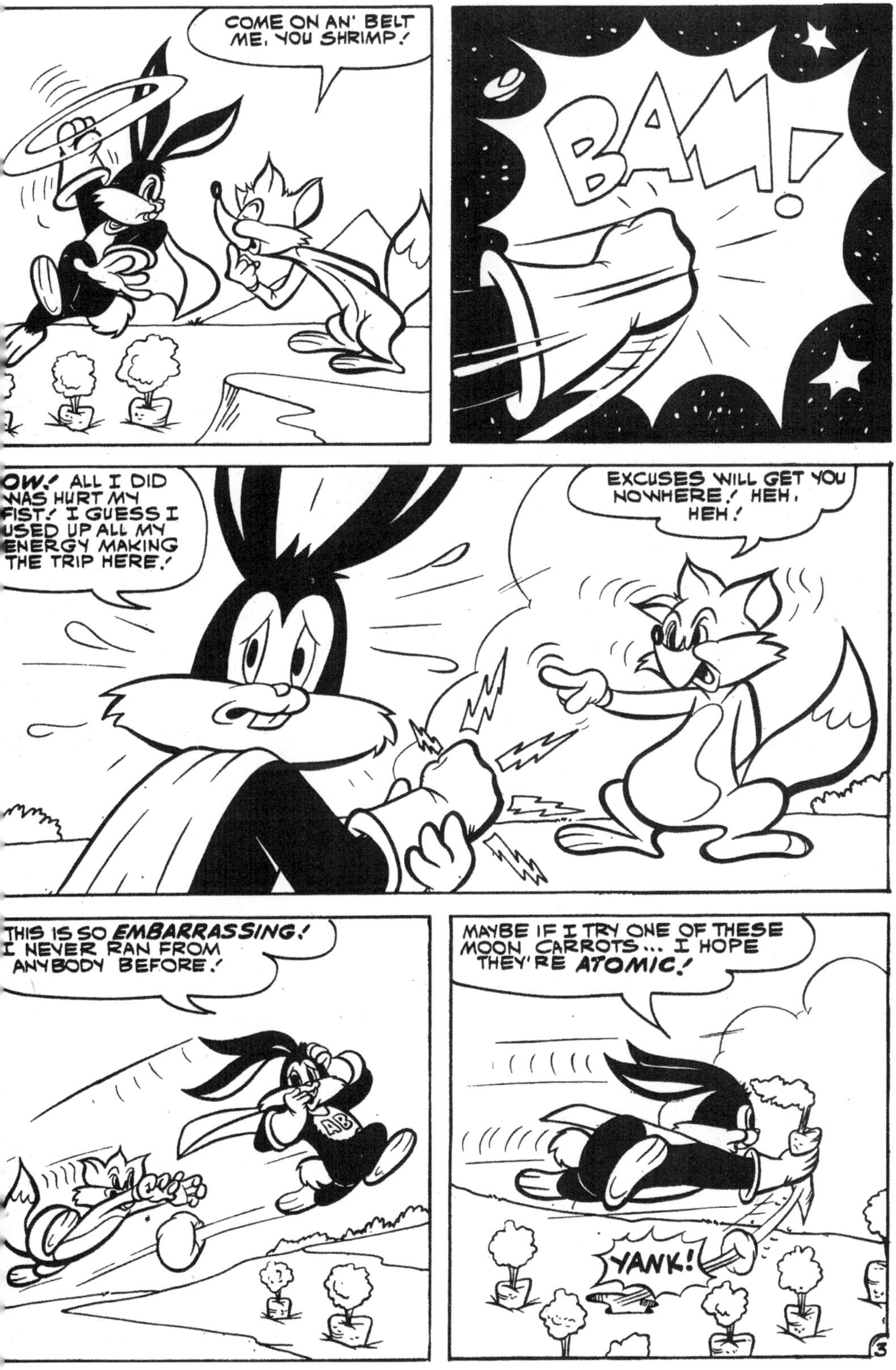
COME ON AN' BELT ME, YOU SHRIMP!
BAM!
OW! ALL I DID WAS HURT MY FIST! I GUESS I USED UP ALL MY ENERGY MAKING THE TRIP HERE!
EXCUSES WILL GET YOU NOWHERE! HEH, HEH!
THIS IS SO EMBARRASSING! I NEVER RAN FROM ANYBODY BEFORE!
MAYBE IF I TRY ONE OF THESE MOON CARROTS... I HOPE THEY'RE ATOMIC!
YANK!
3

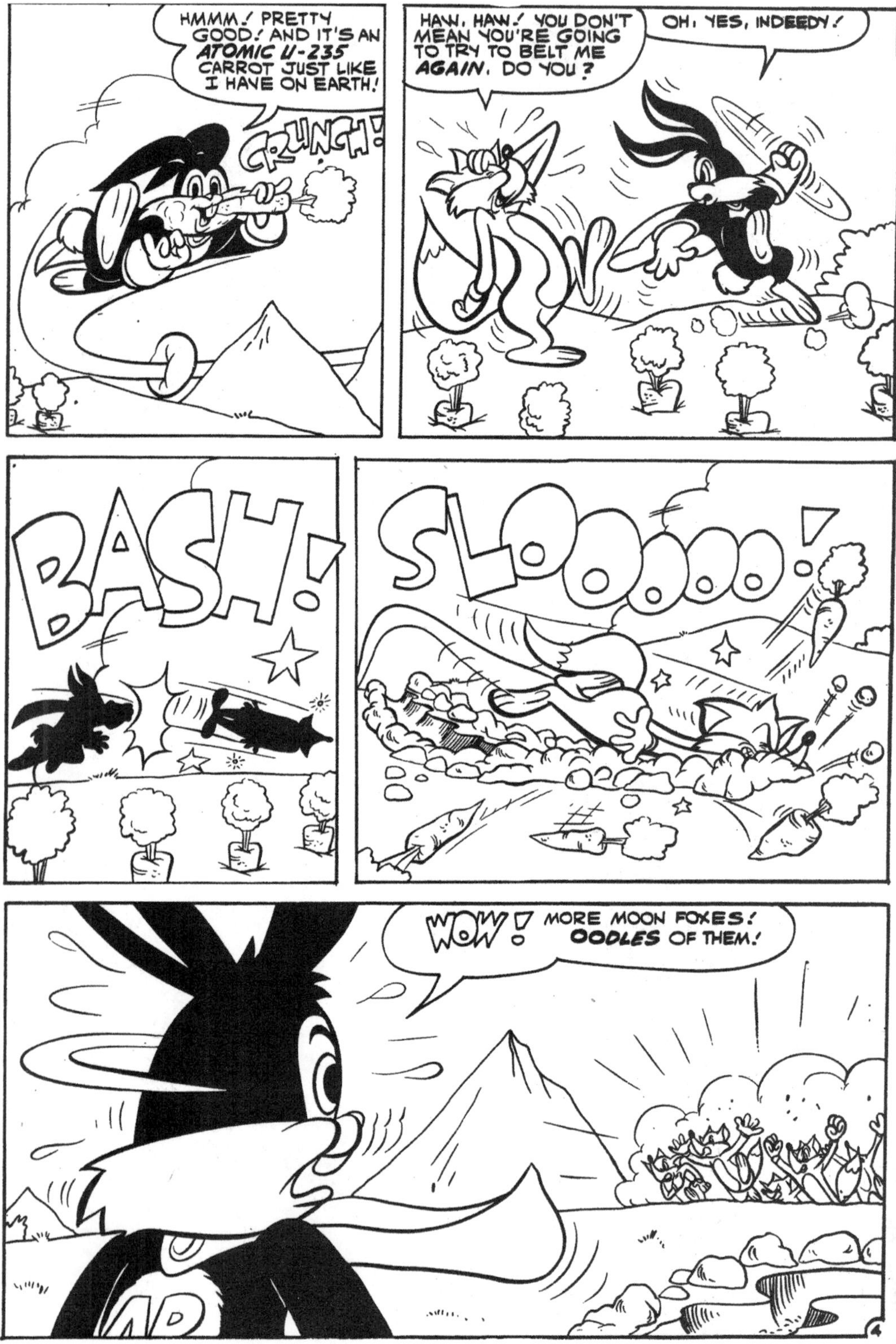
HMMM! PRETTY GOOD! AND IT'S AN ATOMIC U-235 CARROT JUST LIKE I HAVE ON EARTH!
CRUNCH!
HAW, HAW! YOU DON'T MEAN YOU'RE GOING TO TRY TO BELT ME AGAIN, DO YOU?
OH, YES, INDEEDY!
BASH!
SLOOOOOO!
WOW! MORE MOON FOXES! OODLES OF THEM!
4

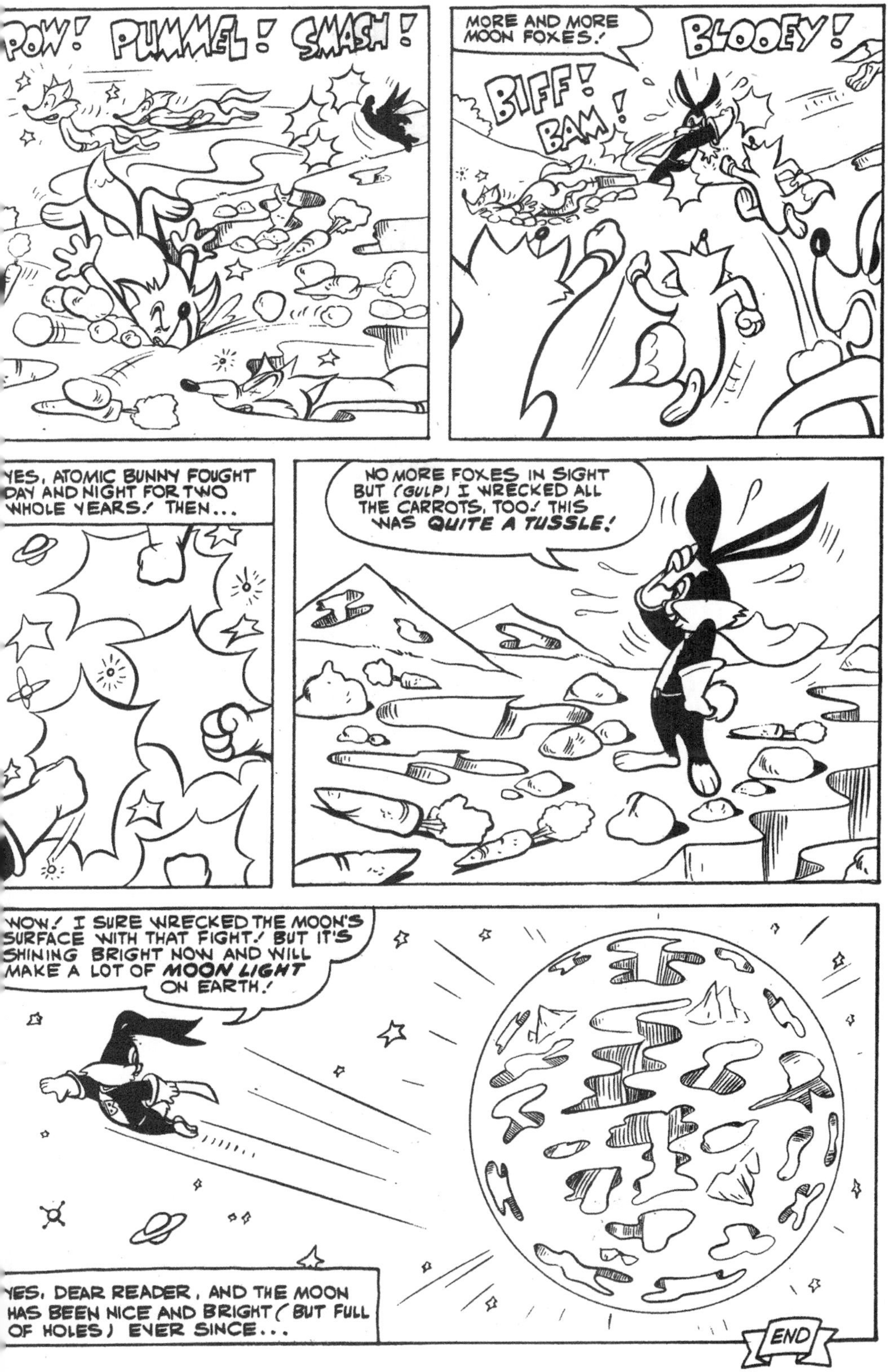
POW! PUMMEL! SMASH!
MORE AND MORE MOON FOXES.!
BLOOEY!
BIFF!
BAM!
YES, ATOMIC BUNNY FOUGHT DAY AND NIGHT FOR TWO WHOLE YEARS! THEN...
NO MORE FOXES IN SIGHT BUT (GULP) I WRECKED ALL THE CARROTS, TOO! THIS WAS QUITE A TUSSLE!
WOW! I SURE WRECKED THE MOON'S SURFACE WITH THAT FIGHT! BUT IT'S SHINING BRIGHT NOW AND WILL MAKE A LOT OF MOON LIGHT ON EARTH!
YES, DEAR READER, AND THE MOON HAS BEEN NICE AND BRIGHT (BUT FULL OF HOLES) EVER SINCE...
END

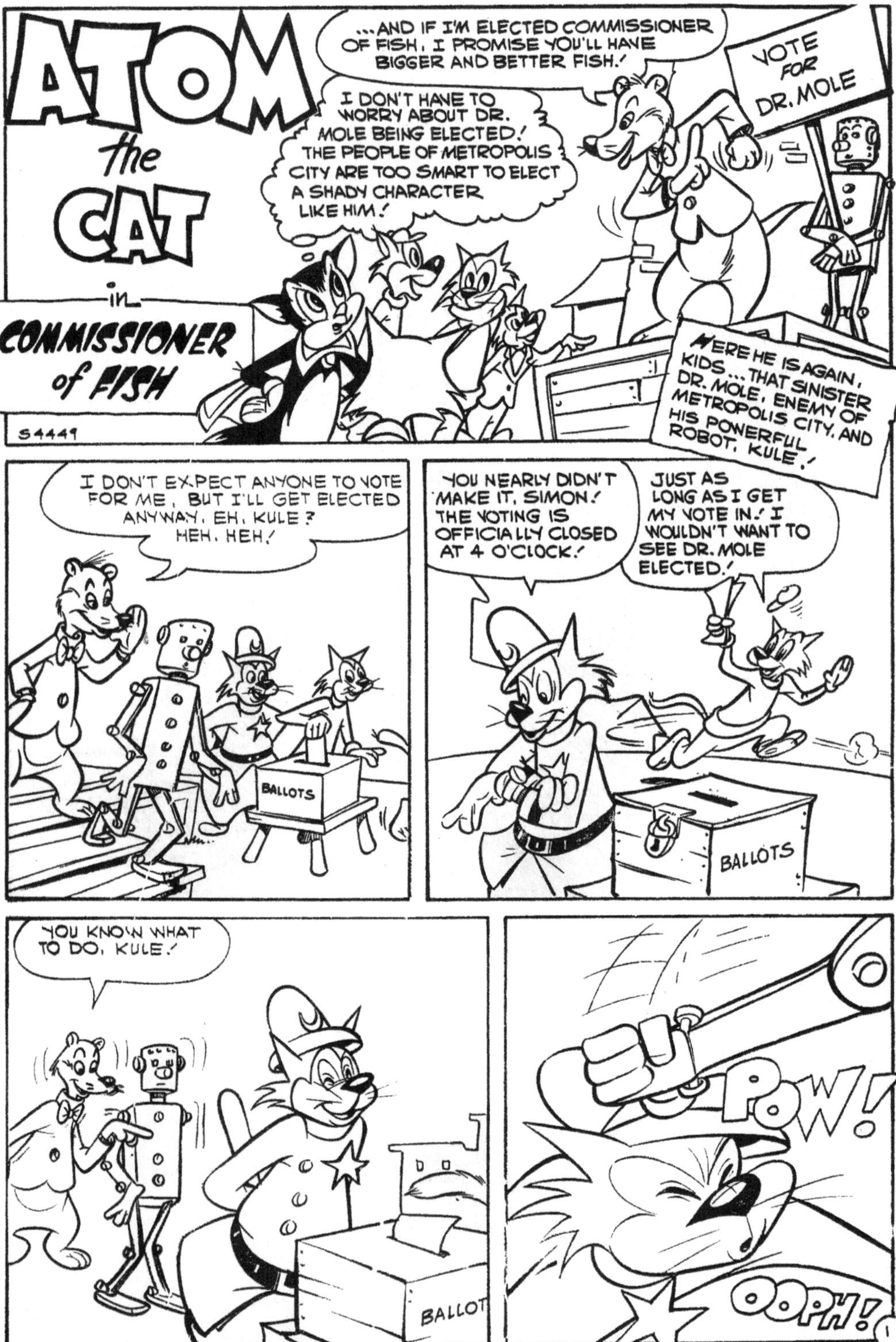
ATOM the CAT
in
COMMISSIONER of FISH
S4449
...AND IF I'M ELECTED COMMISSIONER OF FISH, I PROMISE YOU'LL HAVE BIGGER AND BETTER FISH!
VOTE FOR DR. MOLE
I DON'T HAVE TO WORRY ABOUT DR. MOLE BEING ELECTED! THE PEOPLE OF METROPOLIS CITY ARE TOO SMART TO ELECT A SHADY CHARACTER LIKE HIM!
HERE HE IS AGAIN, KIDS... THAT SINISTER DR. MOLE, ENEMY OF METROPOLIS CITY, AND HIS POWERFUL ROBOT, KULE!
I DON'T EXPECT ANYONE TO VOTE FOR ME, BUT I'LL GET ELECTED ANYWAY, EH, KULE? HEH, HEH!
BALLOTS
YOU NEARLY DIDN'T MAKE IT, SIMON! THE VOTING IS OFFICIALLY CLOSED AT 4 O'CLOCK!
JUST AS LONG AS I GET MY VOTE IN! I WOULDN'T WANT TO SEE DR. MOLE ELECTED!
BALLOTS
YOU KNOW WHAT TO DO, KULE!
BALLOT
POW!
OOPH!
1

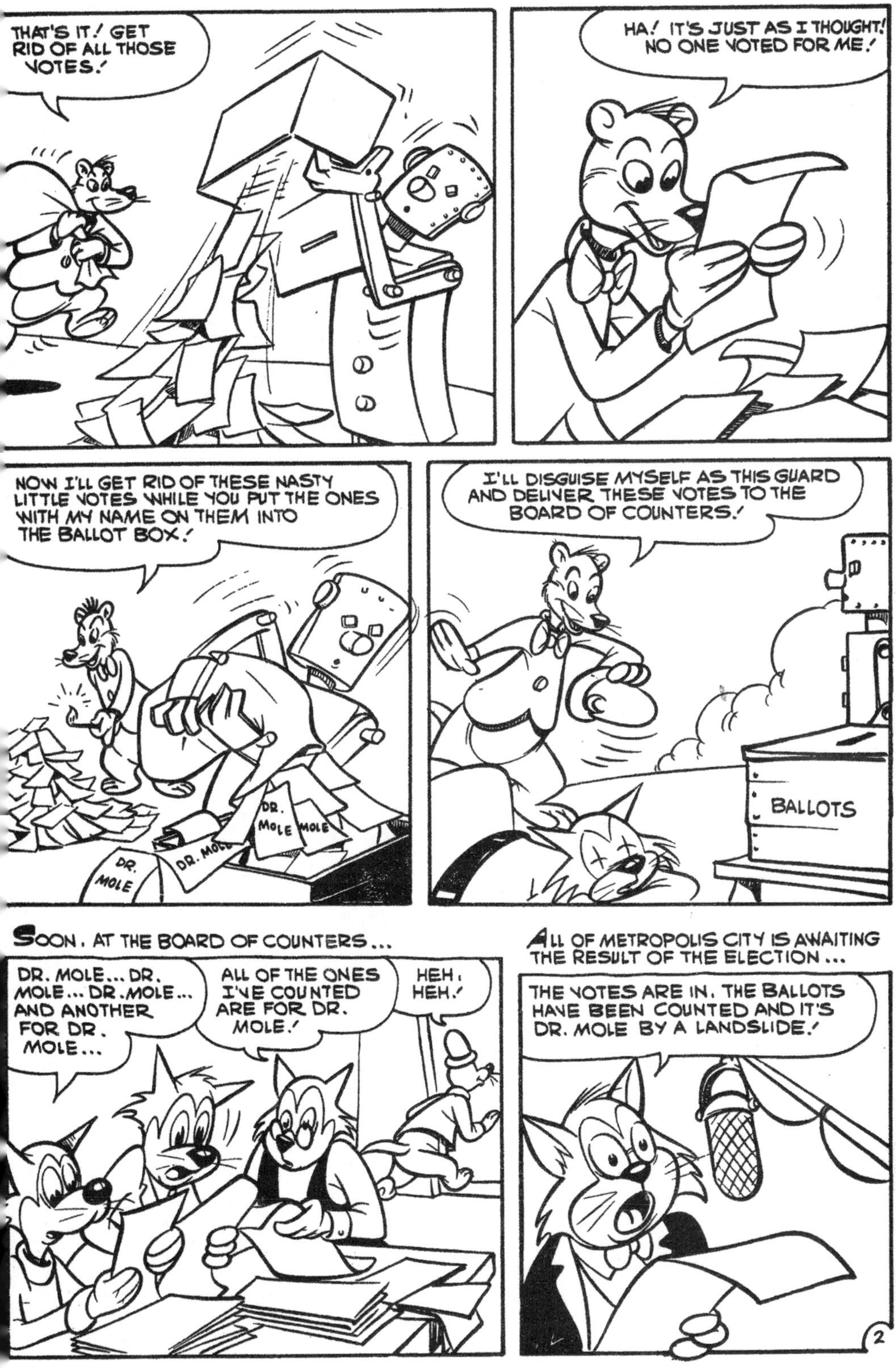
THAT'S IT! GET RID OF ALL THOSE VOTES!
HA! IT'S JUST AS I THOUGHT! NO ONE VOTED FOR ME!
NOW I'LL GET RID OF THESE NASTY LITTLE VOTES WHILE YOU PUT THE ONES WITH MY NAME ON THEM INTO THE BALLOT BOX!
DR. MOLE
DR. MOLE
MOLE
DR. MOLE
I'LL DISGUISE MYSELF AS THIS GUARD AND DELIVER THESE VOTES TO THE BOARD OF COUNTERS!
BALLOTS
SOON, AT THE BOARD OF COUNTERS...
DR. MOLE... DR. MOLE... DR. MOLE... AND ANOTHER FOR DR. MOLE...
ALL OF THE ONES I'VE COUNTED ARE FOR DR. MOLE!
HEH, HEH!
ALL OF METROPOLIS CITY IS AWAITING THE RESULT OF THE ELECTION...
THE VOTES ARE IN, THE BALLOTS HAVE BEEN COUNTED AND IT'S DR. MOLE BY A LANDSLIDE!
2

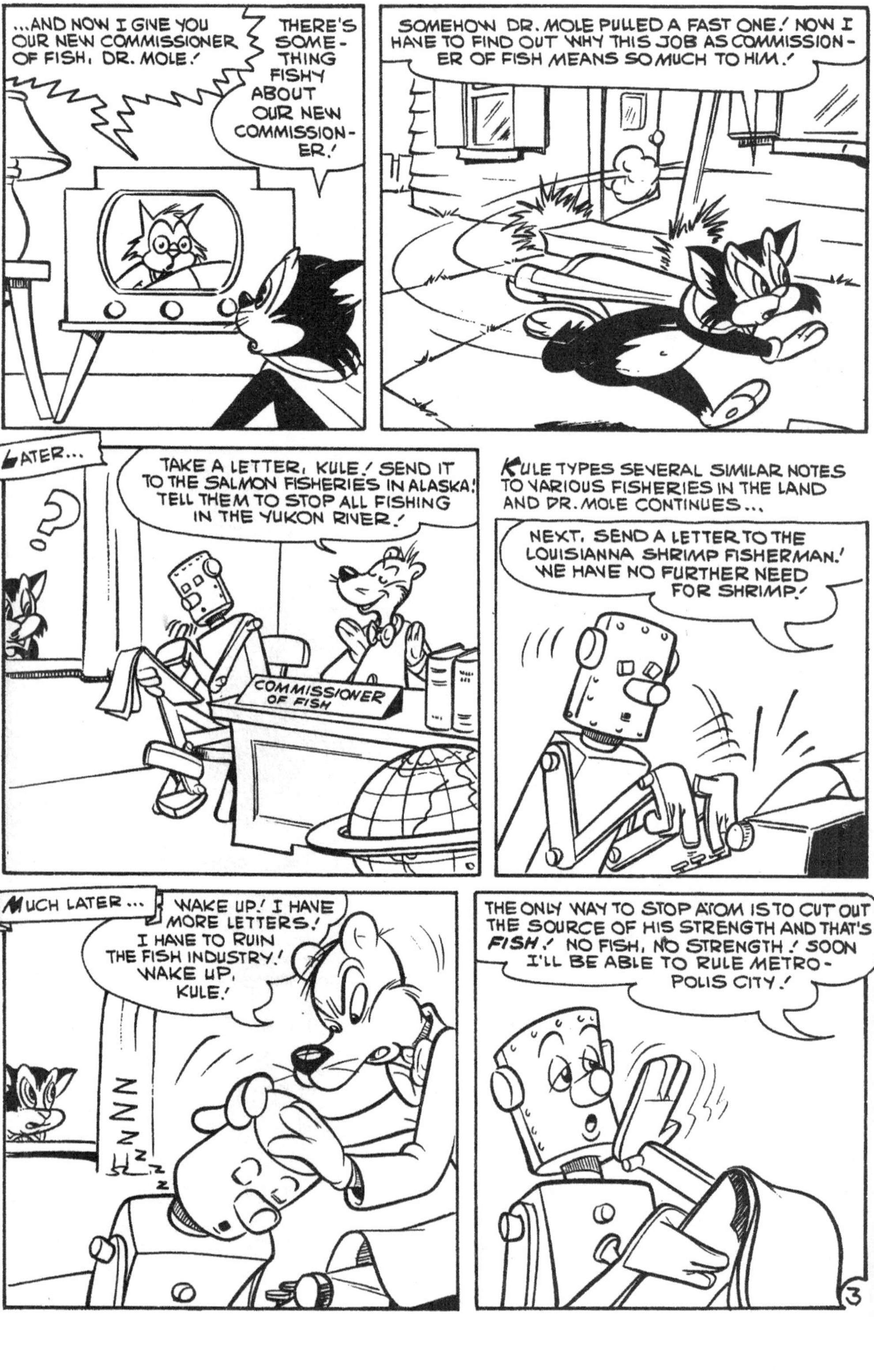
...AND NOW I GIVE YOU OUR NEW COMMISSIONER OF FISH, DR. MOLE!
THERE'S SOME-THING FISHY ABOUT OUR NEW COMMISSION-ER!
SOMEHOW DR. MOLE PULLED A FAST ONE! NOW I HAVE TO FIND OUT WHY THIS JOB AS COMMISSION-ER OF FISH MEANS SO MUCH TO HIM!
LATER...
TAKE A LETTER, KULE! SEND IT TO THE SALMON FISHERIES IN ALASKA! TELL THEM TO STOP ALL FISHING IN THE YUKON RIVER!
COMMISSIONER OF FISH
KULE TYPES SEVERAL SIMILAR NOTES TO VARIOUS FISHERIES IN THE LAND AND DR. MOLE CONTINUES...
NEXT, SEND A LETTER TO THE LOUISIANNA SHRIMP FISHERMAN! WE HAVE NO FURTHER NEED FOR SHRIMP!
MUCH LATER...
WAKE UP! I HAVE MORE LETTERS! I HAVE TO RUIN THE FISH INDUSTRY! WAKE UP, KULE!
ZZZ
THE ONLY WAY TO STOP ATOM IS TO CUT OUT THE SOURCE OF HIS STRENGTH AND THAT'S FISH! NO FISH, NO STRENGTH! SOON I'LL BE ABLE TO RULE METRO-POLIS CITY!

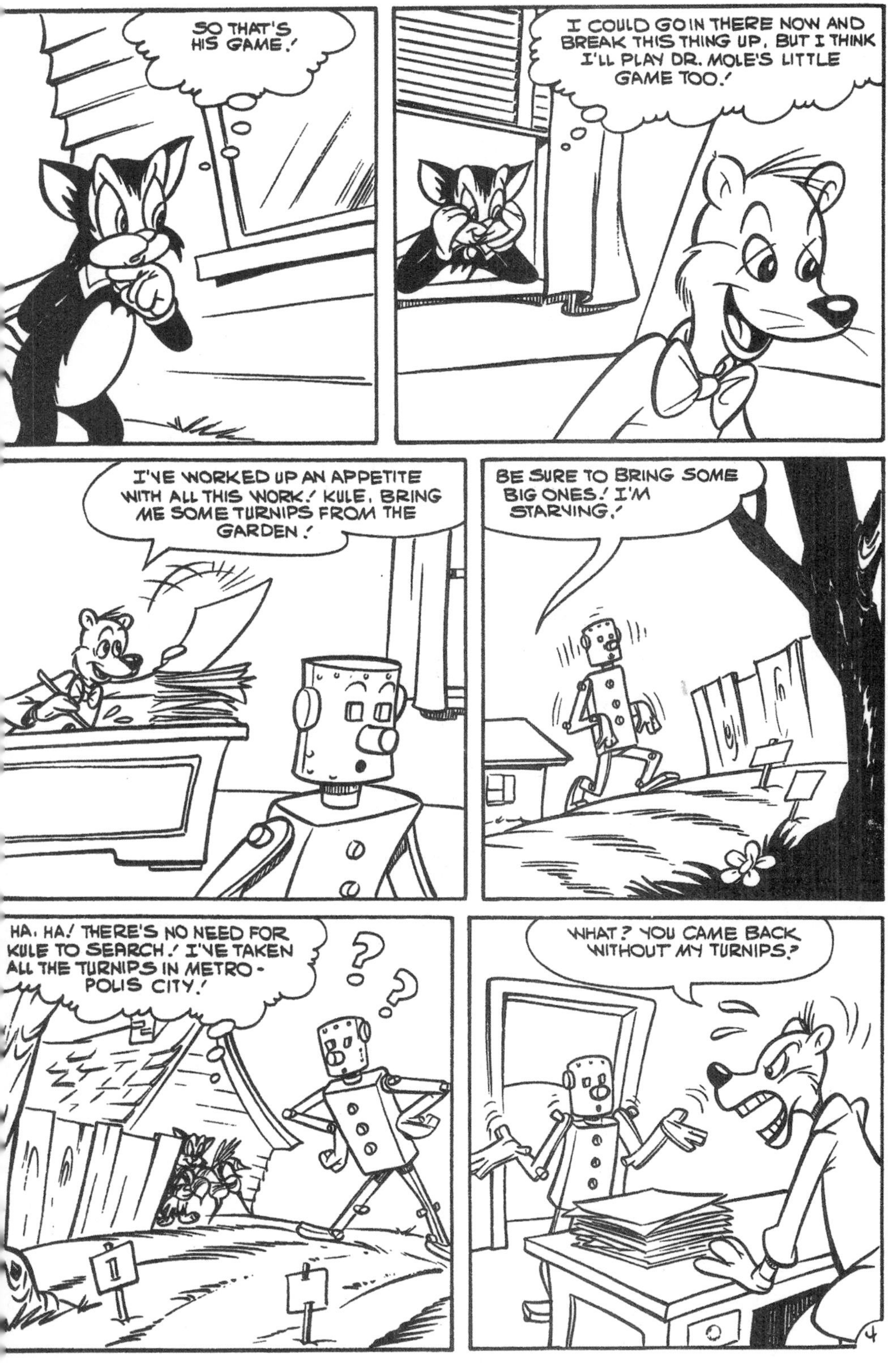
SO THAT'S HIS GAME!
I COULD GO IN THERE NOW AND BREAK THIS THING UP, BUT I THINK I'LL PLAY DR. MOLE'S LITTLE GAME TOO!
I'VE WORKED UP AN APPETITE WITH ALL THIS WORK! KULE, BRING ME SOME TURNIPS FROM THE GARDEN!
BE SURE TO BRING SOME BIG ONES! I'M STARVING!
HA, HA! THERE'S NO NEED FOR KULE TO SEARCH! I'VE TAKEN ALL THE TURNIPS IN METRO-POLIS CITY!
??
WHAT? YOU CAME BACK WITHOUT MY TURNIPS?
4

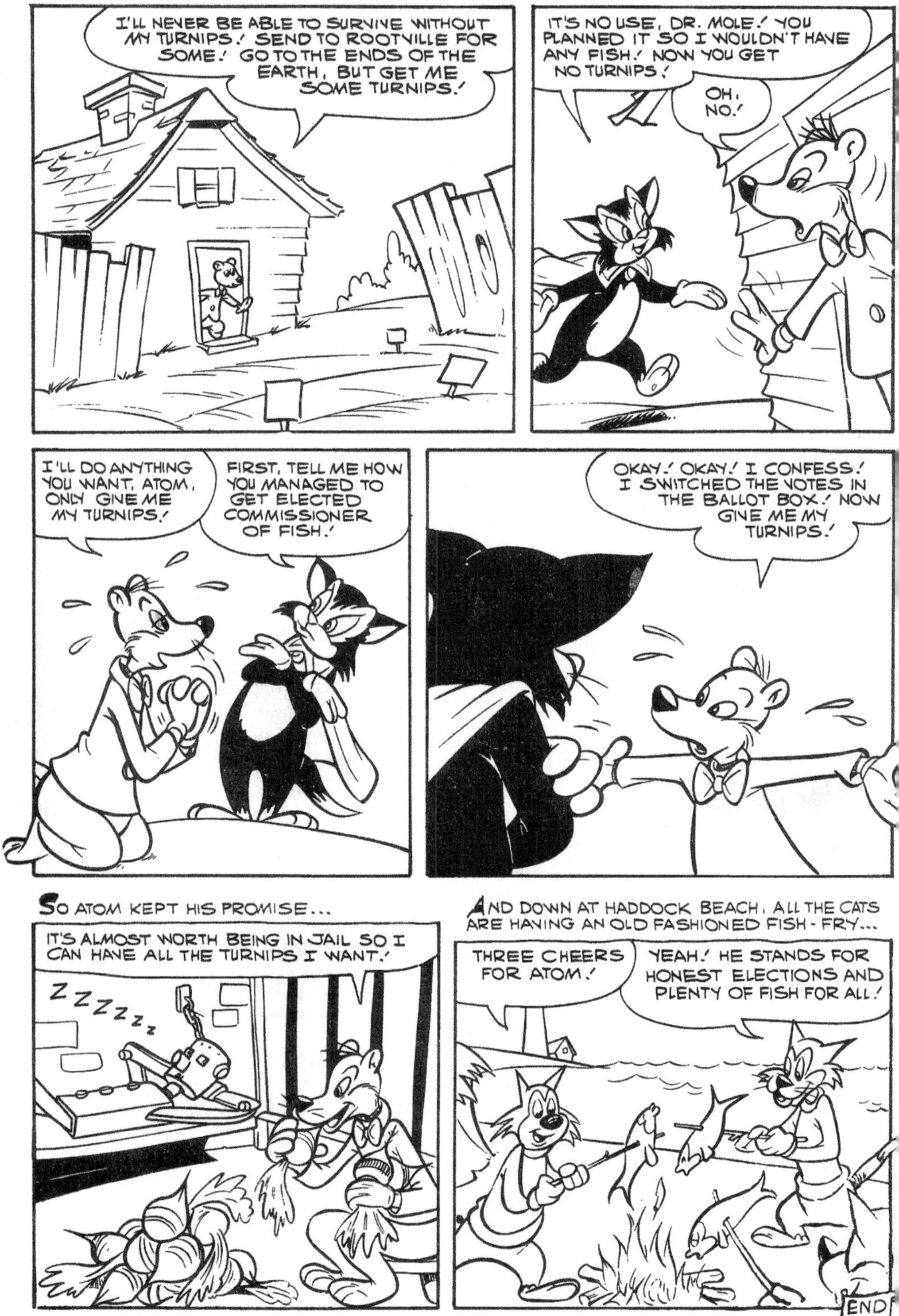

I'LL NEVER BE ABLE TO SURVIVE WITHOUT MY TURNIPS! SEND TO ROOTVILLE FOR SOME! GO TO THE ENDS OF THE EARTH, BUT GET ME SOME TURNIPS!
IT'S NO USE, DR. MOLE! YOU PLANNED IT SO I WOULDN'T HAVE ANY FISH! NOW YOU GET NO TURNIPS!
OH, NO!
I'LL DO ANYTHING YOU WANT, ATOM, ONLY GIVE ME MY TURNIPS!
FIRST, TELL ME HOW YOU MANAGED TO GET ELECTED COMMISSIONER OF FISH!
OKAY! OKAY! I CONFESS! I SWITCHED THE VOTES IN THE BALLOT BOX! NOW GIVE ME MY TURNIPS!
SO ATOM KEPT HIS PROMISE...
IT'S ALMOST WORTH BEING IN JAIL SO I CAN HAVE ALL THE TURNIPS I WANT!
Z Z Z Z Z Z Z
AND DOWN AT HADDOCK BEACH, ALL THE CATS ARE HAVING AN OLD FASHIONED FISH-FRY...
THREE CHEERS FOR ATOM!
YEAH! HE STANDS FOR HONEST ELECTIONS AND PLENTY OF FISH FOR ALL!
END

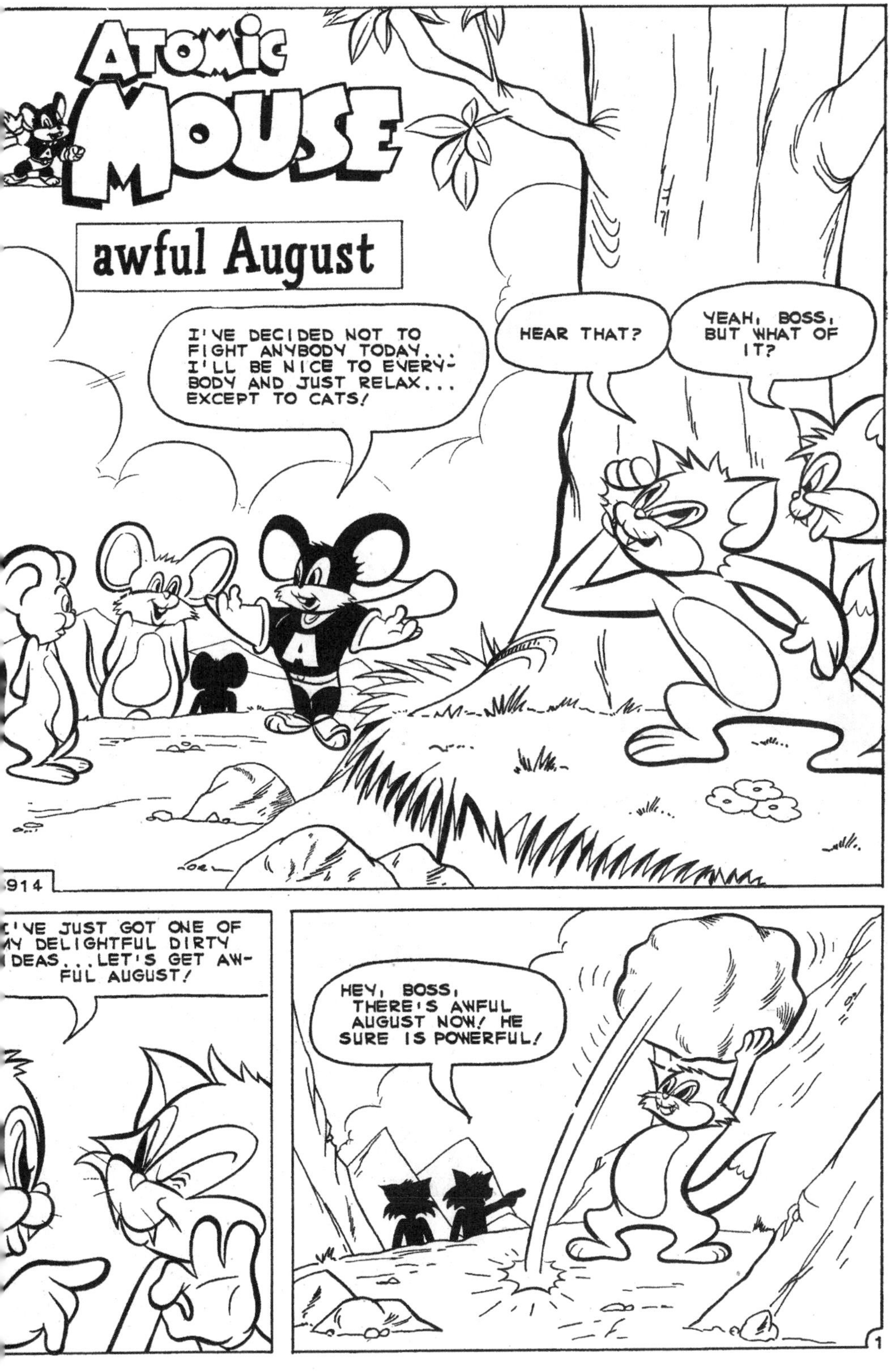
ATOMIC MOUSE
awful August
I'VE DECIDED NOT TO FIGHT ANYBODY TODAY... I'LL BE NICE TO EVERY-BODY AND JUST RELAX... EXCEPT TO CATS!
HEAR THAT?
YEAH, BOSS, BUT WHAT OF IT?
914
'VE JUST GOT ONE OF
Y DELIGHTFUL DIRTY
DEAS...LET'S GET AW-
FUL AUGUST!
HEY, BOSS, THERE'S AWFUL AUGUST NOW! HE SURE IS POWERFUL!

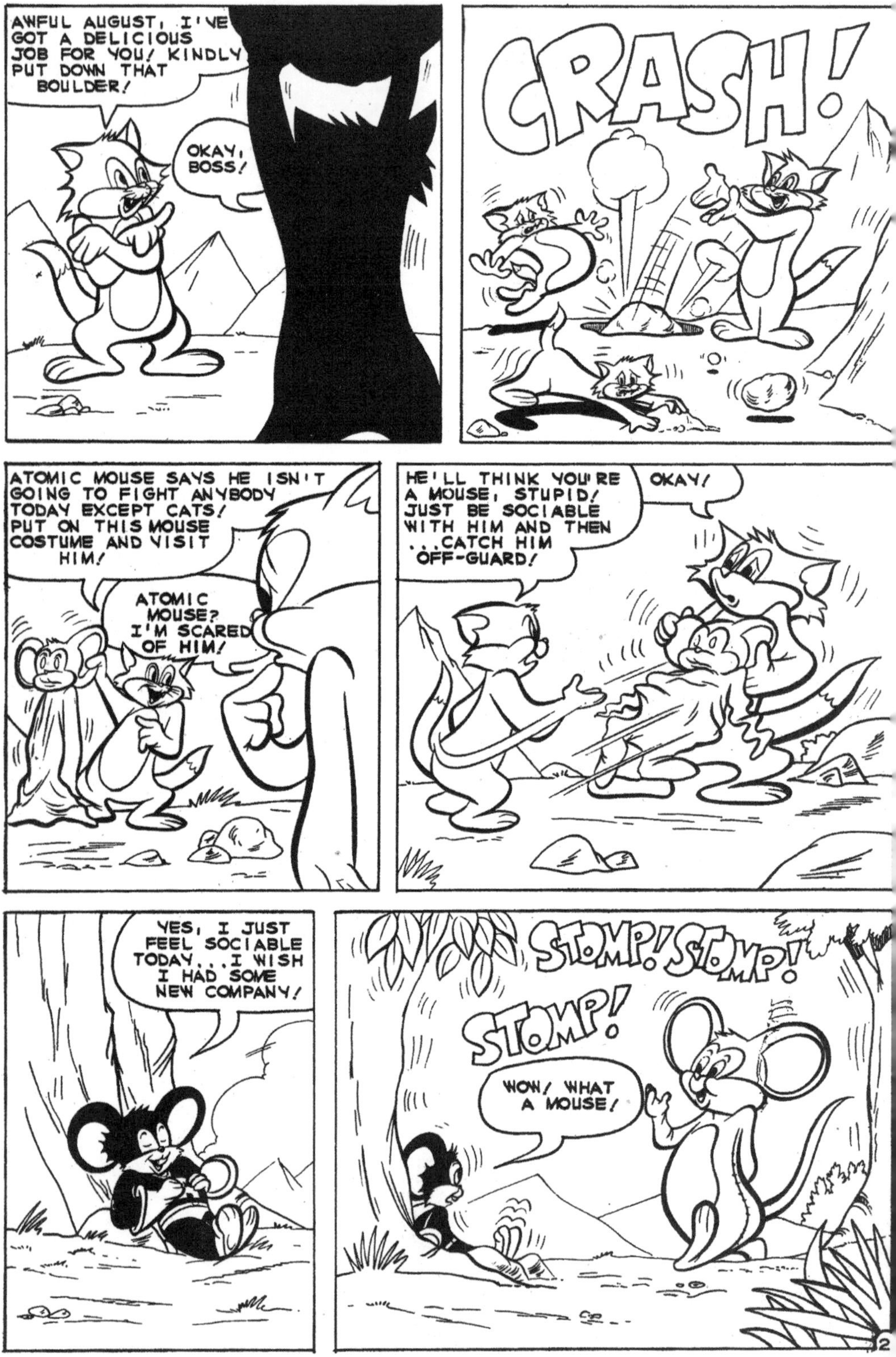
AWFUL AUGUST, I'VE GOT A DELICIOUS JOB FOR YOU! KINDLY PUT DOWN THAT BOULDER!
OKAY, BOSS!
CRASH!
ATOMIC MOUSE SAYS HE ISN'T GOING TO FIGHT ANYBODY TODAY EXCEPT CATS! PUT ON THIS MOUSE COSTUME AND VISIT HIM!
ATOMIC MOUSE? I'M SCARED OF HIM!
HE'LL THINK YOU'RE A MOUSE, STUPID! JUST BE SOCIABLE WITH HIM AND THEN ...CATCH HIM OFF-GUARD!
OKAY!
YES, I JUST FEEL SOCIABLE TODAY...I WISH I HAD SOME NEW COMPANY!
STOMP! STOMP!
STOMP!
WOW! WHAT A MOUSE!
2

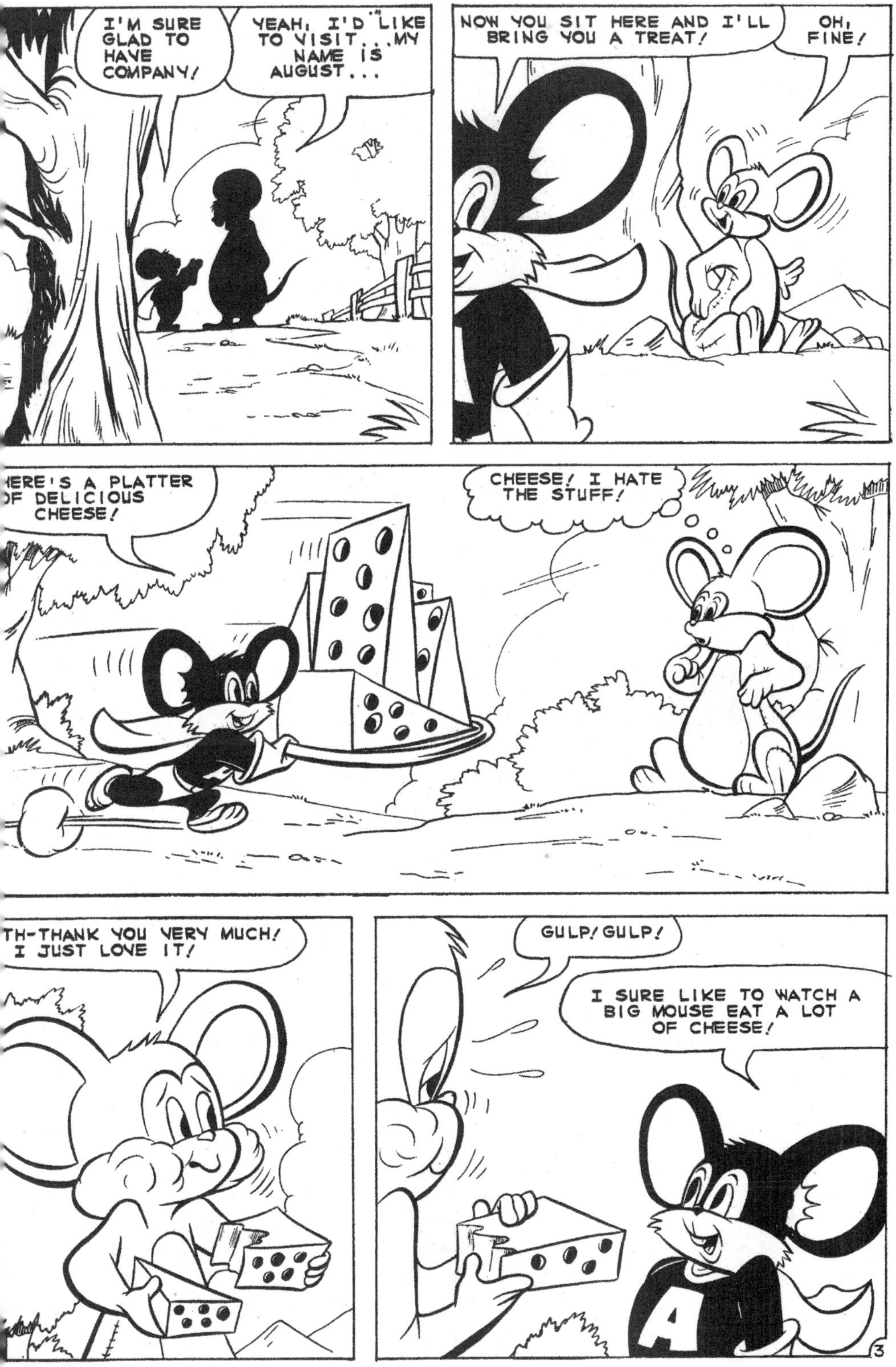

I'M SURE GLAD TO HAVE COMPANY!
YEAH, I'D LIKE TO VISIT...MY NAME IS AUGUST...
NOW YOU SIT HERE AND I'LL BRING YOU A TREAT!
OH, FINE!
HERE'S A PLATTER OF DELICIOUS CHEESE!
CHEESE! I HATE THE STUFF!
TH-THANK YOU VERY MUCH! I JUST LOVE IT!
GULP! GULP!
I SURE LIKE TO WATCH A BIG MOUSE EAT A LOT OF CHEESE!
A
3

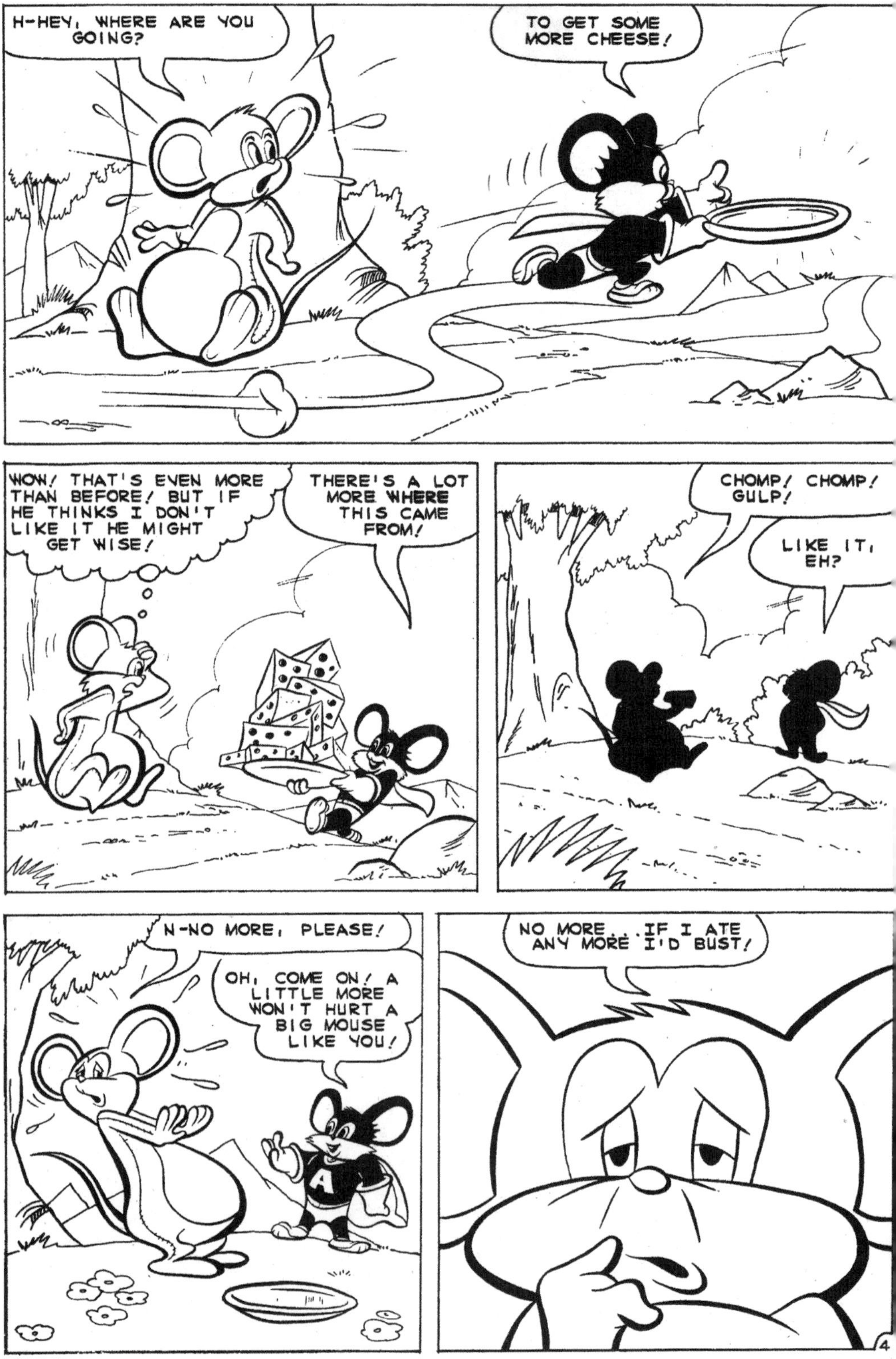
H-HEY, WHERE ARE YOU GOING?
TO GET SOME MORE CHEESE!
WOW! THAT'S EVEN MORE THAN BEFORE! BUT IF HE THINKS I DON'T LIKE IT HE MIGHT GET WISE!
THERE'S A LOT MORE WHERE THIS CAME FROM!
CHOMP! CHOMP! GULP!
LIKE IT, EH?
N-NO MORE, PLEASE!
OH, COME ON! A LITTLE MORE WON'T HURT A BIG MOUSE LIKE YOU!
NO MORE...IF I ATE ANY MORE I'D BUST!
4

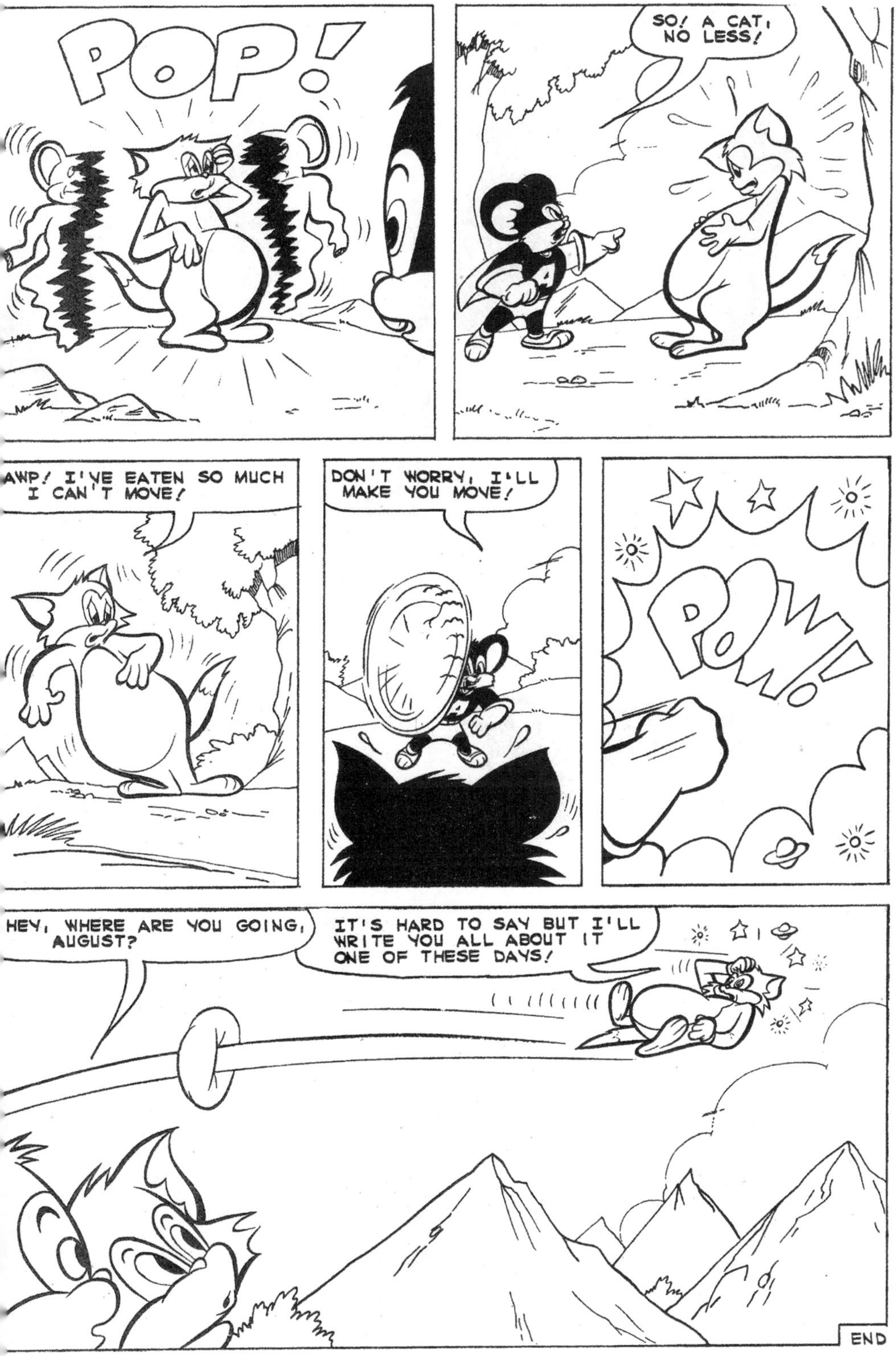
POP!
SO! A CAT, NO LESS!
AWP! I'VE EATEN SO MUCH I CAN'T MOVE!
DON'T WORRY, I'LL MAKE YOU MOVE!
POW!
HEY, WHERE ARE YOU GOING, AUGUST?
IT'S HARD TO SAY BUT I'LL WRITE YOU ALL ABOUT IT ONE OF THESE DAYS!
END

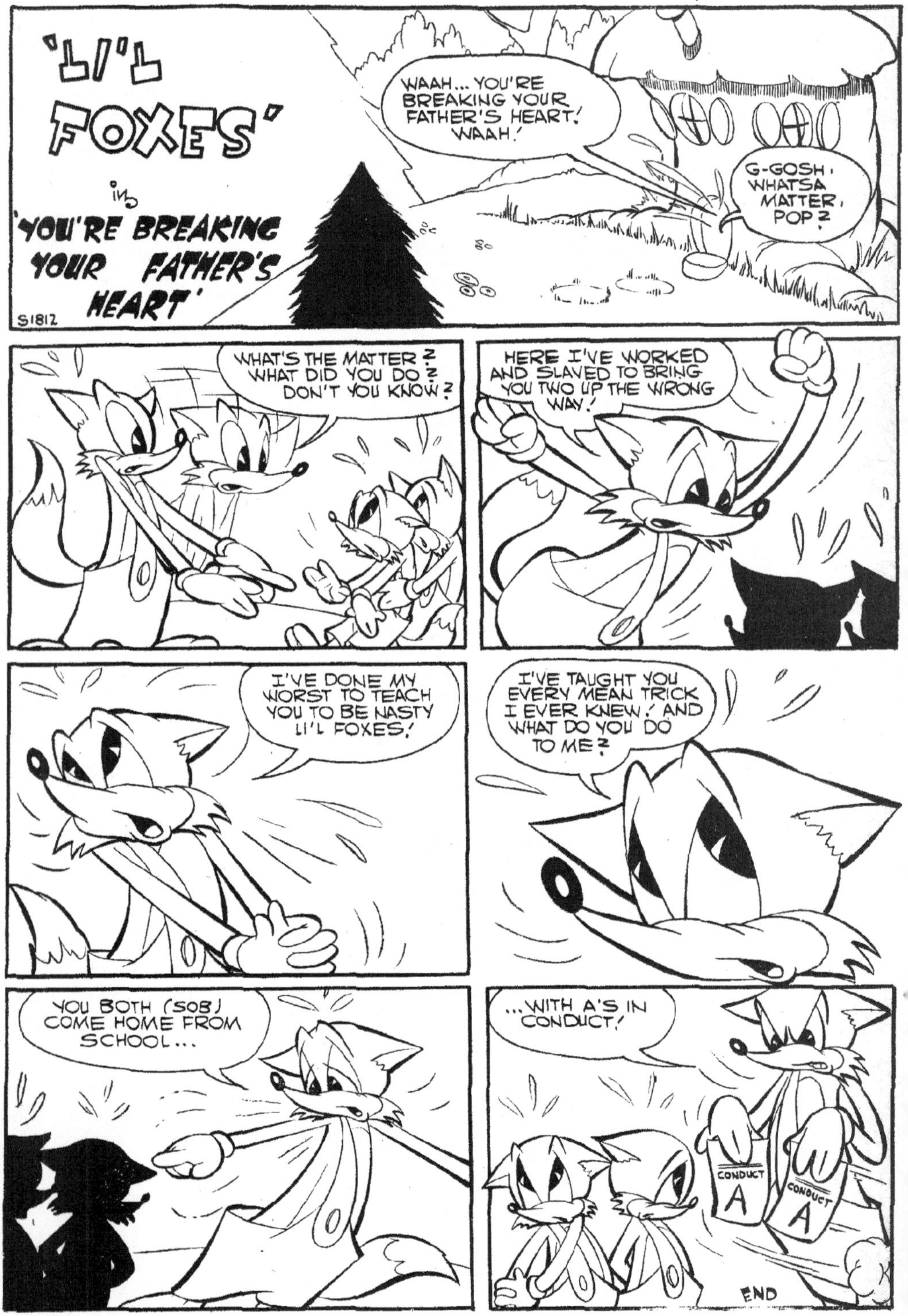
'LI'L FOXES'
in
'YOU'RE BREAKING YOUR FATHER'S HEART'
S1812
WAAH... YOU'RE BREAKING YOUR FATHER'S HEART! WAAH!
G-GOSH, WHATSA MATTER, POP?
WHAT'S THE MATTER? WHAT DID YOU DO? DON'T YOU KNOW?
HERE I'VE WORKED AND SLAVED TO BRING YOU TWO UP THE WRONG WAY!
I'VE DONE MY WORST TO TEACH YOU TO BE NASTY LI'L FOXES!
I'VE TAUGHT YOU EVERY MEAN TRICK I EVER KNEW! AND WHAT DO YOU DO TO ME?
YOU BOTH (SOB) COME HOME FROM SCHOOL...
...WITH A'S IN CONDUCT!
CONDUCT A
CONDUCT A
END

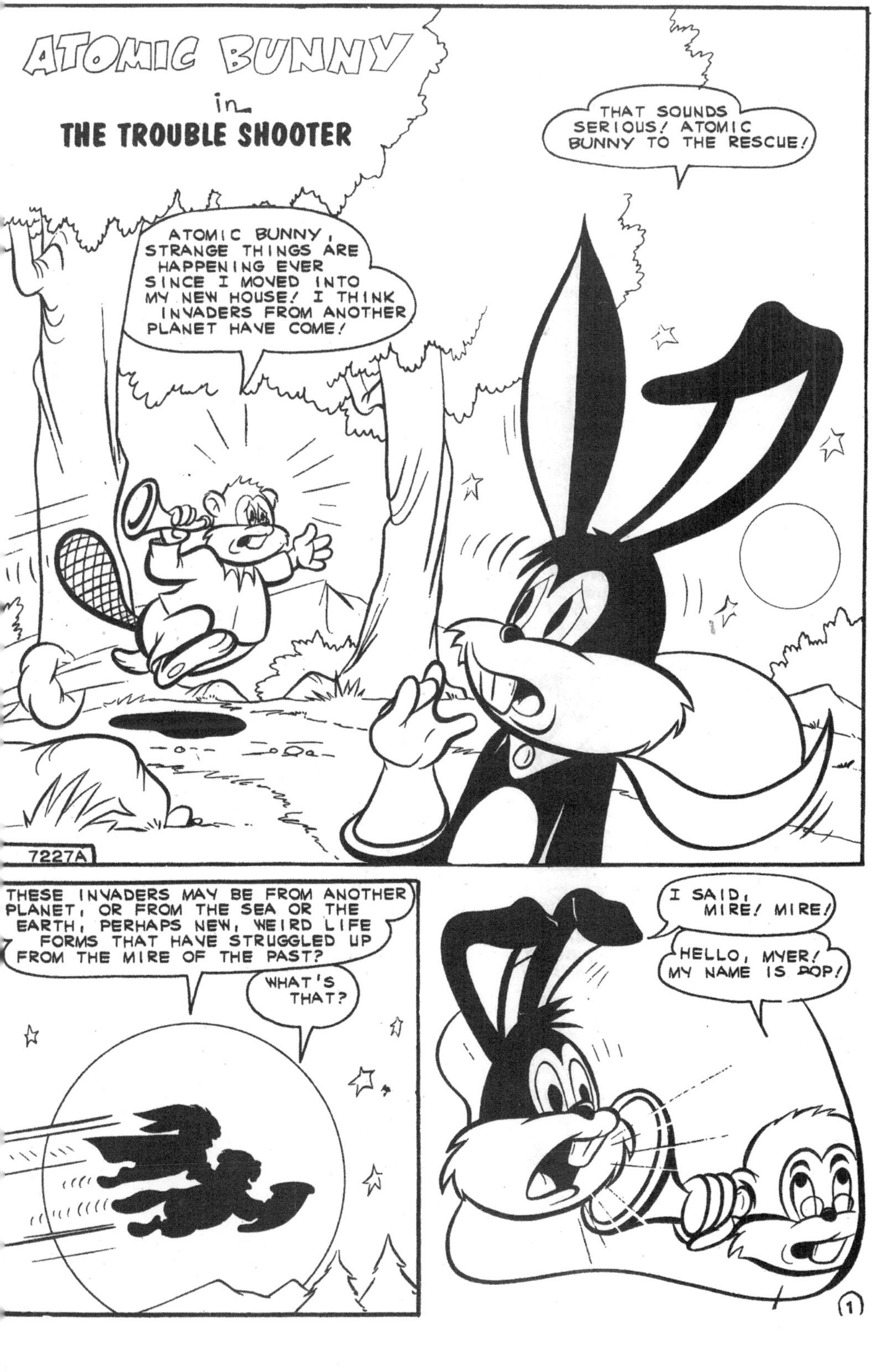
ATOMIC BUNNY
in
THE TROUBLE SHOOTER
ATOMIC BUNNY, STRANGE THINGS ARE HAPPENING EVER SINCE I MOVED INTO MY NEW HOUSE! I THINK INVADERS FROM ANOTHER PLANET HAVE COME!
THAT SOUNDS SERIOUS! ATOMIC BUNNY TO THE RESCUE!
7227A
THESE INVADERS MAY BE FROM ANOTHER PLANET, OR FROM THE SEA OR THE EARTH, PERHAPS NEW, WEIRD LIFE FORMS THAT HAVE STRUGGLED UP FROM THE MIRE OF THE PAST?
WHAT'S THAT?
I SAID, MIRE! MIRE!
HELLO, MYER! MY NAME IS POP!

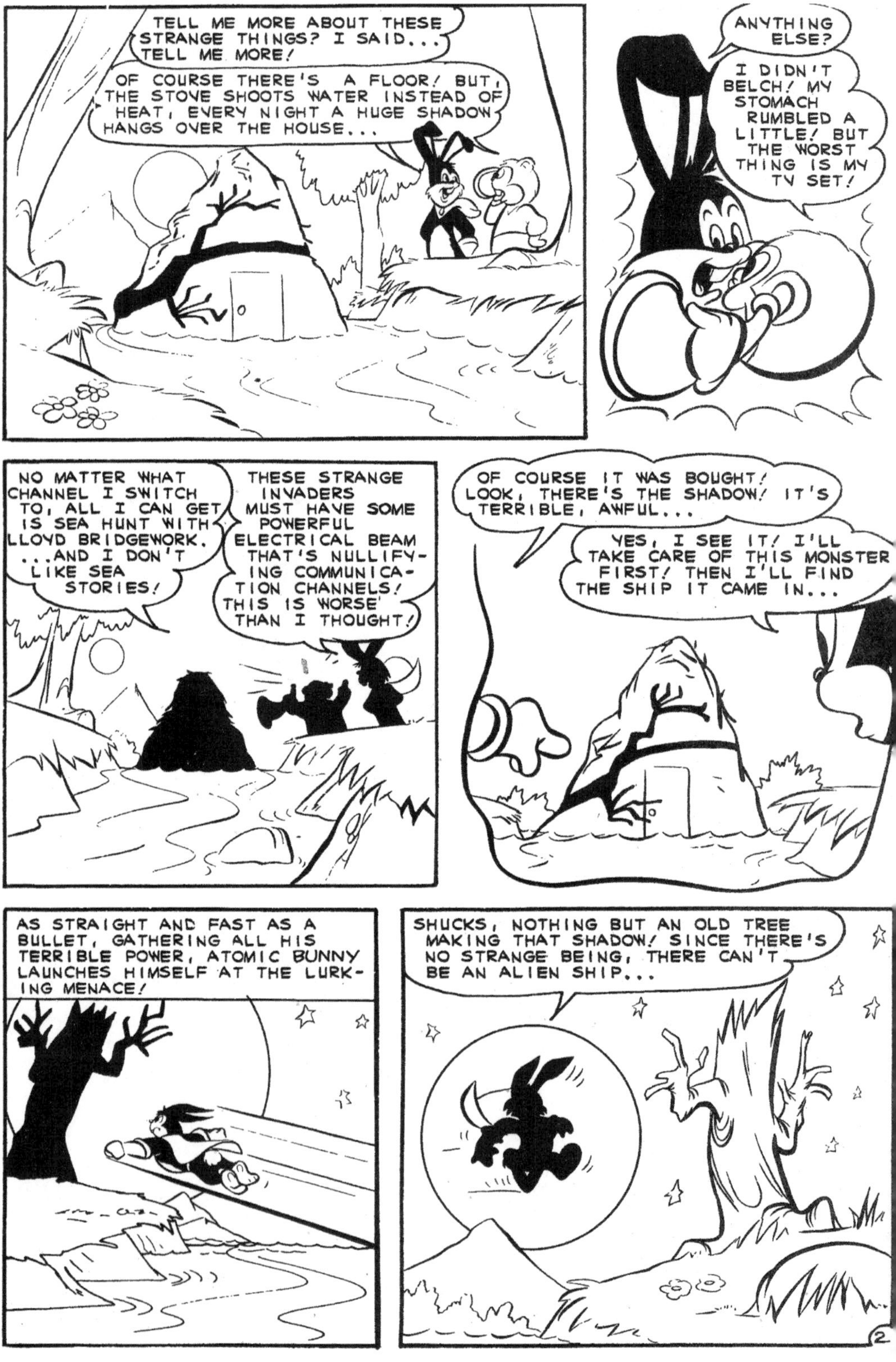
TELL ME MORE ABOUT THESE STRANGE THINGS? I SAID... TELL ME MORE!
OF COURSE THERE'S A FLOOR! BUT, THE STOVE SHOOTS WATER INSTEAD OF HEAT, EVERY NIGHT A HUGE SHADOW HANGS OVER THE HOUSE...
ANYTHING ELSE?
I DIDN'T BELCH! MY STOMACH RUMBLED A LITTLE! BUT THE WORST THING IS MY TV SET!
NO MATTER WHAT CHANNEL I SWITCH TO, ALL I CAN GET IS SEA HUNT WITH LLOYD BRIDGEWORK. ...AND I DON'T LIKE SEA STORIES!
THESE STRANGE INVADERS MUST HAVE SOME POWERFUL ELECTRICAL BEAM THAT'S NULLIFYING COMMUNICATION CHANNELS! THIS IS WORSE THAN I THOUGHT!
OF COURSE IT WAS BOUGHT! LOOK, THERE'S THE SHADOW! IT'S TERRIBLE, AWFUL...
YES, I SEE IT! I'LL TAKE CARE OF THIS MONSTER FIRST! THEN I'LL FIND THE SHIP IT CAME IN...
AS STRAIGHT AND FAST AS A BULLET, GATHERING ALL HIS TERRIBLE POWER, ATOMIC BUNNY LAUNCHES HIMSELF AT THE LURKING MENACE!
SHUCKS, NOTHING BUT AN OLD TREE MAKING THAT SHADOW! SINCE THERE'S NO STRANGE BEING, THERE CAN'T BE AN ALIEN SHIP...
2

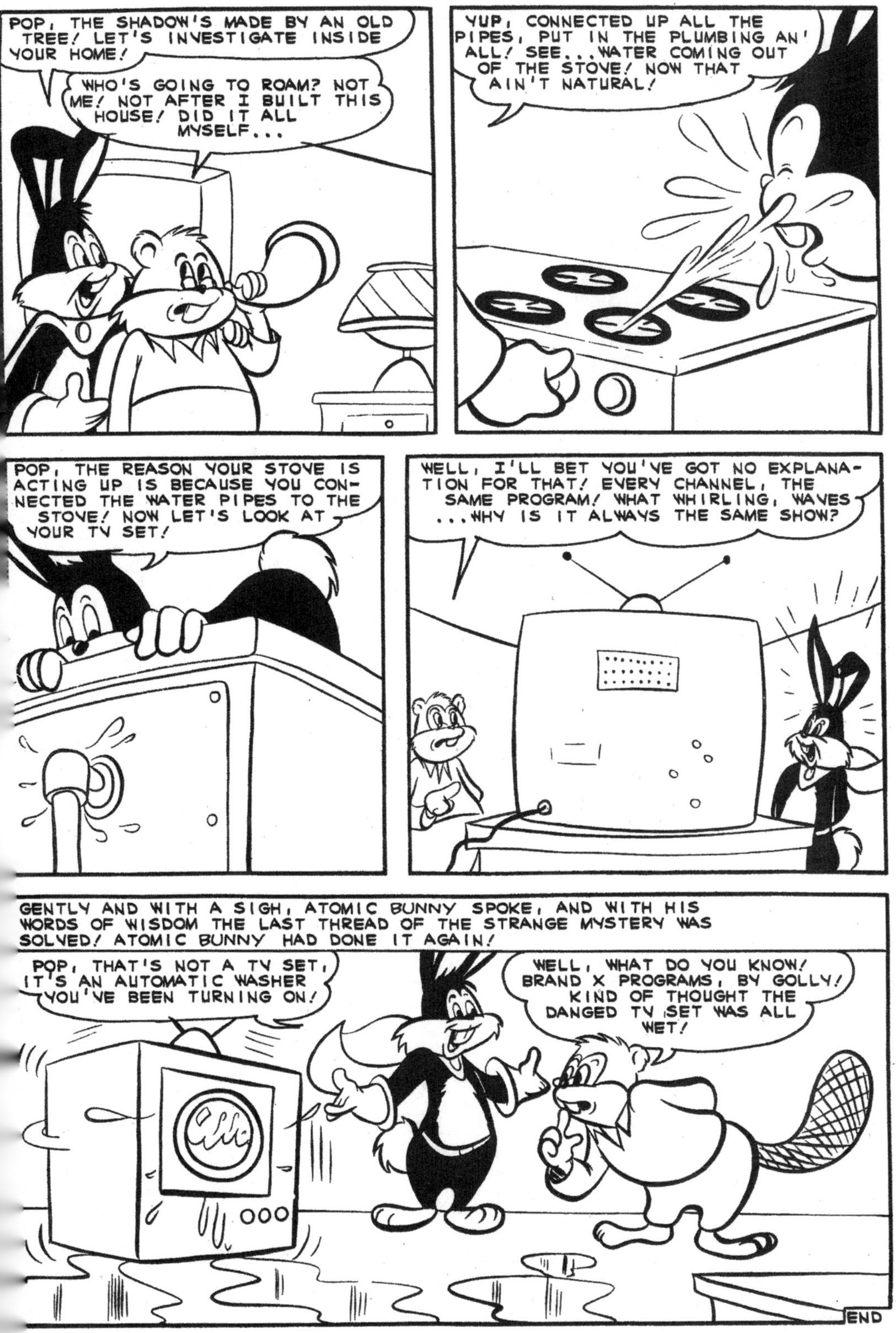
POP, THE SHADOW'S MADE BY AN OLD TREE! LET'S INVESTIGATE INSIDE YOUR HOME!
WHO'S GOING TO ROAM? NOT ME! NOT AFTER I BUILT THIS HOUSE! DID IT ALL MYSELF...
YUP, CONNECTED UP ALL THE PIPES, PUT IN THE PLUMBING AN' ALL! SEE...WATER COMING OUT OF THE STOVE! NOW THAT AIN'T NATURAL!
POP, THE REASON YOUR STOVE IS ACTING UP IS BECAUSE YOU CONNECTED THE WATER PIPES TO THE STOVE! NOW LET'S LOOK AT YOUR TV SET!
WELL, I'LL BET YOU'VE GOT NO EXPLANATION FOR THAT! EVERY CHANNEL, THE SAME PROGRAM! WHAT WHIRLING, WAVES ...WHY IS IT ALWAYS THE SAME SHOW?
GENTLY AND WITH A SIGH, ATOMIC BUNNY SPOKE, AND WITH HIS WORDS OF WISDOM THE LAST THREAD OF THE STRANGE MYSTERY WAS SOLVED! ATOMIC BUNNY HAD DONE IT AGAIN!
POP, THAT'S NOT A TV SET, IT'S AN AUTOMATIC WASHER YOU'VE BEEN TURNING ON!
WELL, WHAT DO YOU KNOW! BRAND X PROGRAMS, BY GOLLY! KIND OF THOUGHT THE DANGED TV SET WAS ALL WET!
END

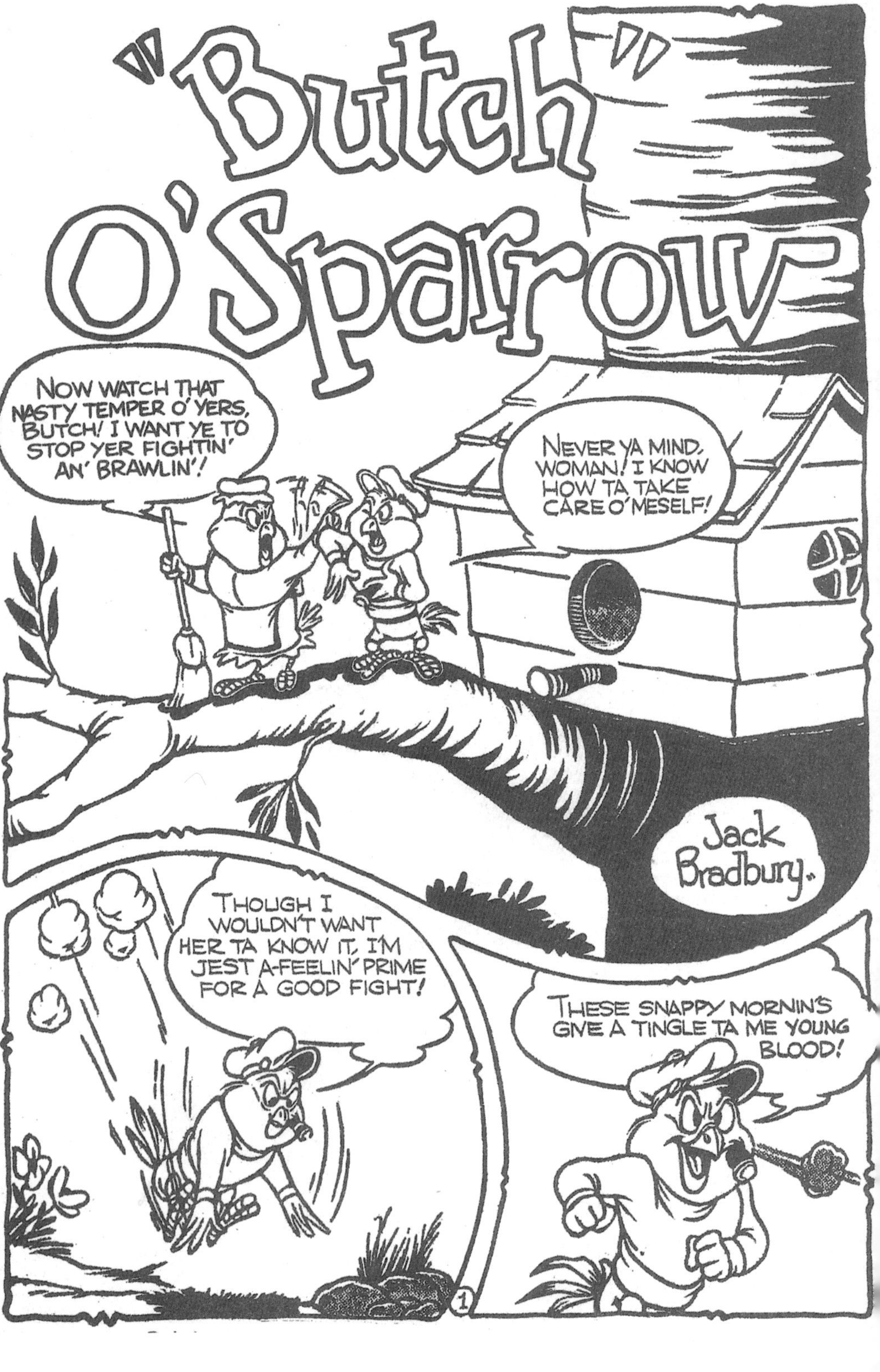
"Butch" O'Sparrow
NOW WATCH THAT NASTY TEMPER O'YERS, BUTCH! I WANT YE TO STOP YER FIGHTIN' AN' BRAWLIN'!
NEVER YA MIND, WOMAN! I KNOW HOW TA TAKE CARE O'MESELF!
Jack Bradbury.
THOUGH I WOULDN'T WANT HER TA KNOW IT, I'M JEST A-FEELIN' PRIME FOR A GOOD FIGHT!
THESE SNAPPY MORNIN'S GIVE A TINGLE TA ME YOUNG BLOOD!
1

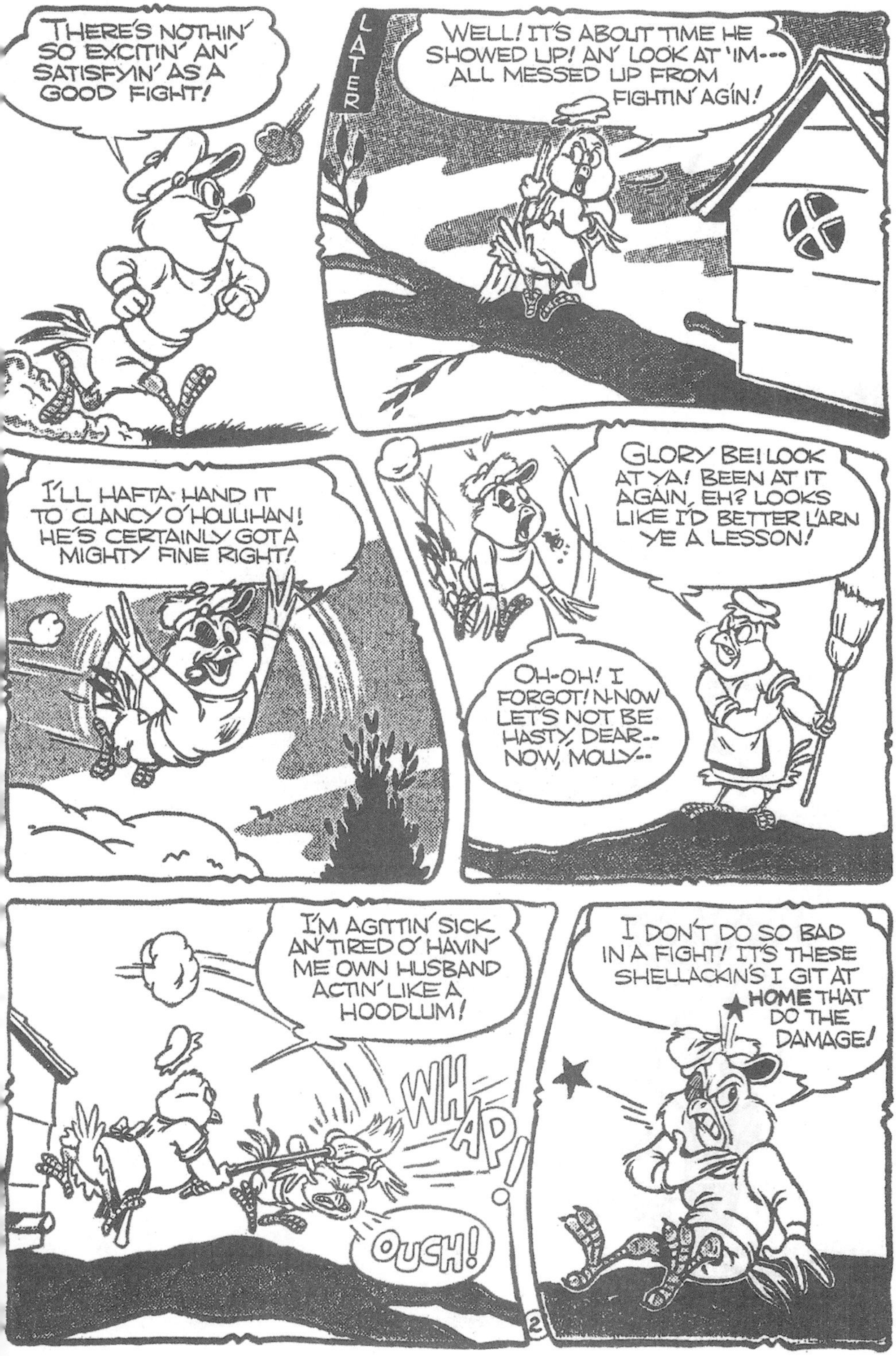
THERE'S NOTHIN' SO EXCITIN' AN' SATISFYIN' AS A GOOD FIGHT!
LATER
WELL! IT'S ABOUT TIME HE SHOWED UP! AN' LOOK AT 'IM--- ALL MESSED UP FROM FIGHTIN' AGIN!
I'LL HAFTA HAND IT TO CLANCY O'HOULIHAN! HE'S CERTAINLY GOT A MIGHTY FINE RIGHT!
GLORY BE! LOOK AT YA! BEEN AT IT AGAIN, EH? LOOKS LIKE I'D BETTER L'ARN YE A LESSON!
OH-OH! I FORGOT! N-NOW LET'S NOT BE HASTY, DEAR-- NOW, MOLLY--
I'M AGITTIN' SICK AN' TIRED O' HAVIN' ME OWN HUSBAND ACTIN' LIKE A HOODLUM!
WHAP!
OUCH!
I DON'T DO SO BAD IN A FIGHT! IT'S THESE SHELLACKIN'S I GIT AT HOME THAT DO THE DAMAGE!
2

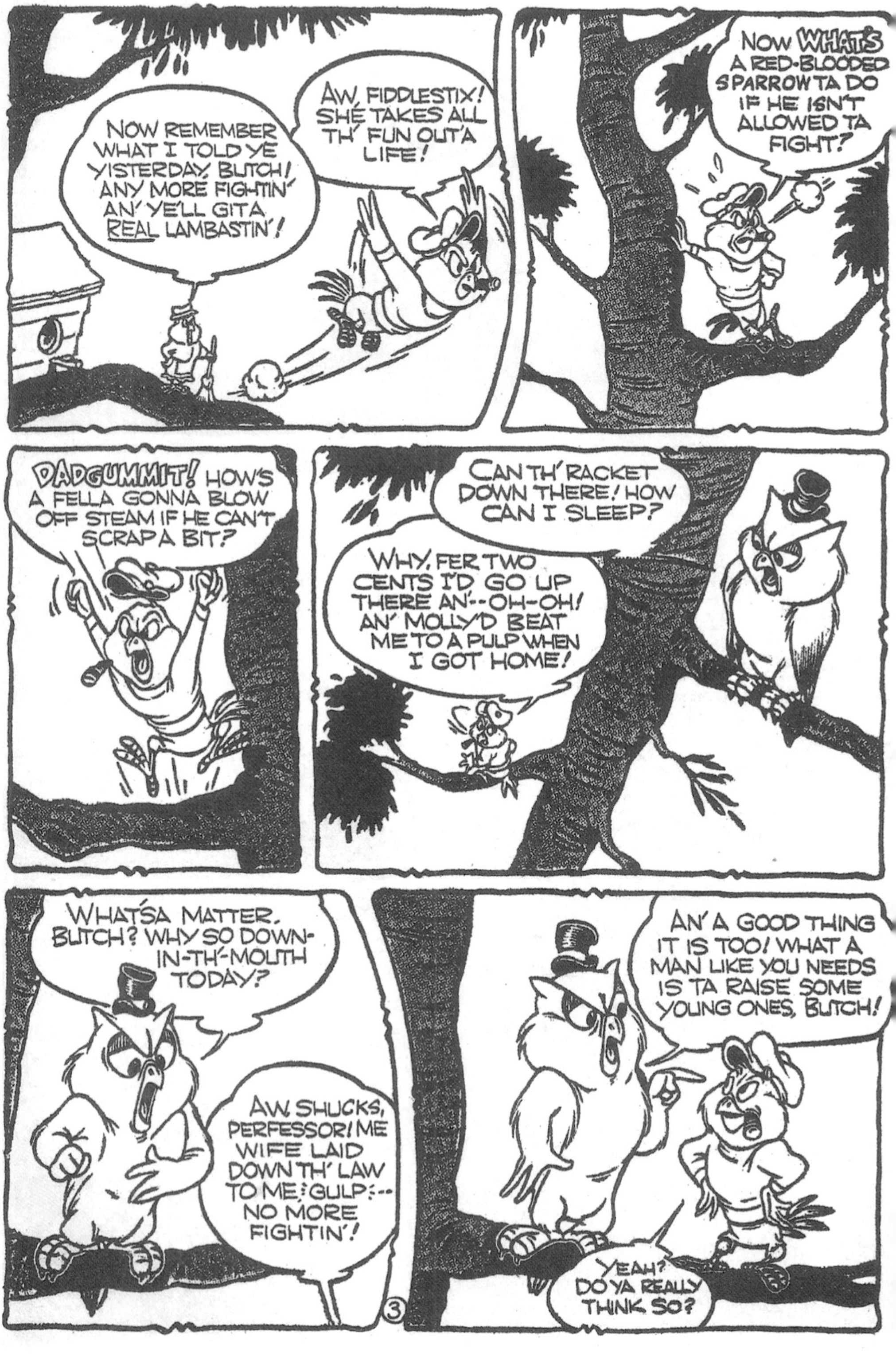
NOW REMEMBER WHAT I TOLD YE YISTERDAY, BUTCH! ANY MORE FIGHTIN' AN' YE'LL GIT A REAL LAMBASTIN'!
AW, FIDDLESTIX! SHE TAKES ALL TH' FUN OUT'A LIFE!
NOW WHAT'S A RED-BLOODED SPARROW TA DO IF HE ISN'T ALLOWED TA FIGHT?
DADGUMMIT! HOW'S A FELLA GONNA BLOW OFF STEAM IF HE CAN'T SCRAP A BIT?
CAN TH' RACKET DOWN THERE! HOW CAN I SLEEP?
WHY, FER TWO CENTS I'D GO UP THERE AN'--OH-OH! AN' MOLLY'D BEAT ME TO A PULP WHEN I GOT HOME!
WHAT'SA MATTER, BUTCH? WHY SO DOWN-IN-TH'-MOUTH TODAY?
AW, SHUCKS, PERFESSOR! ME WIFE LAID DOWN TH' LAW TO ME: GULP:-- NO MORE FIGHTIN'!
AN' A GOOD THING IT IS TOO! WHAT A MAN LIKE YOU NEEDS IS TA RAISE SOME YOUNG ONES, BUTCH!
YEAH? DO YA REALLY THINK SO?
3

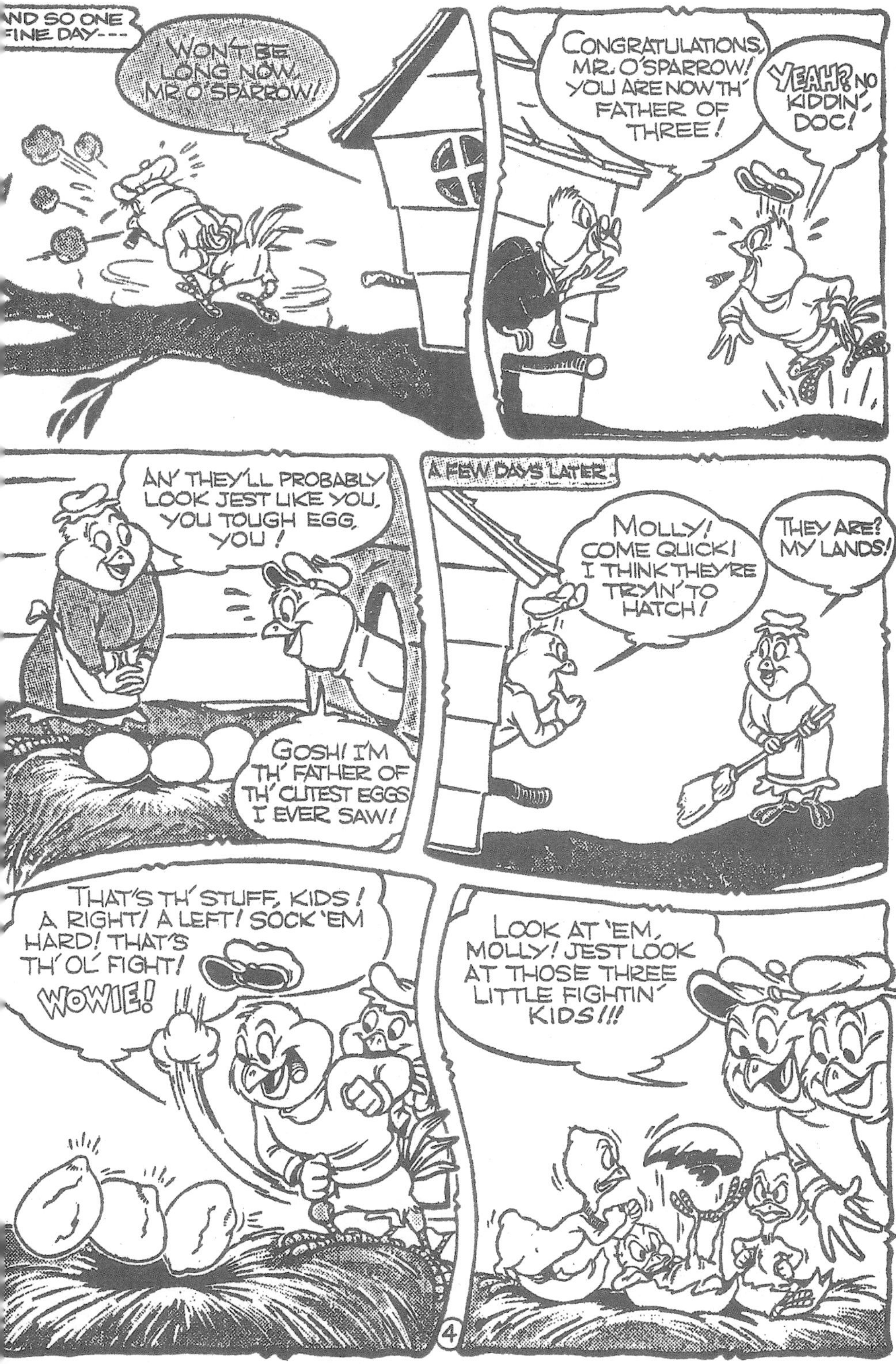

ND SO ONE FINE DAY---
WON'T BE LONG NOW, MR. O'SPARROW!
CONGRATULATIONS, MR. O'SPARROW! YOU ARE NOW TH' FATHER OF THREE!
YEAH? NO KIDDIN', DOC!
AN' THEY'LL PROBABLY LOOK JEST LIKE YOU, YOU TOUGH EGG, YOU!
GOSH! I'M TH' FATHER OF TH' CUTEST EGGS I EVER SAW!
A FEW DAYS LATER
MOLLY! COME QUICK! I THINK THEY'RE TRYIN' TO HATCH!
THEY ARE? MY LANDS!
THAT'S TH' STUFF, KIDS! A RIGHT! A LEFT! SOCK 'EM HARD! THAT'S TH' OL' FIGHT!
WOWIE!
LOOK AT 'EM, MOLLY! JEST LOOK AT THOSE THREE LITTLE FIGHTIN' KIDS!!!
4

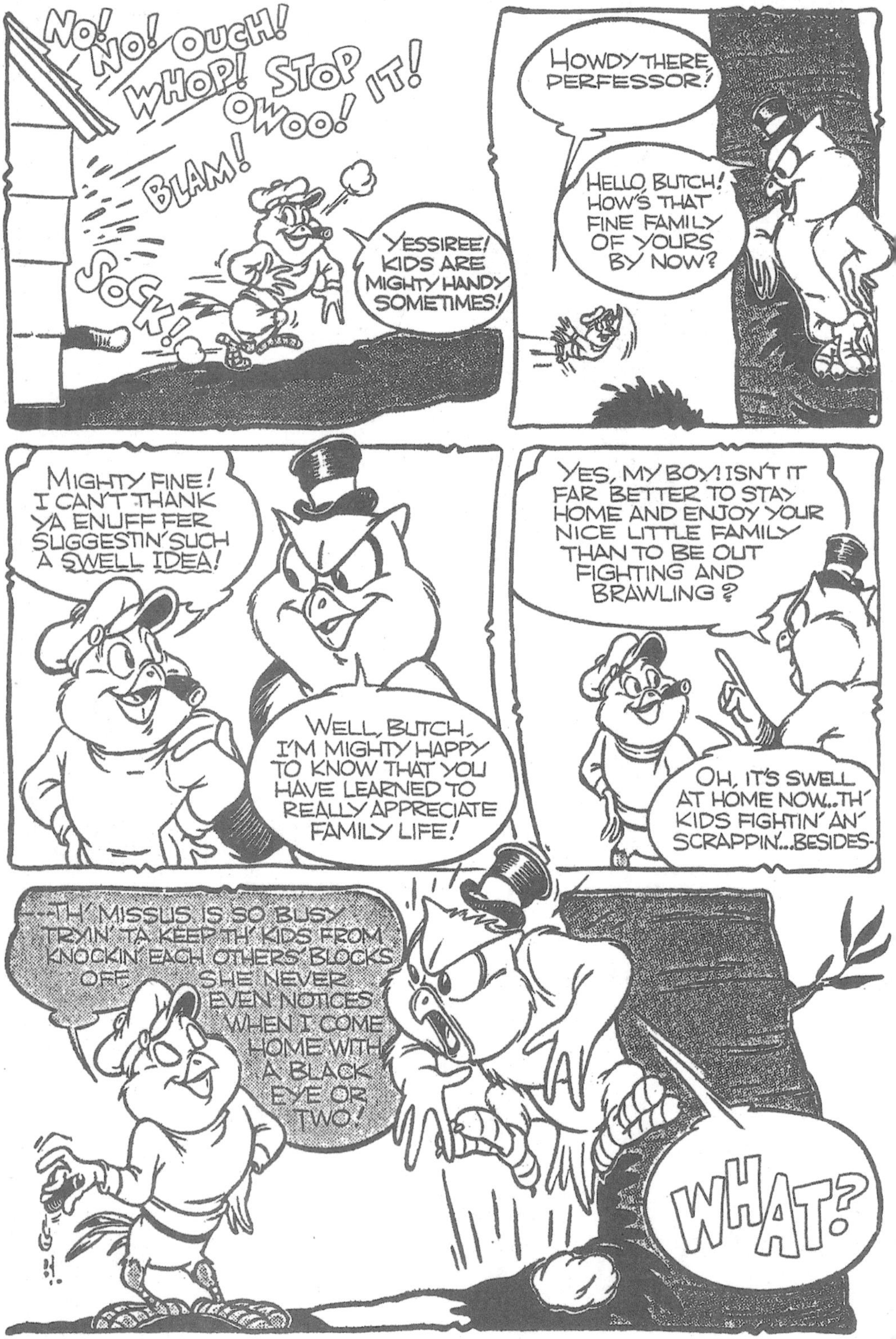
NO! NO! OUCH!
WHOP! STOP IT!
OWOO!
BLAM!
SOCK!
YESSIREE! KIDS ARE MIGHTY HANDY SOMETIMES!
HOWDY THERE, PERFESSOR!
HELLO, BUTCH! HOW'S THAT FINE FAMILY OF YOURS BY NOW?
MIGHTY FINE! I CAN'T THANK YA ENUFF FER SUGGESTIN' SUCH A SWELL IDEA!
WELL, BUTCH, I'M MIGHTY HAPPY TO KNOW THAT YOU HAVE LEARNED TO REALLY APPRECIATE FAMILY LIFE!
YES, MY BOY! ISN'T IT FAR BETTER TO STAY HOME AND ENJOY YOUR NICE LITTLE FAMILY THAN TO BE OUT FIGHTING AND BRAWLING?
OH, IT'S SWELL AT HOME NOW..TH' KIDS FIGHTIN' AN' SCRAPPIN'...BESIDES-
--TH' MISSUS IS SO BUSY TRYIN' TA KEEP TH' KIDS FROM KNOCKIN' EACH OTHERS' BLOCKS OFF, SHE NEVER EVEN NOTICES WHEN I COME HOME WITH A BLACK EYE OR TWO!
WHAT?

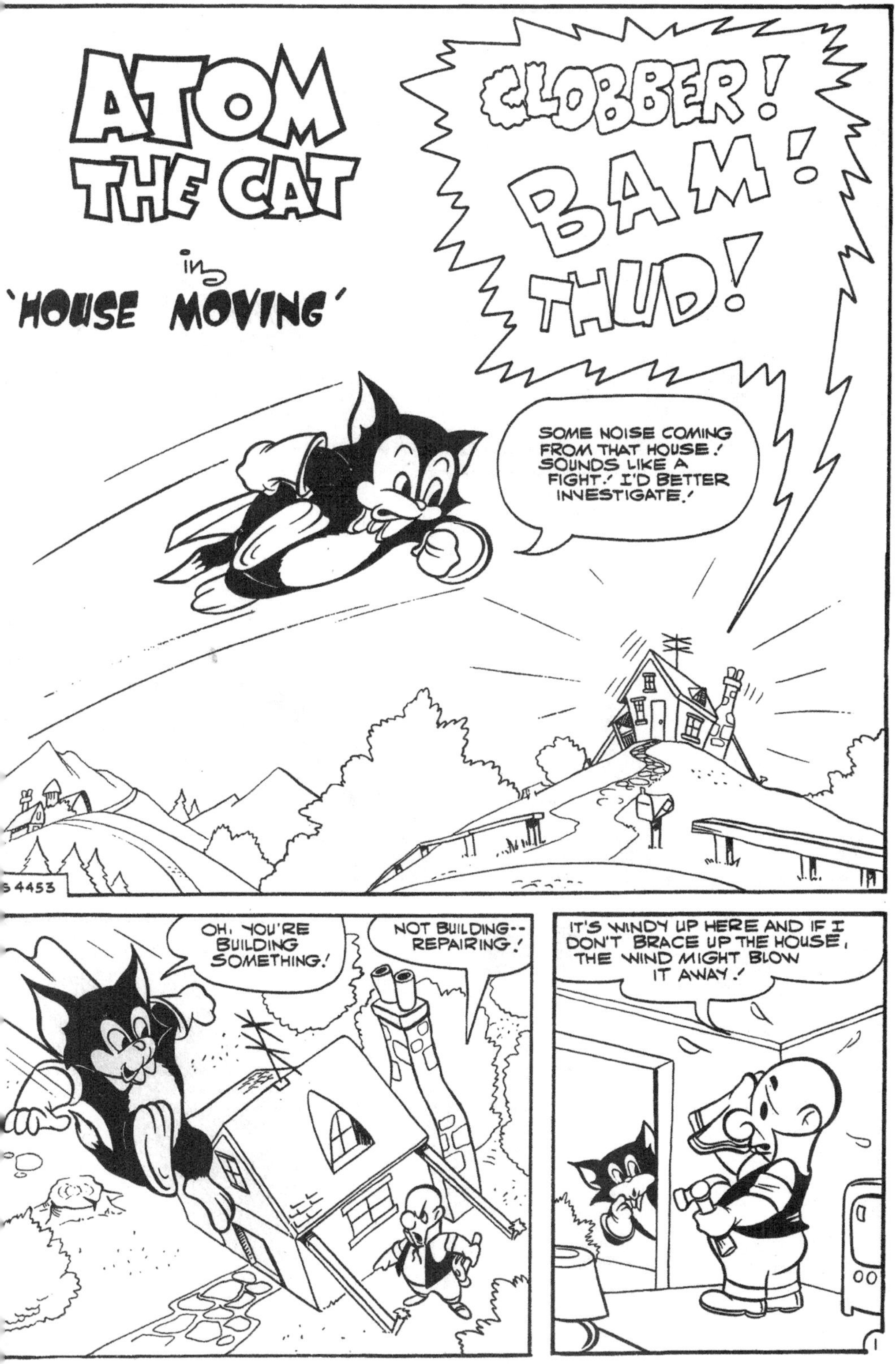
ATOM THE CAT
in 'HOUSE MOVING'
CLOBBER! BAM! THUD!
SOME NOISE COMING FROM THAT HOUSE! SOUNDS LIKE A FIGHT! I'D BETTER INVESTIGATE!
S 4453
OH, YOU'RE BUILDING SOMETHING!
NOT BUILDING--REPAIRING!
IT'S WINDY UP HERE AND IF I DON'T BRACE UP THE HOUSE, THE WIND MIGHT BLOW IT AWAY!
1

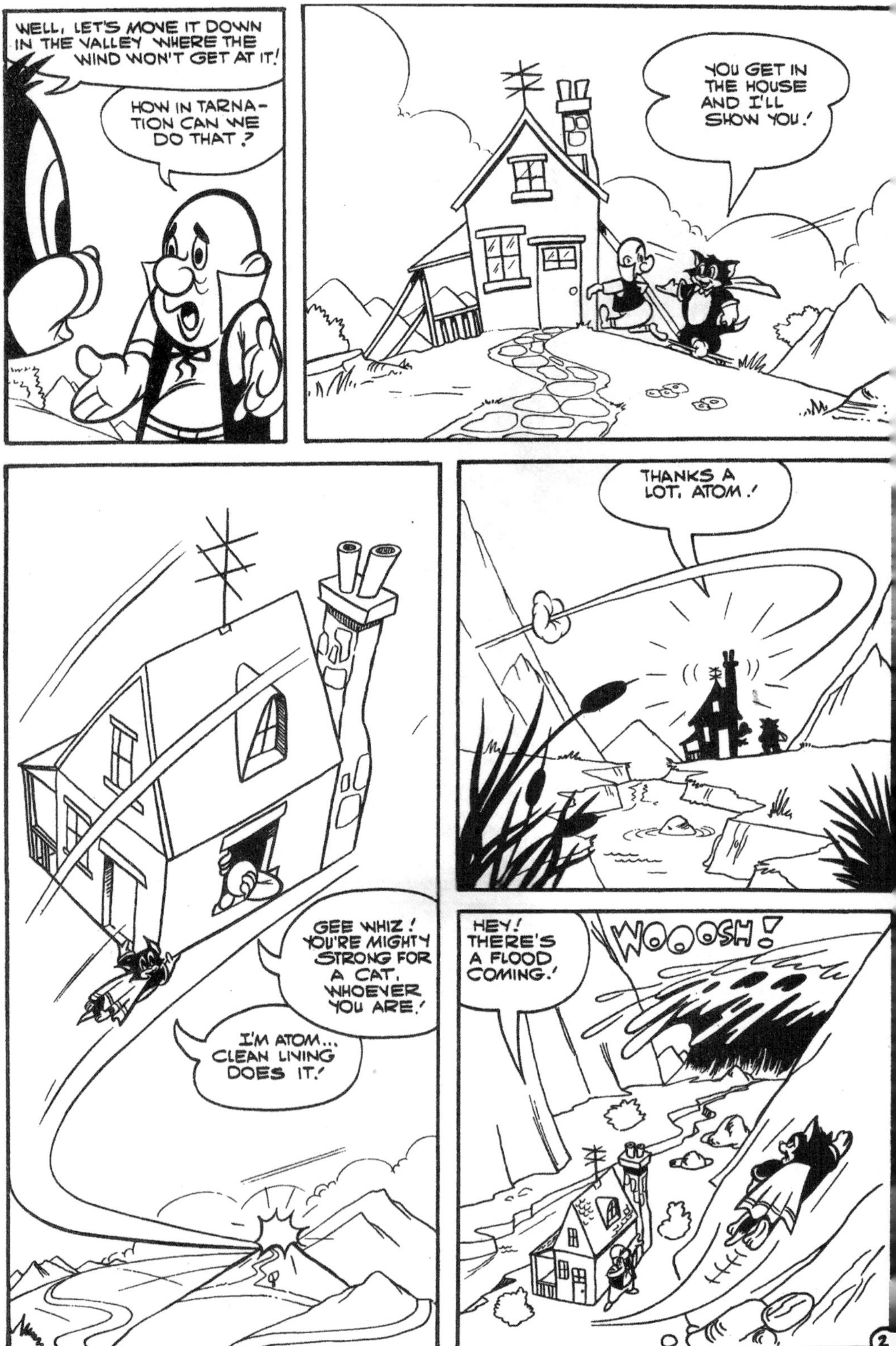

WELL, LET'S MOVE IT DOWN IN THE VALLEY WHERE THE WIND WON'T GET AT IT!
HOW IN TARNATION CAN WE DO THAT?
YOU GET IN THE HOUSE AND I'LL SHOW YOU!
GEE WHIZ! YOU'RE MIGHTY STRONG FOR A CAT, WHOEVER YOU ARE!
I'M ATOM... CLEAN LIVING DOES IT!
THANKS A LOT, ATOM!
HEY! THERE'S A FLOOD COMING!
WOOOSH!

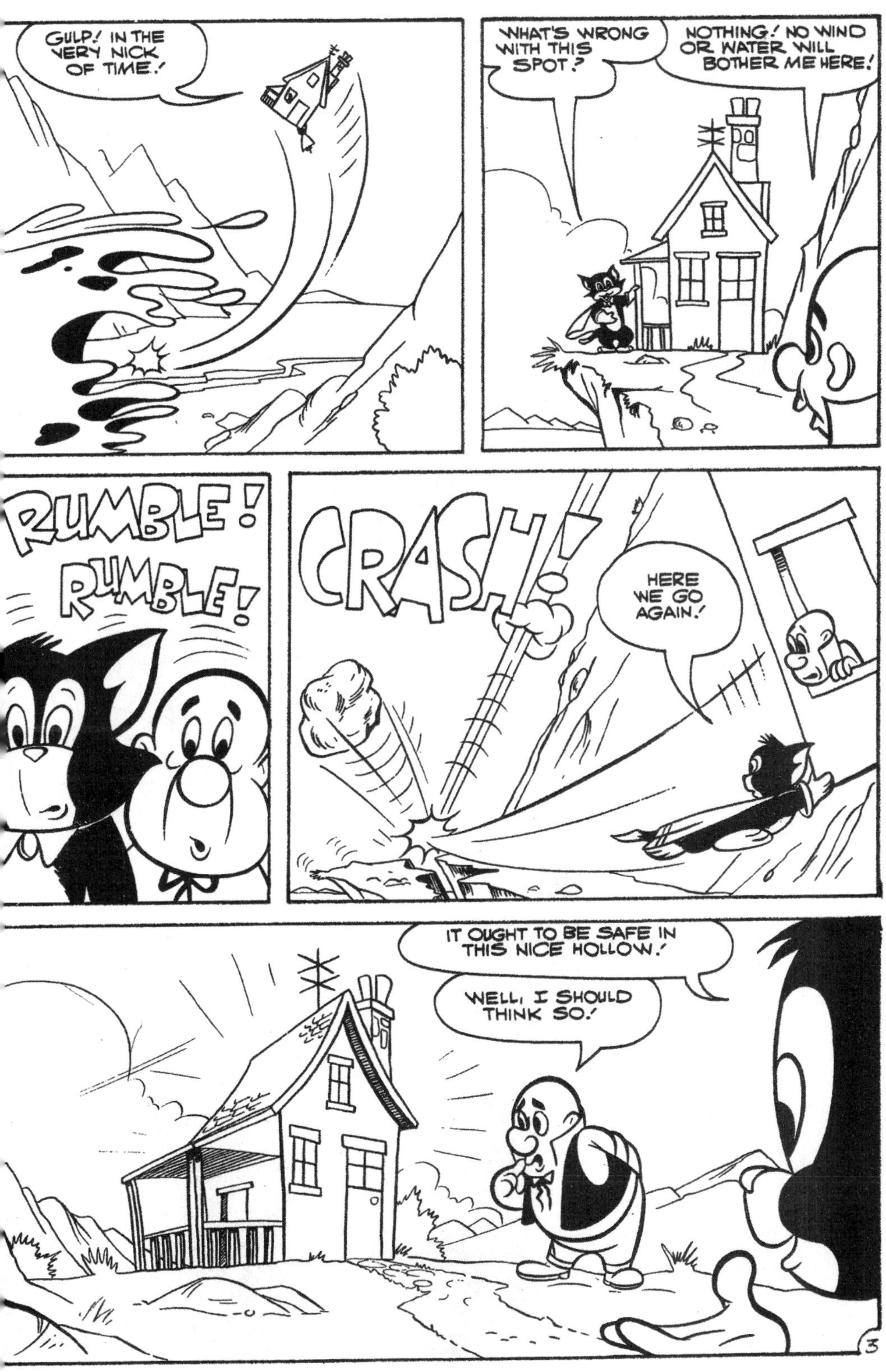
GULP! IN THE VERY NICK OF TIME!
WHAT'S WRONG WITH THIS SPOT?
NOTHING! NO WIND OR WATER WILL BOTHER ME HERE!
RUMBLE! RUMBLE!
CRASH!
HERE WE GO AGAIN!
IT OUGHT TO BE SAFE IN THIS NICE HOLLOW!
WELL, I SHOULD THINK SO!
3

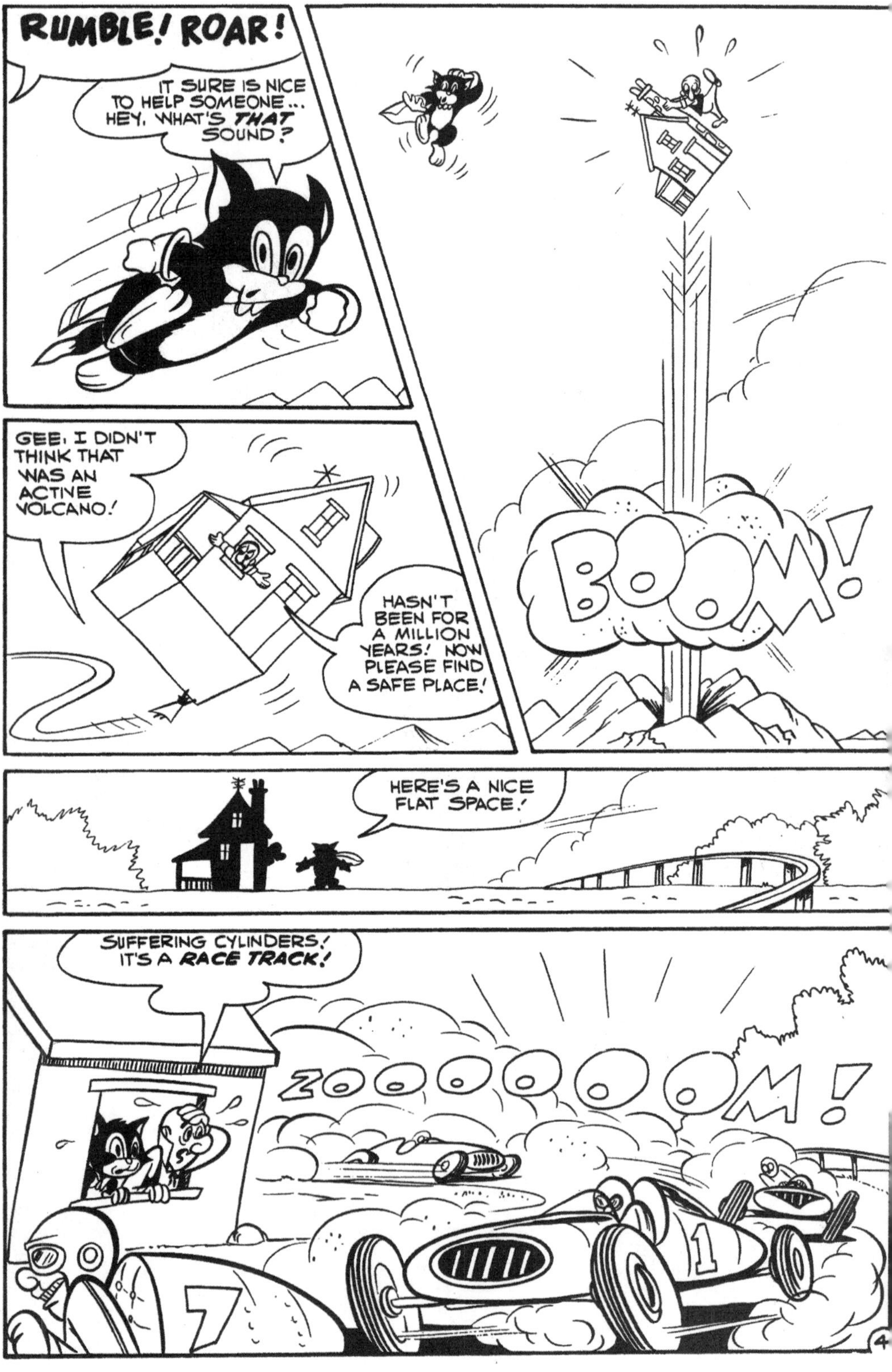
RUMBLE! ROAR!
IT SURE IS NICE TO HELP SOMEONE... HEY, WHAT'S *THAT* SOUND?
BOOM!
GEE, I DIDN'T THINK THAT WAS AN ACTIVE VOLCANO!
HASN'T BEEN FOR A MILLION YEARS! NOW PLEASE FIND A SAFE PLACE!
HERE'S A NICE FLAT SPACE!
SUFFERING CYLINDERS! IT'S A *RACE TRACK!*
ZOOOOOOOM!
1
7

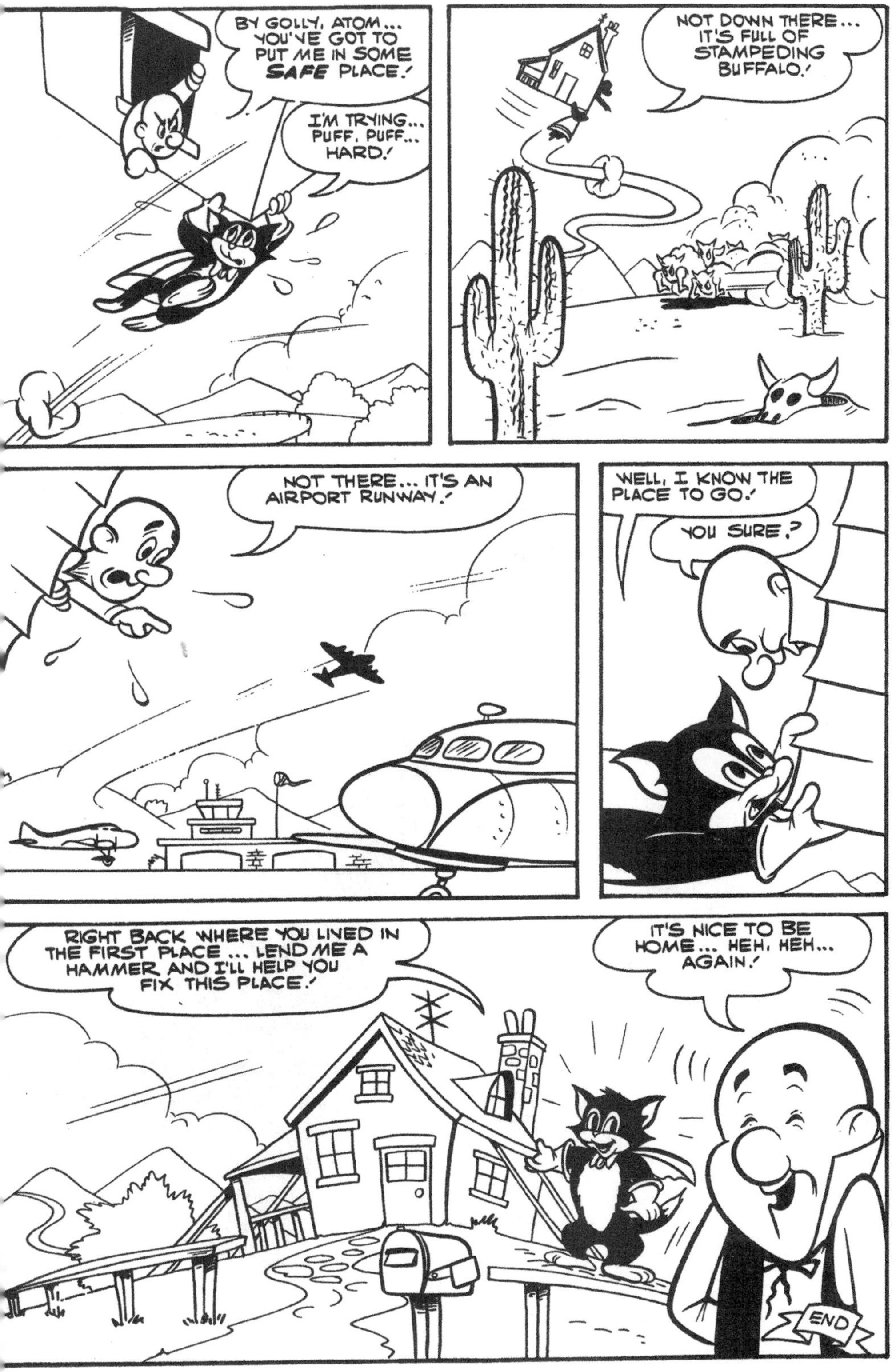
BY GOLLY, ATOM... YOU'VE GOT TO PUT ME IN SOME SAFE PLACE!
I'M TRYING... PUFF, PUFF... HARD!
NOT DOWN THERE... IT'S FULL OF STAMPEDING BUFFALO!
NOT THERE... IT'S AN AIRPORT RUNWAY!
WELL, I KNOW THE PLACE TO GO!
YOU SURE?
RIGHT BACK WHERE YOU LIVED IN THE FIRST PLACE ... LEND ME A HAMMER AND I'LL HELP YOU FIX THIS PLACE!
IT'S NICE TO BE HOME... HEH, HEH... AGAIN!
END

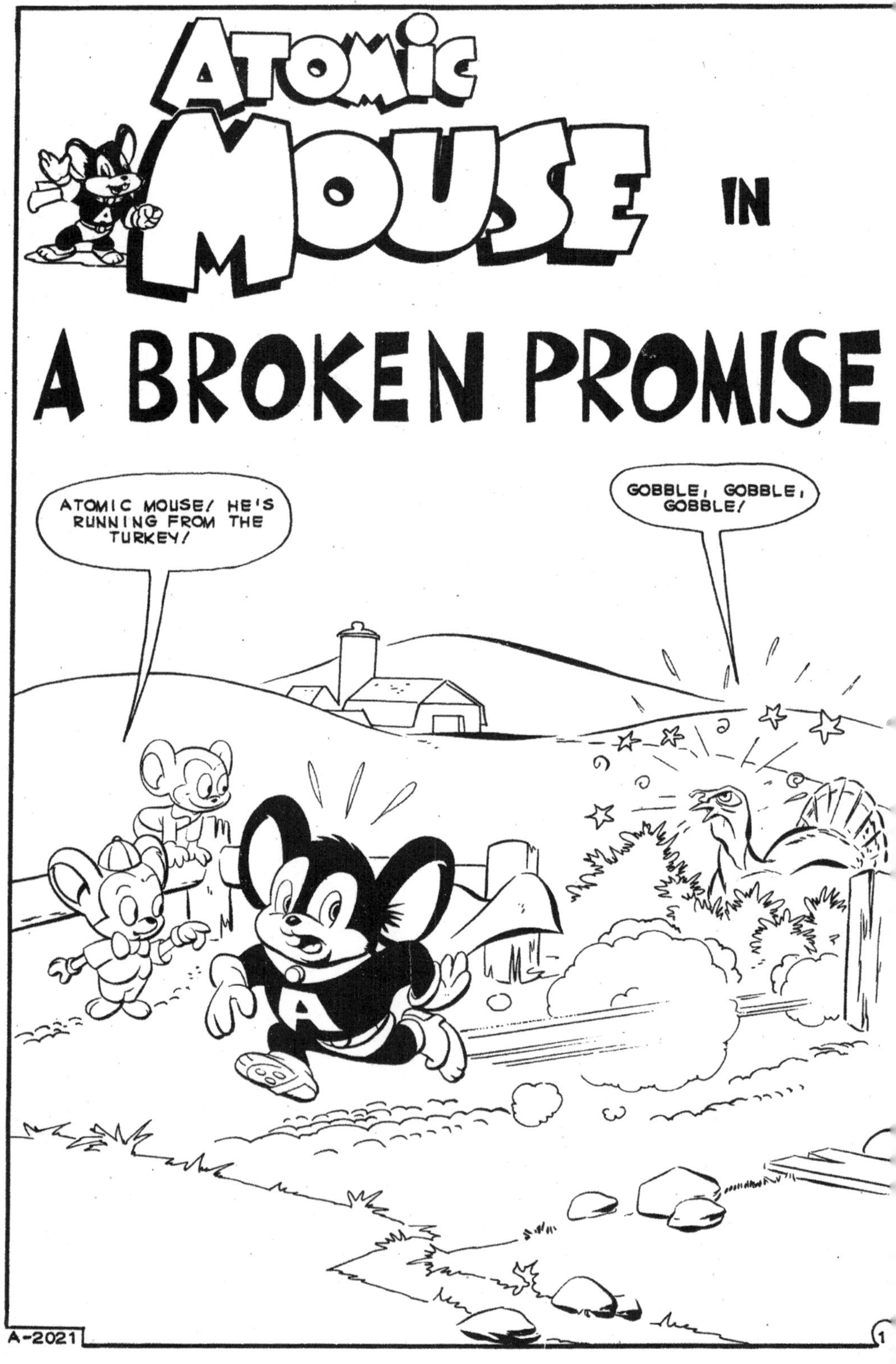
ATOMIC MOUSE IN
A BROKEN PROMISE
ATOMIC MOUSE! HE'S RUNNING FROM THE TURKEY!
GOBBLE, GOBBLE, GOBBLE!

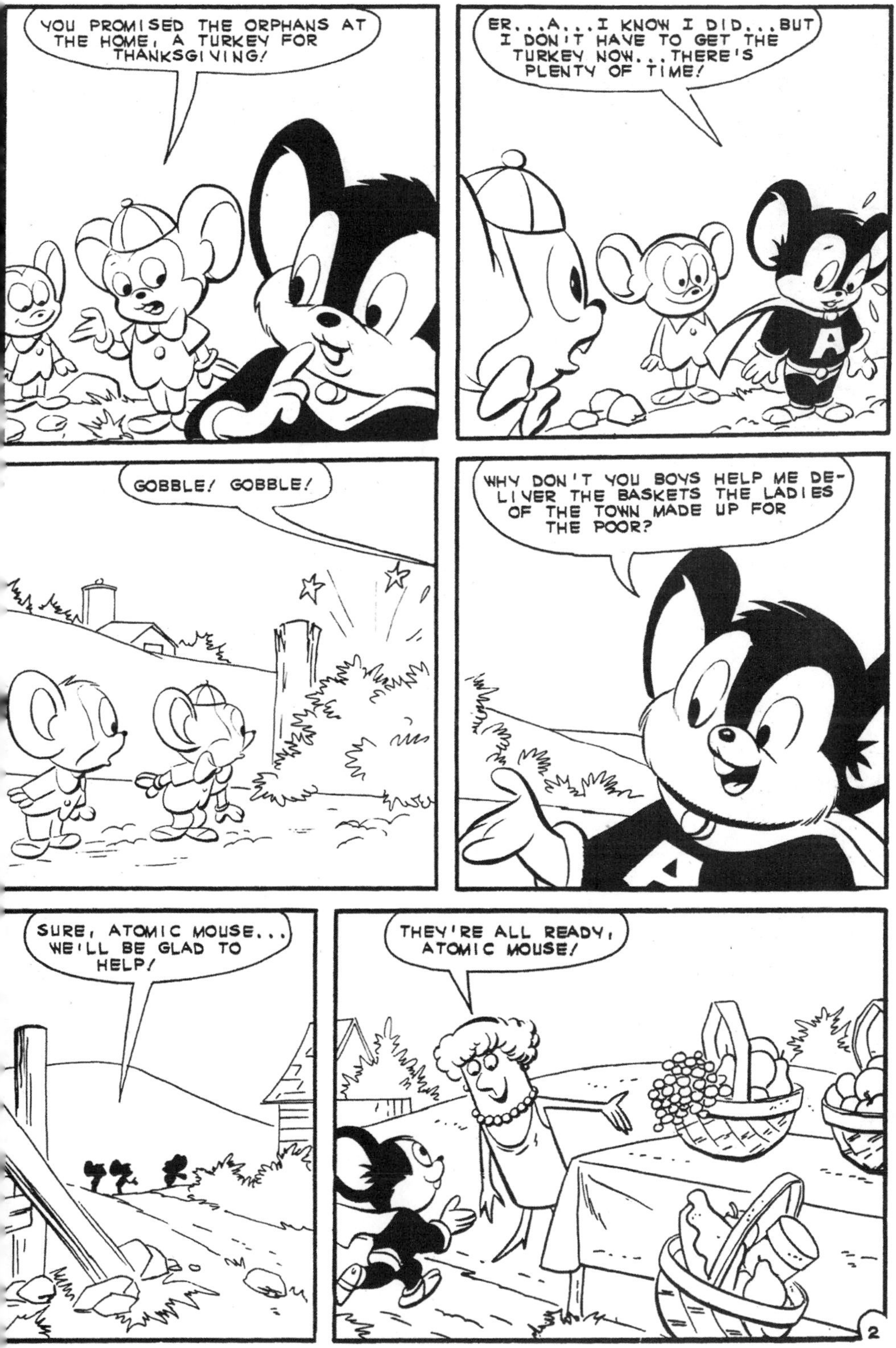
YOU PROMISED THE ORPHANS AT THE HOME, A TURKEY FOR THANKSGIVING!
ER...A...I KNOW I DID...BUT I DON'T HAVE TO GET THE TURKEY NOW...THERE'S PLENTY OF TIME!
GOBBLE! GOBBLE!
WHY DON'T YOU BOYS HELP ME DELIVER THE BASKETS THE LADIES OF THE TOWN MADE UP FOR THE POOR?
SURE, ATOMIC MOUSE... WE'LL BE GLAD TO HELP!
THEY'RE ALL READY, ATOMIC MOUSE!

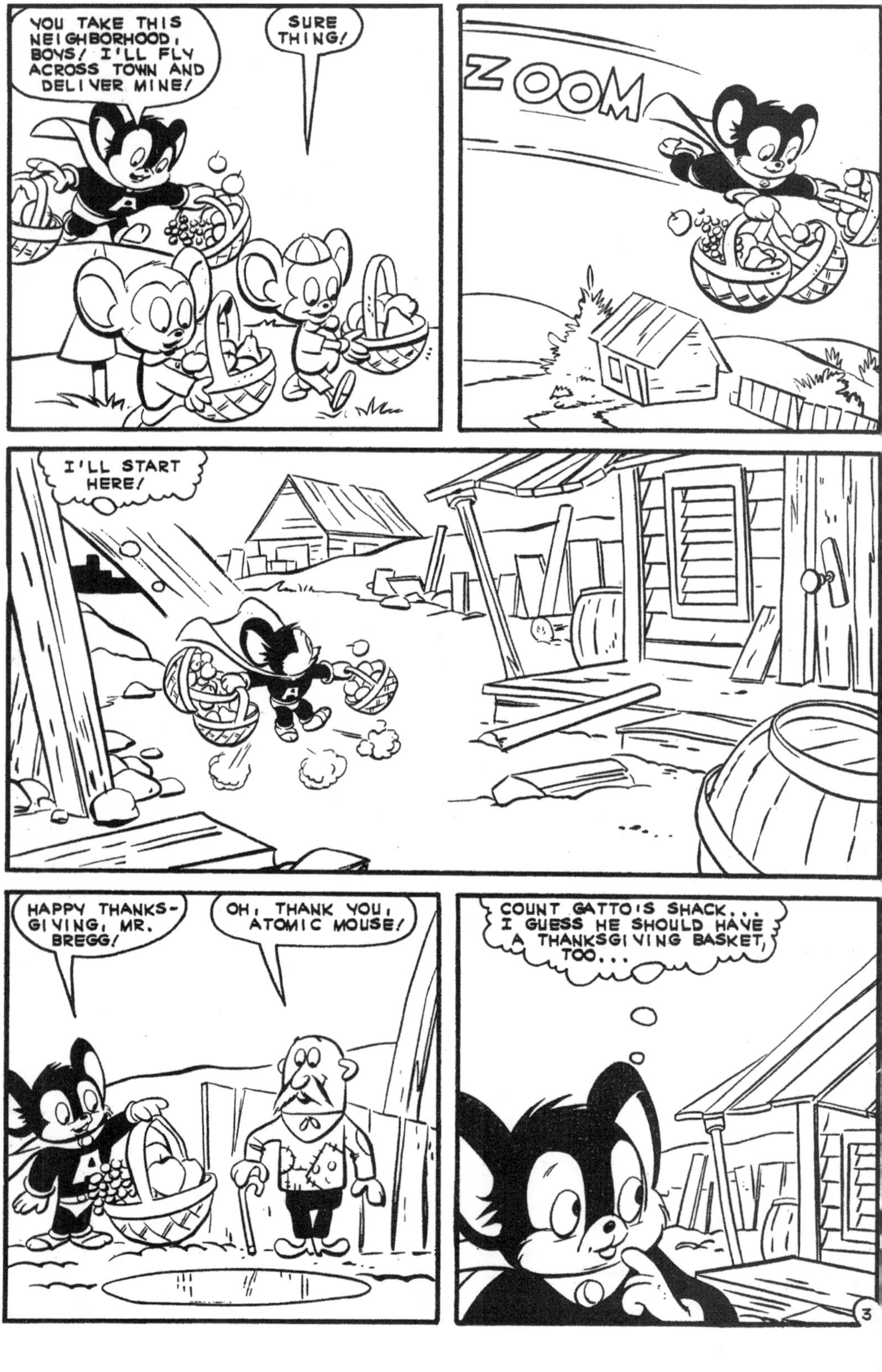

YOU TAKE THIS NEIGHBORHOOD, BOYS! I'LL FLY ACROSS TOWN AND DELIVER MINE!
SURE THING!
ZOOM
I'LL START HERE!
HAPPY THANKS-GIVING, MR. BREGG!
OH, THANK YOU, ATOMIC MOUSE!
COUNT GATTO'S SHACK... I GUESS HE SHOULD HAVE A THANKSGIVING BASKET, TOO...

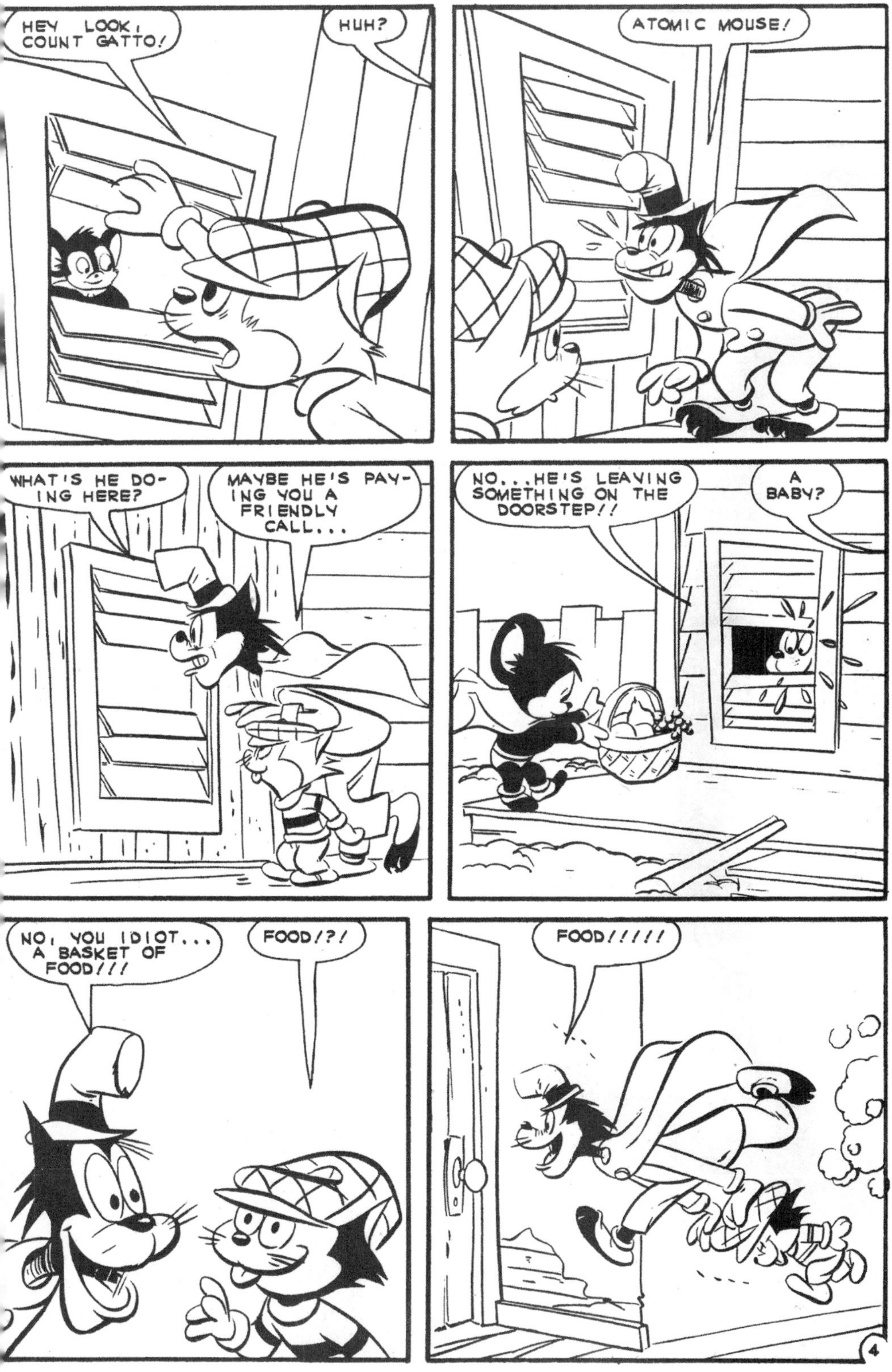
HEY LOOK, COUNT GATTO!
HUH?
ATOMIC MOUSE!
WHAT'S HE DO- ING HERE?
MAYBE HE'S PAY- ING YOU A FRIENDLY CALL...
NO...HE'S LEAVING SOMETHING ON THE DOORSTEP!!
A BABY?
NO, YOU IDIOT... A BASKET OF FOOD!!!
FOOD!?!
FOOD!!!!!

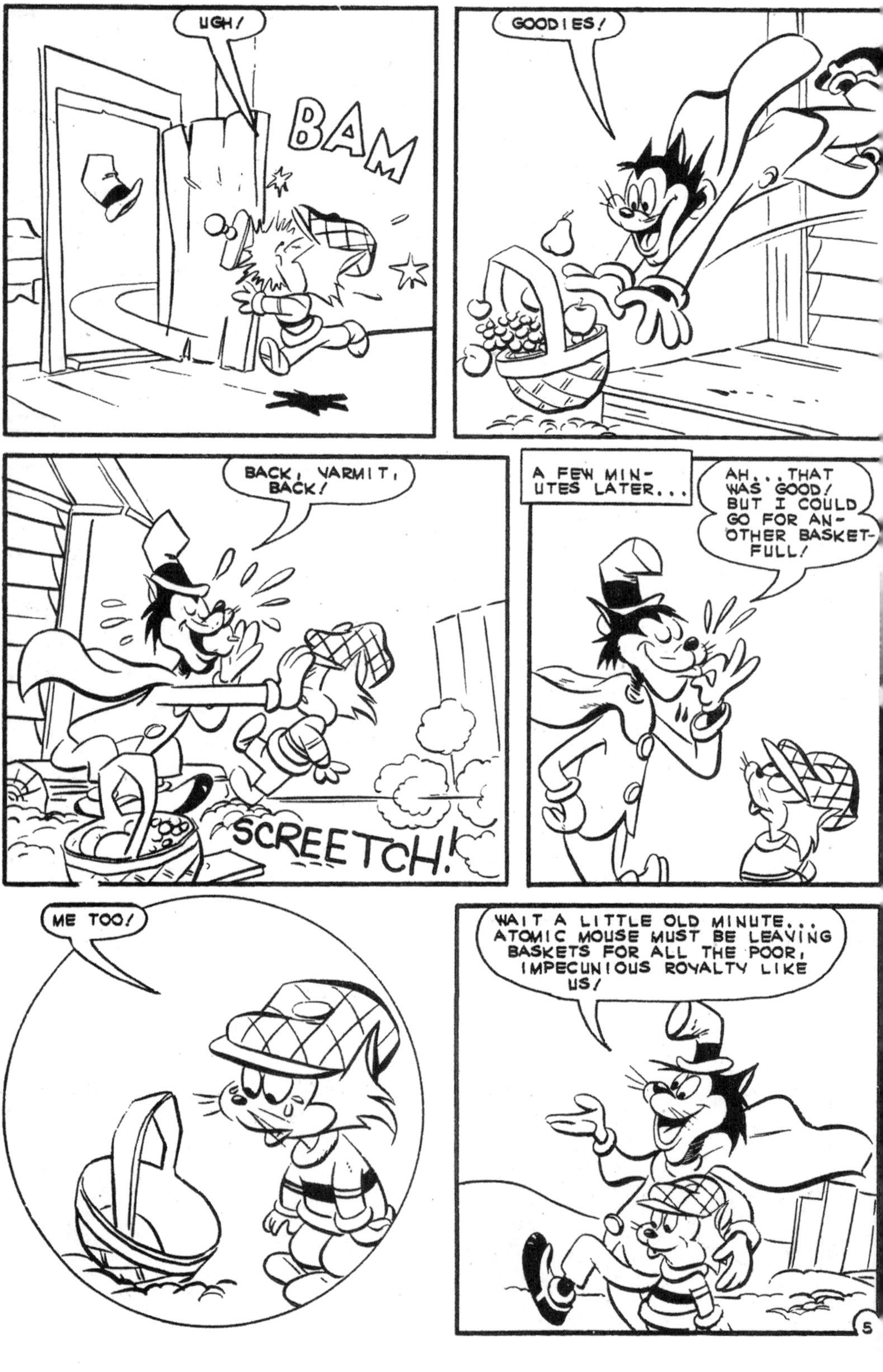
UGH!
BAM
GOODIES!
BACK, VARMIT, BACK!
SCREETCH!
A FEW MIN-UTES LATER...
AH...THAT WAS GOOD! BUT I COULD GO FOR AN-OTHER BASKET-FULL!
ME TOO!
WAIT A LITTLE OLD MINUTE... ATOMIC MOUSE MUST BE LEAVING BASKETS FOR ALL THE POOR, IMPECUNIOUS ROYALTY LIKE US!

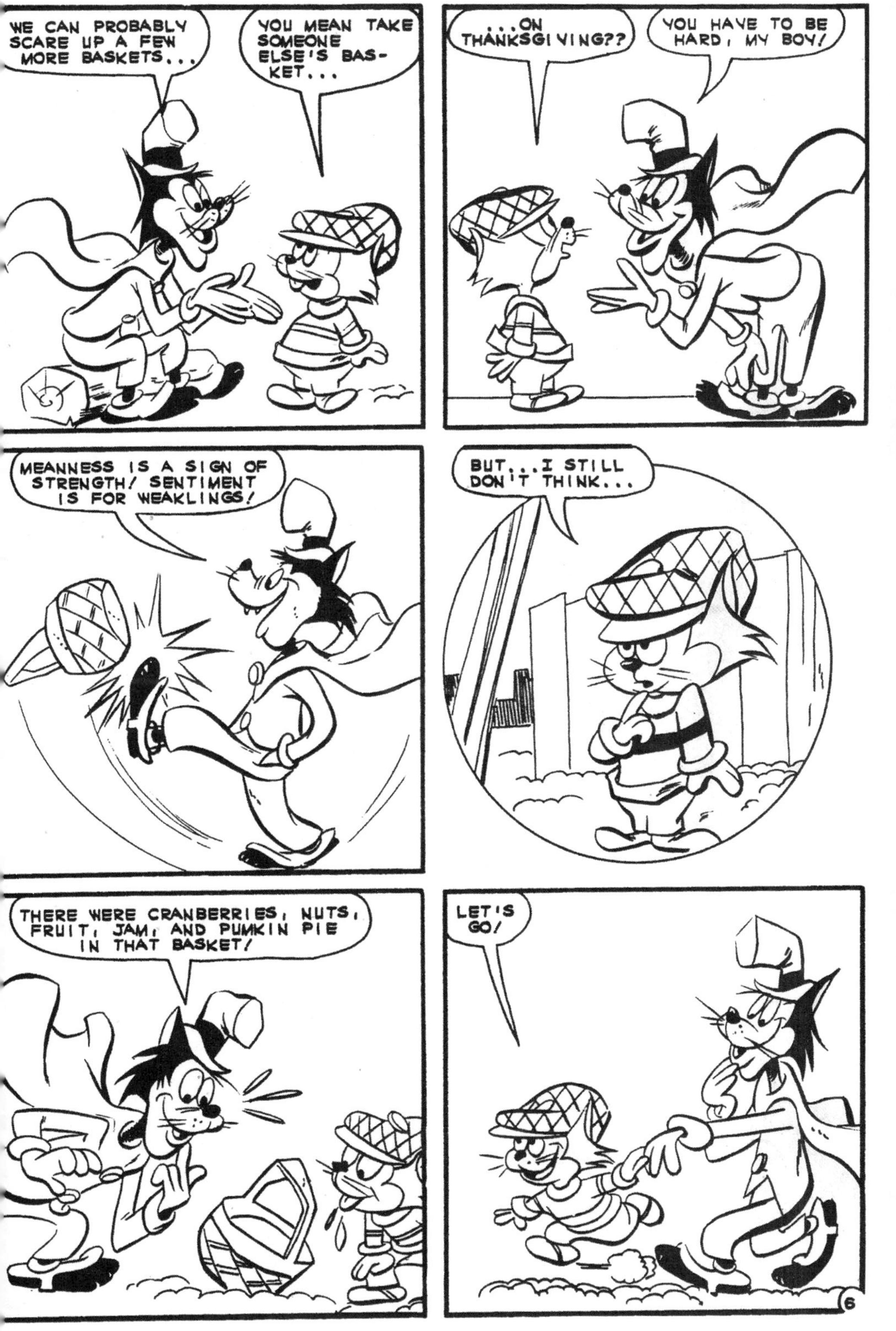
WE CAN PROBABLY SCARE UP A FEW MORE BASKETS...
YOU MEAN TAKE SOMEONE ELSE'S BAS-KET...
...ON THANKSGIVING??
YOU HAVE TO BE HARD, MY BOY!
MEANNESS IS A SIGN OF STRENGTH! SENTIMENT IS FOR WEAKLINGS!
BUT...I STILL DON'T THINK...
THERE WERE CRANBERRIES, NUTS, FRUIT, JAM, AND PUMKIN PIE IN THAT BASKET!
LET'S GO!
6

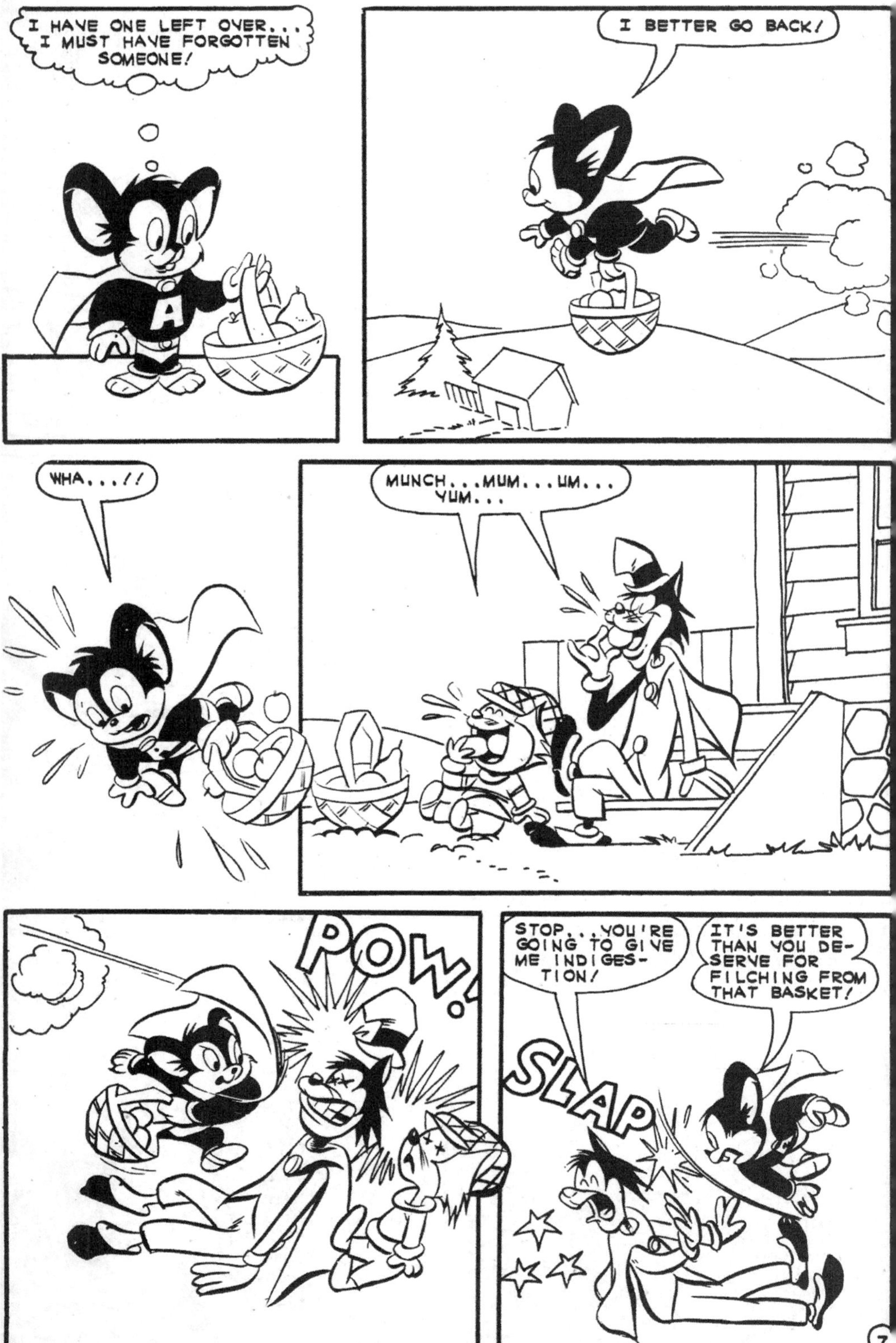
I HAVE ONE LEFT OVER... I MUST HAVE FORGOTTEN SOMEONE!
I BETTER GO BACK!
WHA...!!
MUNCH...MUM...UM... YUM...
POW!
STOP...YOU'RE GOING TO GIVE ME INDIGES- TION!
IT'S BETTER THAN YOU DE- SERVE FOR FILCHING FROM THAT BASKET!
SLAP

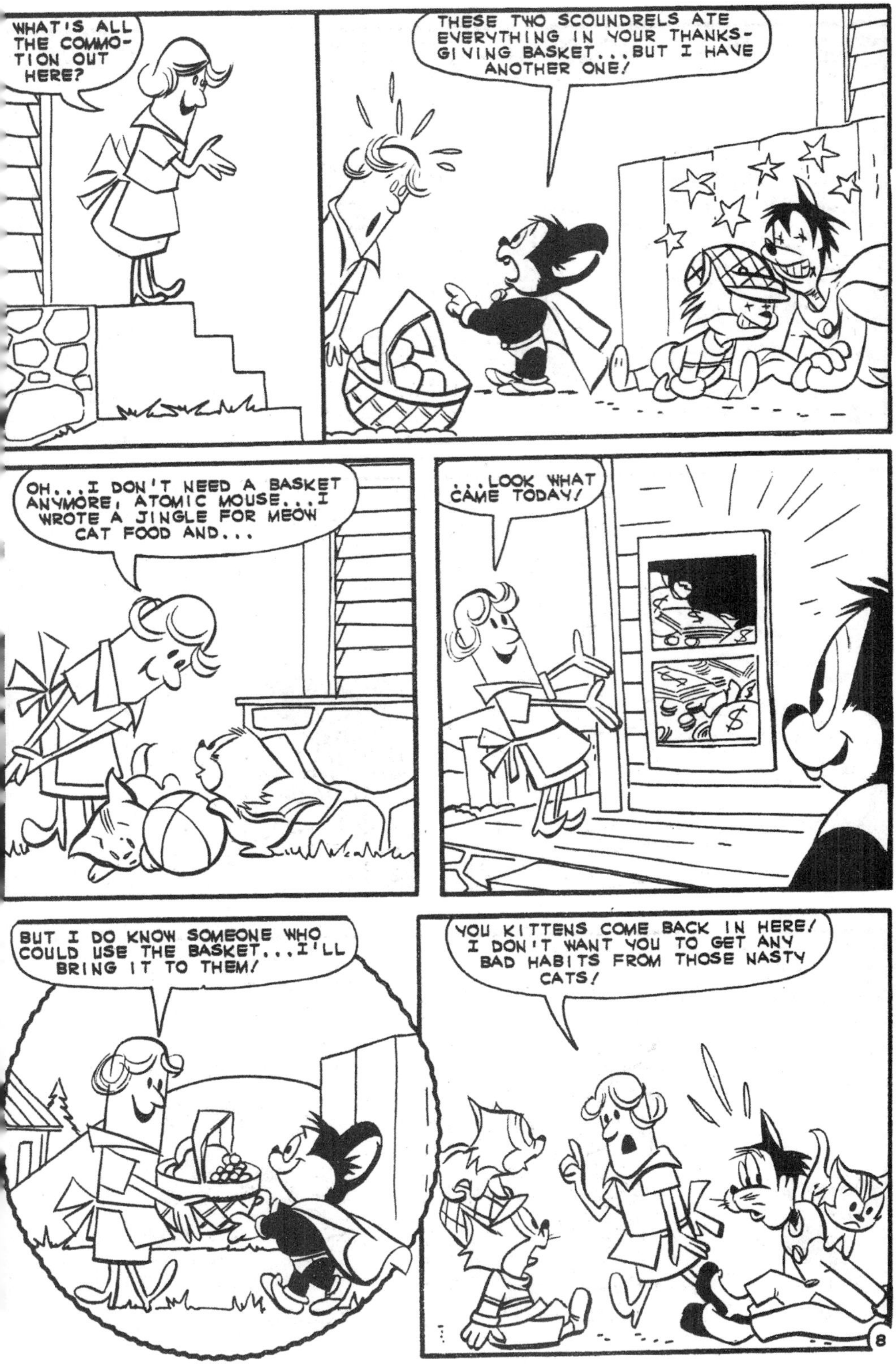
WHAT'S ALL THE COMMOTION OUT HERE?
THESE TWO SCOUNDRELS ATE EVERYTHING IN YOUR THANKSGIVING BASKET...BUT I HAVE ANOTHER ONE!
OH...I DON'T NEED A BASKET ANYMORE, ATOMIC MOUSE...I WROTE A JINGLE FOR MEOW CAT FOOD AND...
...LOOK WHAT CAME TODAY!
BUT I DO KNOW SOMEONE WHO COULD USE THE BASKET...I'LL BRING IT TO THEM!
YOU KITTENS COME BACK IN HERE! I DON'T WANT YOU TO GET ANY BAD HABITS FROM THOSE NASTY CATS!
8

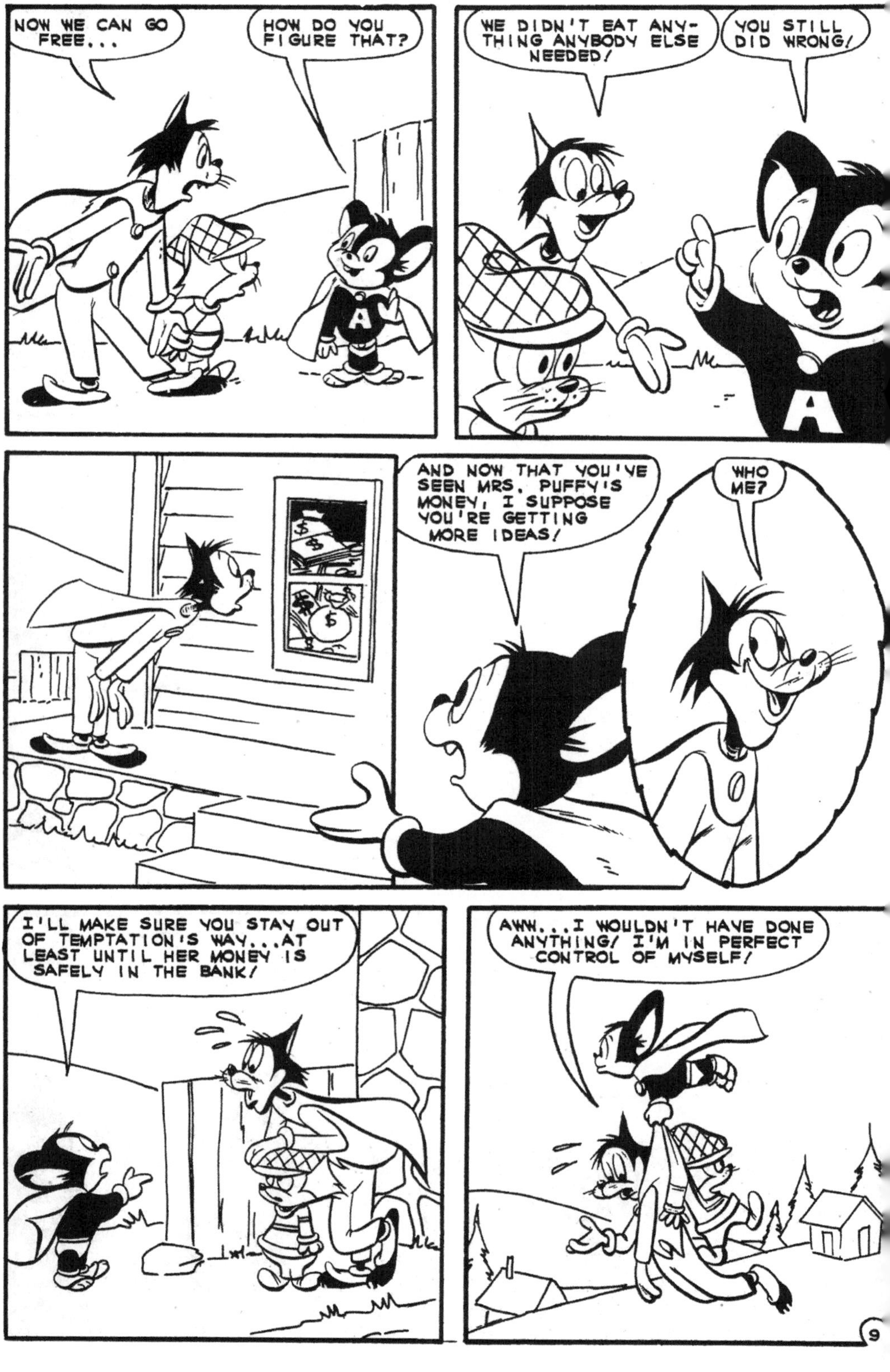
NOW WE CAN GO FREE...
HOW DO YOU FIGURE THAT?
WE DIDN'T EAT ANYTHING ANYBODY ELSE NEEDED!
YOU STILL DID WRONG!
AND NOW THAT YOU'VE SEEN MRS. PUFFY'S MONEY, I SUPPOSE YOU'RE GETTING MORE IDEAS!
WHO ME?
I'LL MAKE SURE YOU STAY OUT OF TEMPTATION'S WAY...AT LEAST UNTIL HER MONEY IS SAFELY IN THE BANK!
AWW...I WOULDN'T HAVE DONE ANYTHING! I'M IN PERFECT CONTROL OF MYSELF!
9

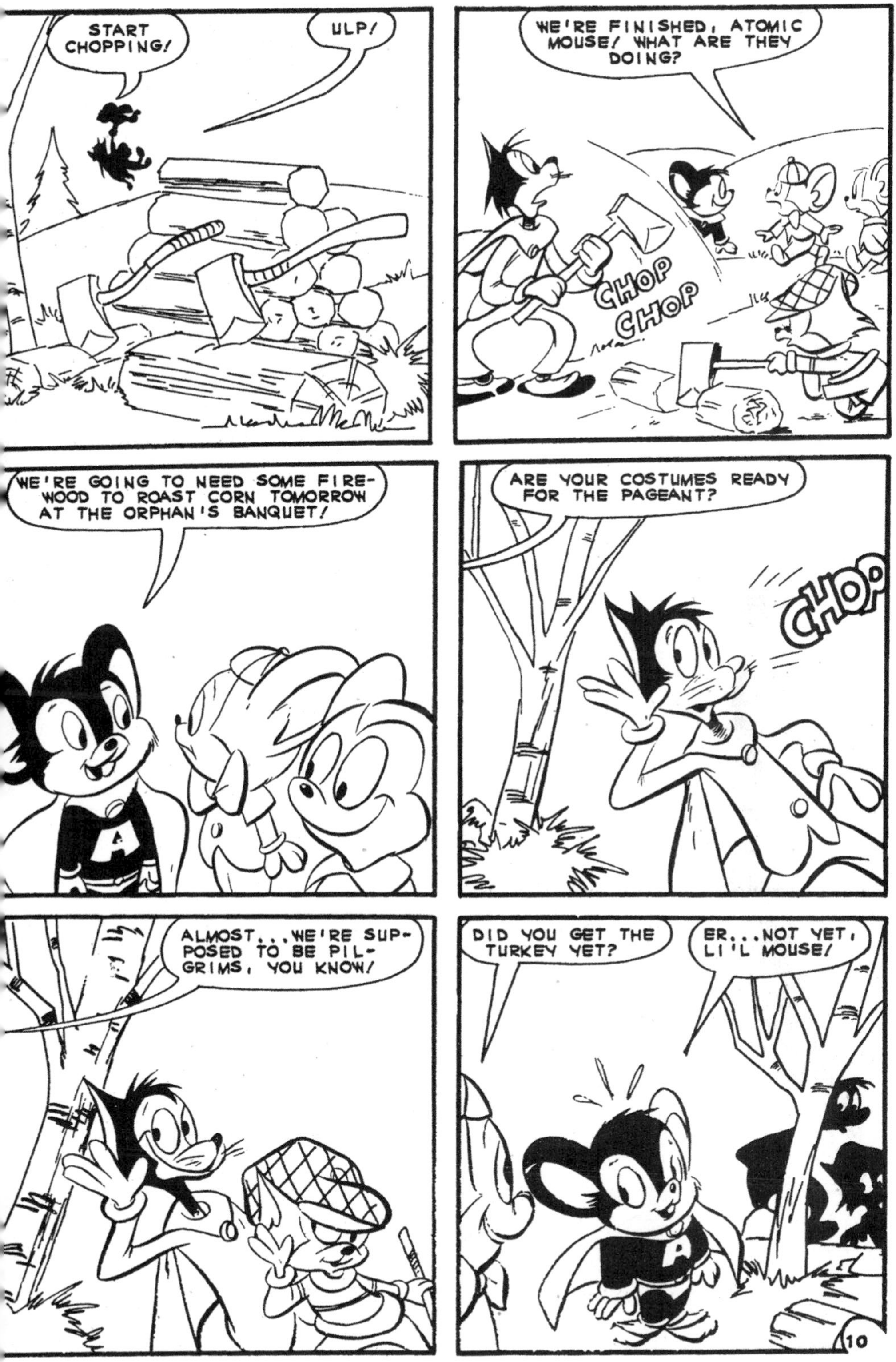
START CHOPPING!
ULP!
WE'RE FINISHED, ATOMIC MOUSE! WHAT ARE THEY DOING?
CHOP
CHOP
WE'RE GOING TO NEED SOME FIRE-WOOD TO ROAST CORN TOMORROW AT THE ORPHAN'S BANQUET!
ARE YOUR COSTUMES READY FOR THE PAGEANT?
CHOP
ALMOST...WE'RE SUP-POSED TO BE PIL-GRIMS, YOU KNOW!
DID YOU GET THE TURKEY YET?
ER...NOT YET, LI'L MOUSE!

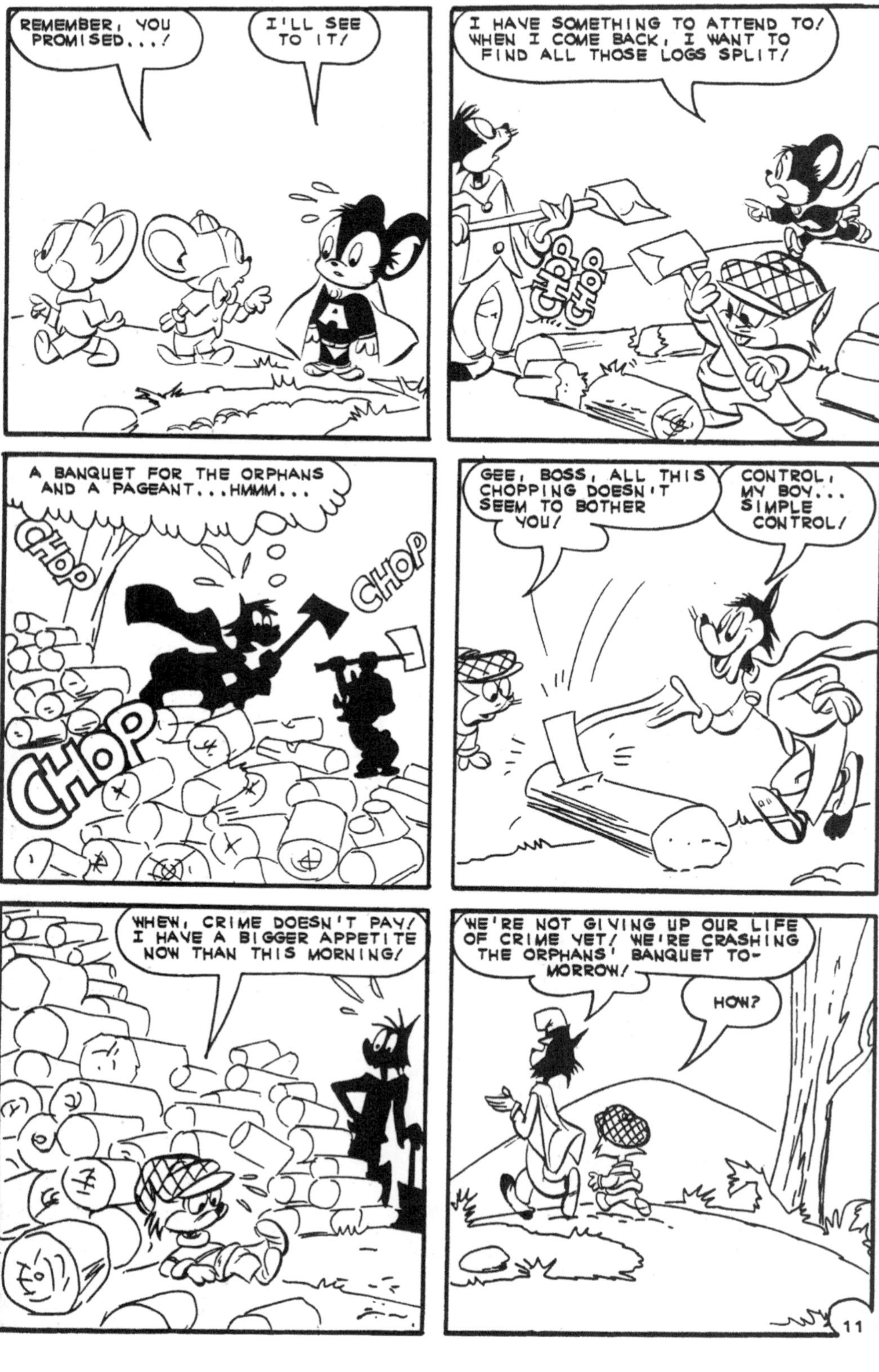
REMEMBER, YOU PROMISED...!
I'LL SEE TO IT!
I HAVE SOMETHING TO ATTEND TO! WHEN I COME BACK, I WANT TO FIND ALL THOSE LOGS SPLIT!
CHOP CHOP
A BANQUET FOR THE ORPHANS AND A PAGEANT...HMMM...
CHOP
CHOP
CHOP
GEE, BOSS, ALL THIS CHOPPING DOESN'T SEEM TO BOTHER YOU!
CONTROL, MY BOY... SIMPLE CONTROL!
WHEW, CRIME DOESN'T PAY! I HAVE A BIGGER APPETITE NOW THAN THIS MORNING!
WE'RE NOT GIVING UP OUR LIFE OF CRIME YET! WE'RE CRASHING THE ORPHANS' BANQUET TO-MORROW!
HOW?

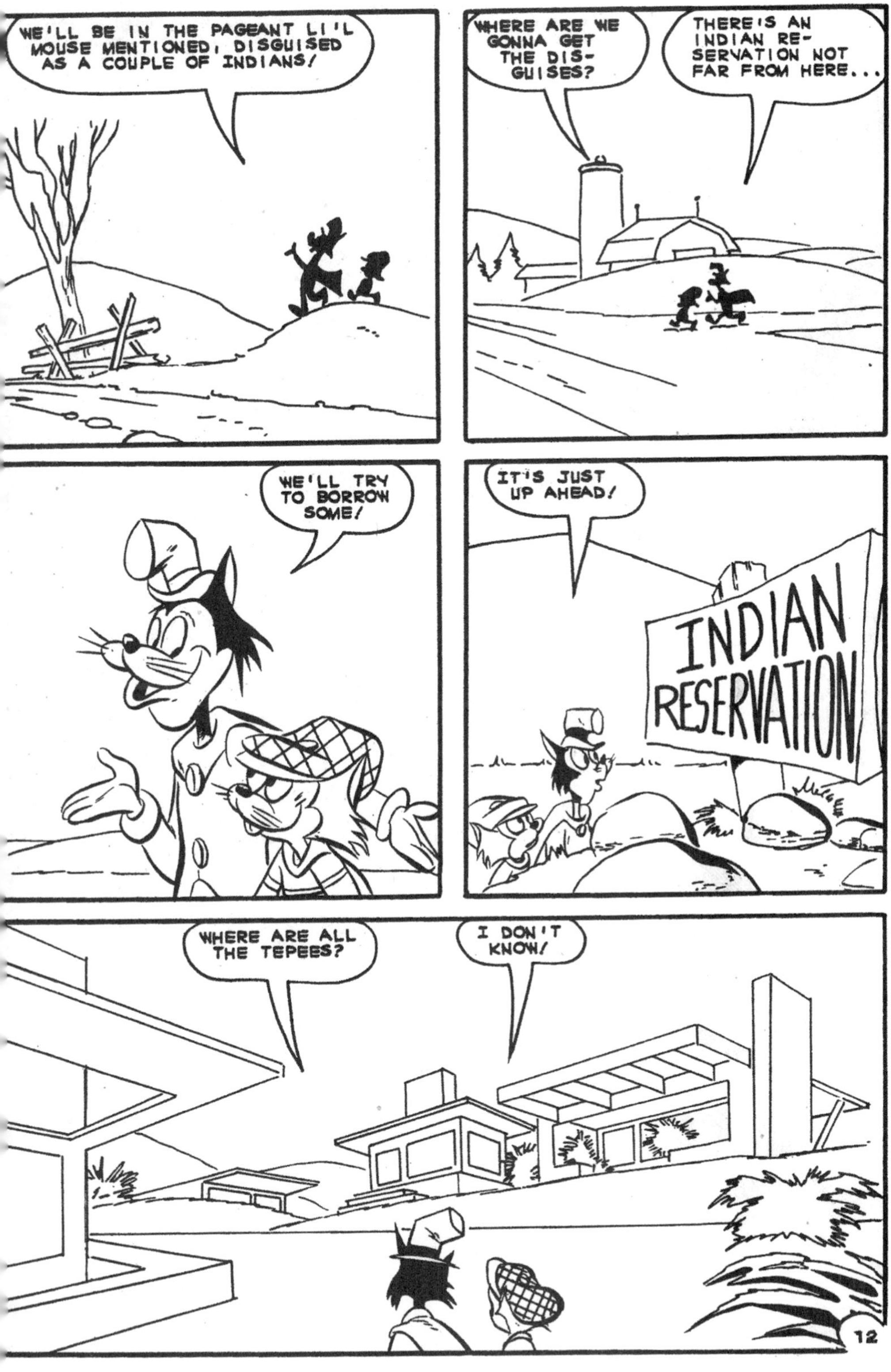
WE'LL BE IN THE PAGEANT LI'L MOUSE MENTIONED, DISGUISED AS A COUPLE OF INDIANS!
WHERE ARE WE GONNA GET THE DIS-GUISES?
THERE'S AN INDIAN RE-SERVATION NOT FAR FROM HERE...
WE'LL TRY TO BORROW SOME!
IT'S JUST UP AHEAD!
INDIAN RESERVATION
WHERE ARE ALL THE TEPEES?
I DON'T KNOW!

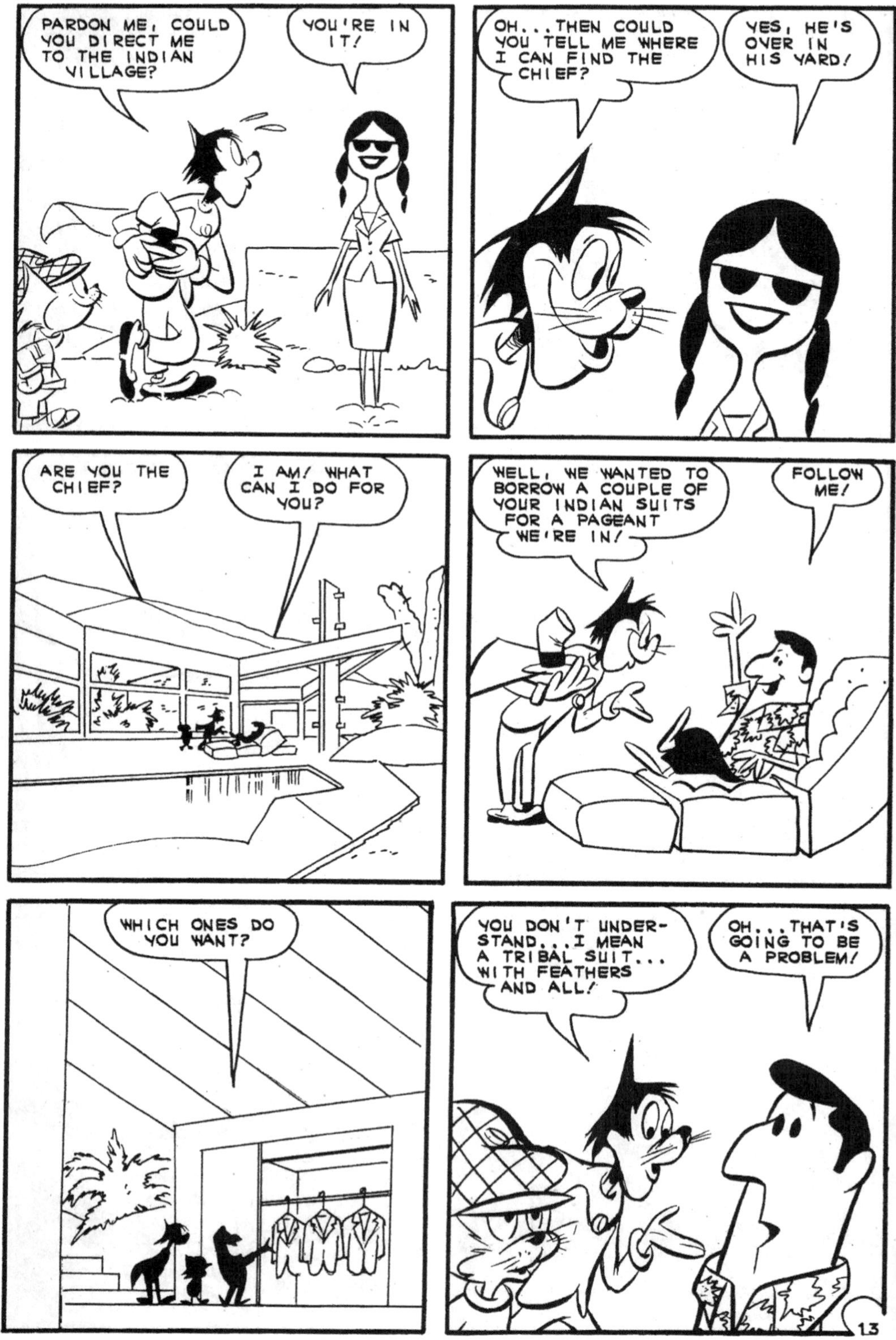
PARDON ME, COULD YOU DIRECT ME TO THE INDIAN VILLAGE?
YOU'RE IN IT!
OH...THEN COULD YOU TELL ME WHERE I CAN FIND THE CHIEF?
YES, HE'S OVER IN HIS YARD!
ARE YOU THE CHIEF?
I AM! WHAT CAN I DO FOR YOU?
WELL, WE WANTED TO BORROW A COUPLE OF YOUR INDIAN SUITS FOR A PAGEANT WE'RE IN!
FOLLOW ME!
WHICH ONES DO YOU WANT?
YOU DON'T UNDER-STAND...I MEAN A TRIBAL SUIT... WITH FEATHERS AND ALL!
OH...THAT'S GOING TO BE A PROBLEM!

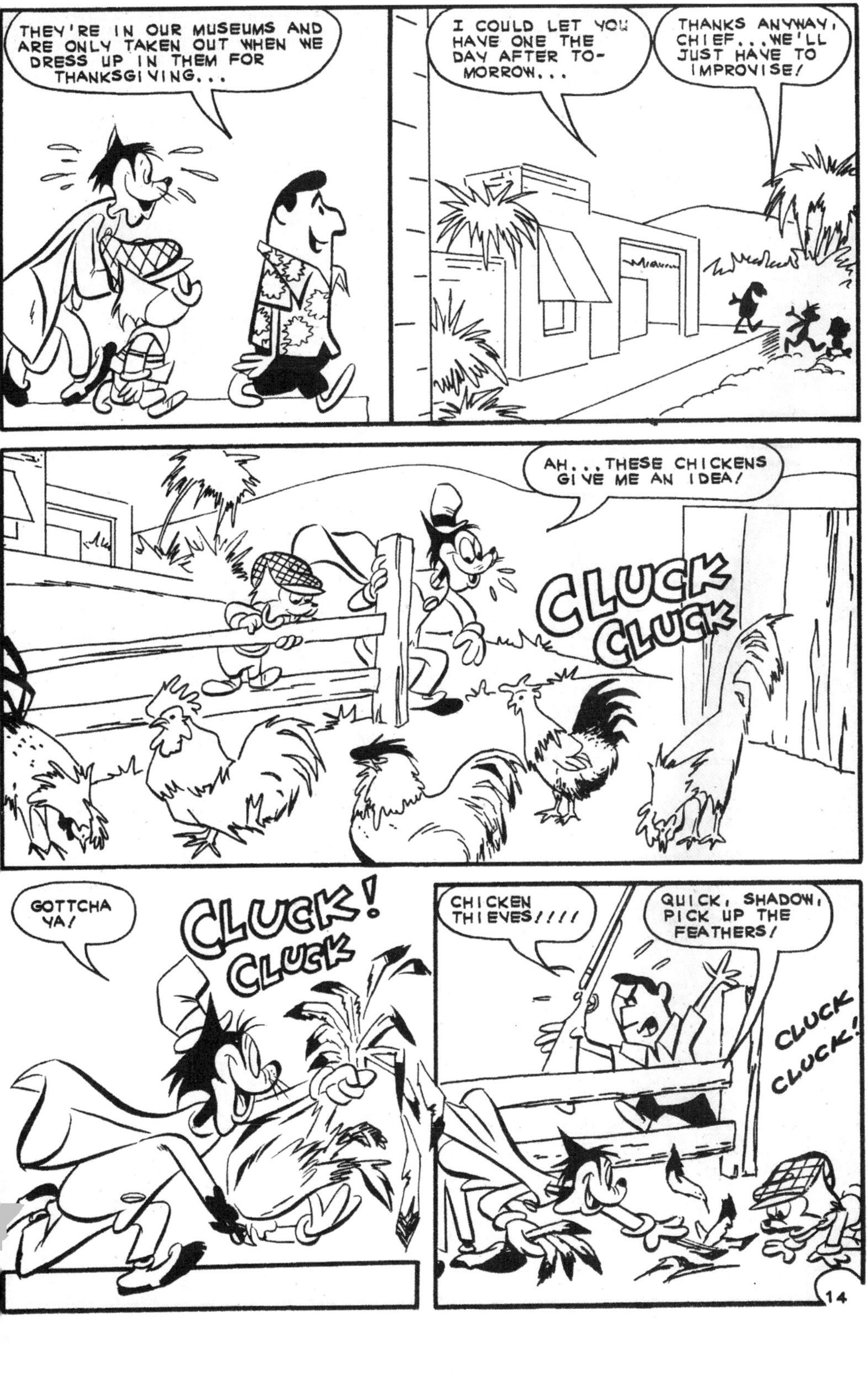
THEY'RE IN OUR MUSEUMS AND ARE ONLY TAKEN OUT WHEN WE DRESS UP IN THEM FOR THANKSGIVING...
I COULD LET YOU HAVE ONE THE DAY AFTER TO-MORROW...
THANKS ANYWAY, CHIEF...WE'LL JUST HAVE TO IMPROVISE!
AH...THESE CHICKENS GIVE ME AN IDEA!
CLUCK CLUCK
GOTTCHA YA!
CLUCK! CLUCK
CHICKEN THIEVES!!!!
QUICK, SHADOW, PICK UP THE FEATHERS!
CLUCK CLUCK!

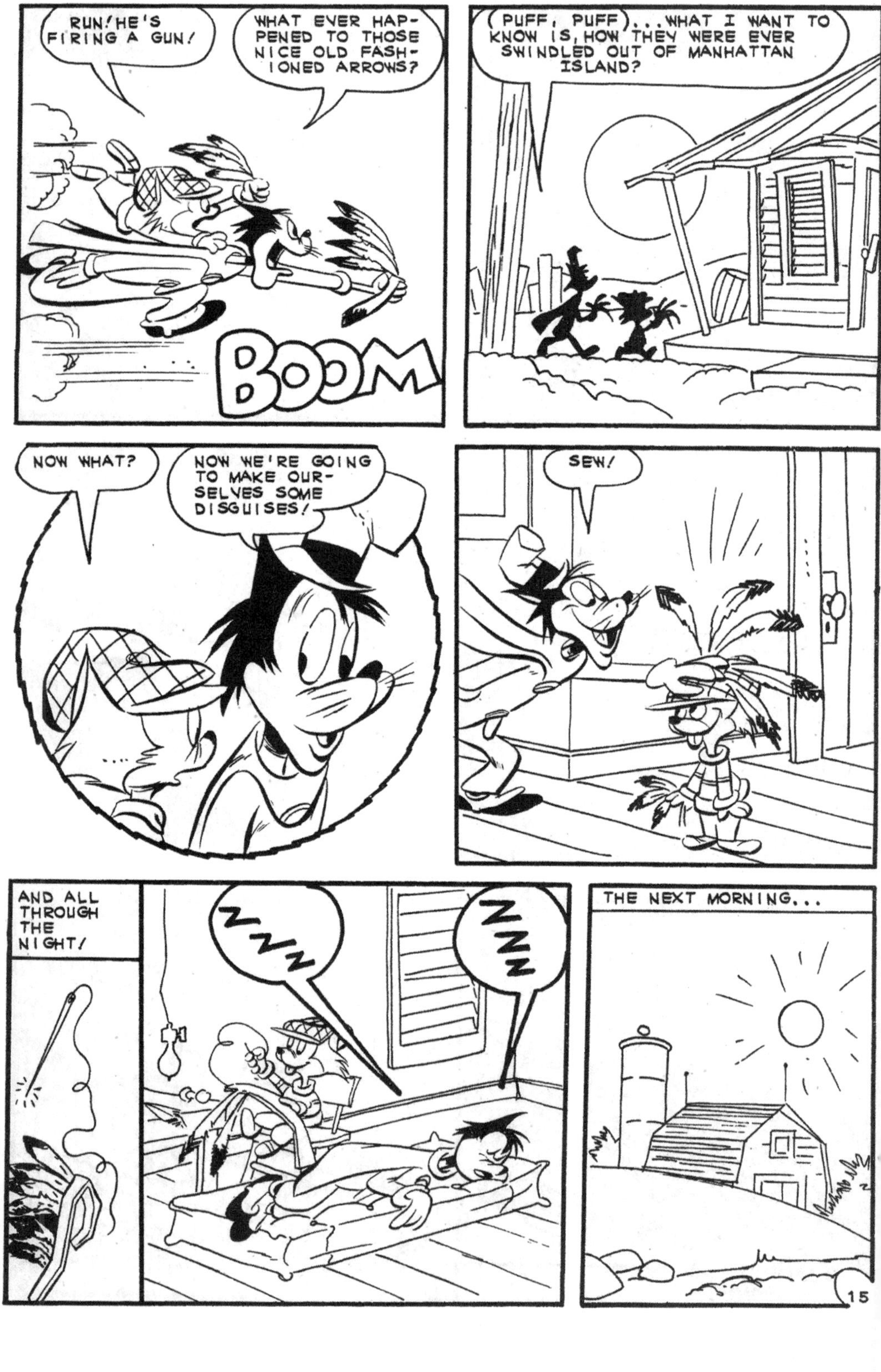
RUN! HE'S FIRING A GUN!
WHAT EVER HAPPENED TO THOSE NICE OLD FASHIONED ARROWS?
BOOM
(PUFF, PUFF)...WHAT I WANT TO KNOW IS, HOW THEY WERE EVER SWINDLED OUT OF MANHATTAN ISLAND?
NOW WHAT?
NOW WE'RE GOING TO MAKE OURSELVES SOME DISGUISES!
....
SEW!
AND ALL THROUGH THE NIGHT!
ZZZ
ZZZ
THE NEXT MORNING...

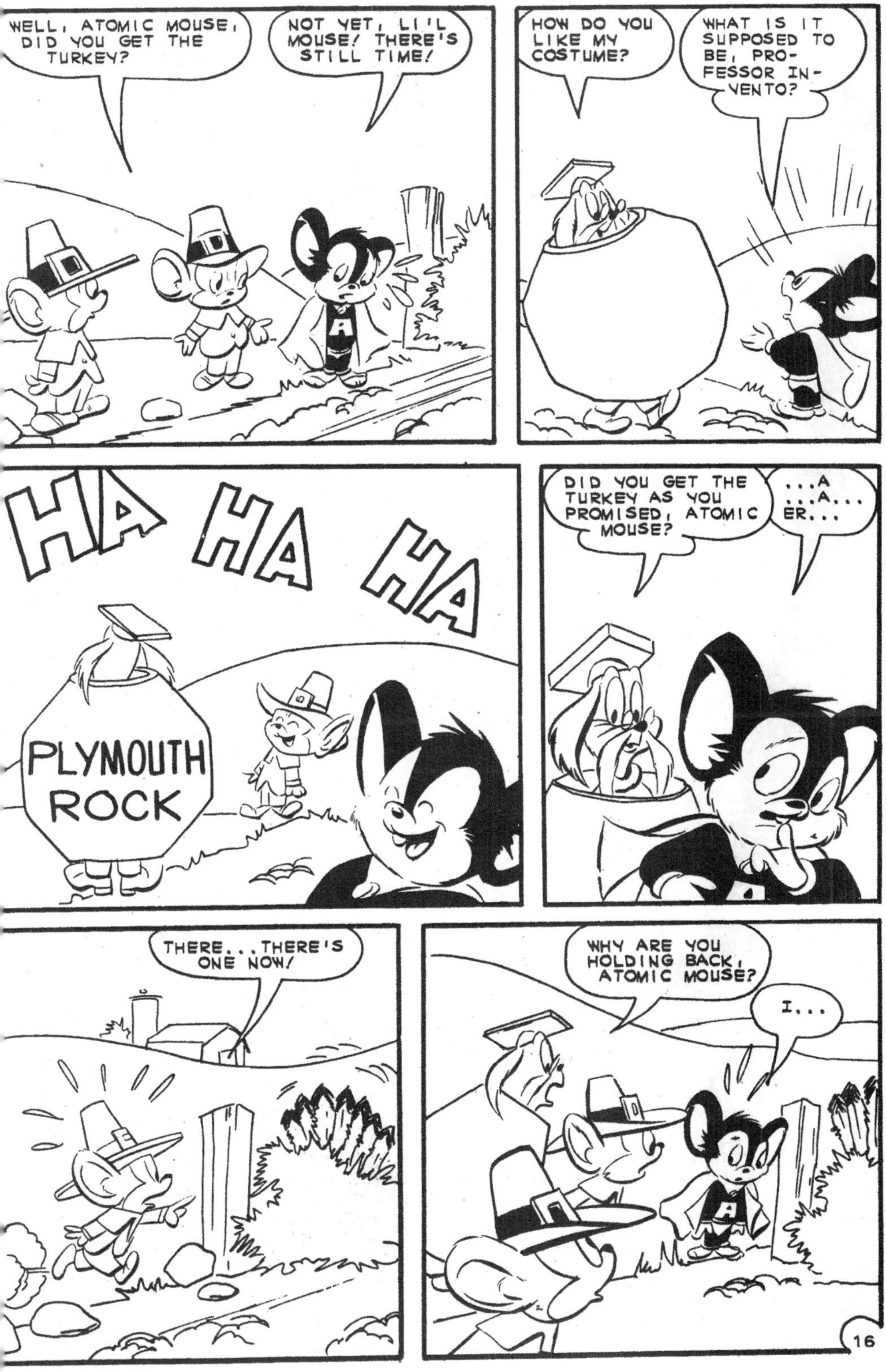

WELL, ATOMIC MOUSE, DID YOU GET THE TURKEY?
NOT YET, LI'L MOUSE! THERE'S STILL TIME!
HOW DO YOU LIKE MY COSTUME?
WHAT IS IT SUPPOSED TO BE, PROFESSOR INVENTO?
HA HA HA
PLYMOUTH ROCK
DID YOU GET THE TURKEY AS YOU PROMISED, ATOMIC MOUSE?
...A ...A... ER...
THERE...THERE'S ONE NOW!
WHY ARE YOU HOLDING BACK, ATOMIC MOUSE?
I...

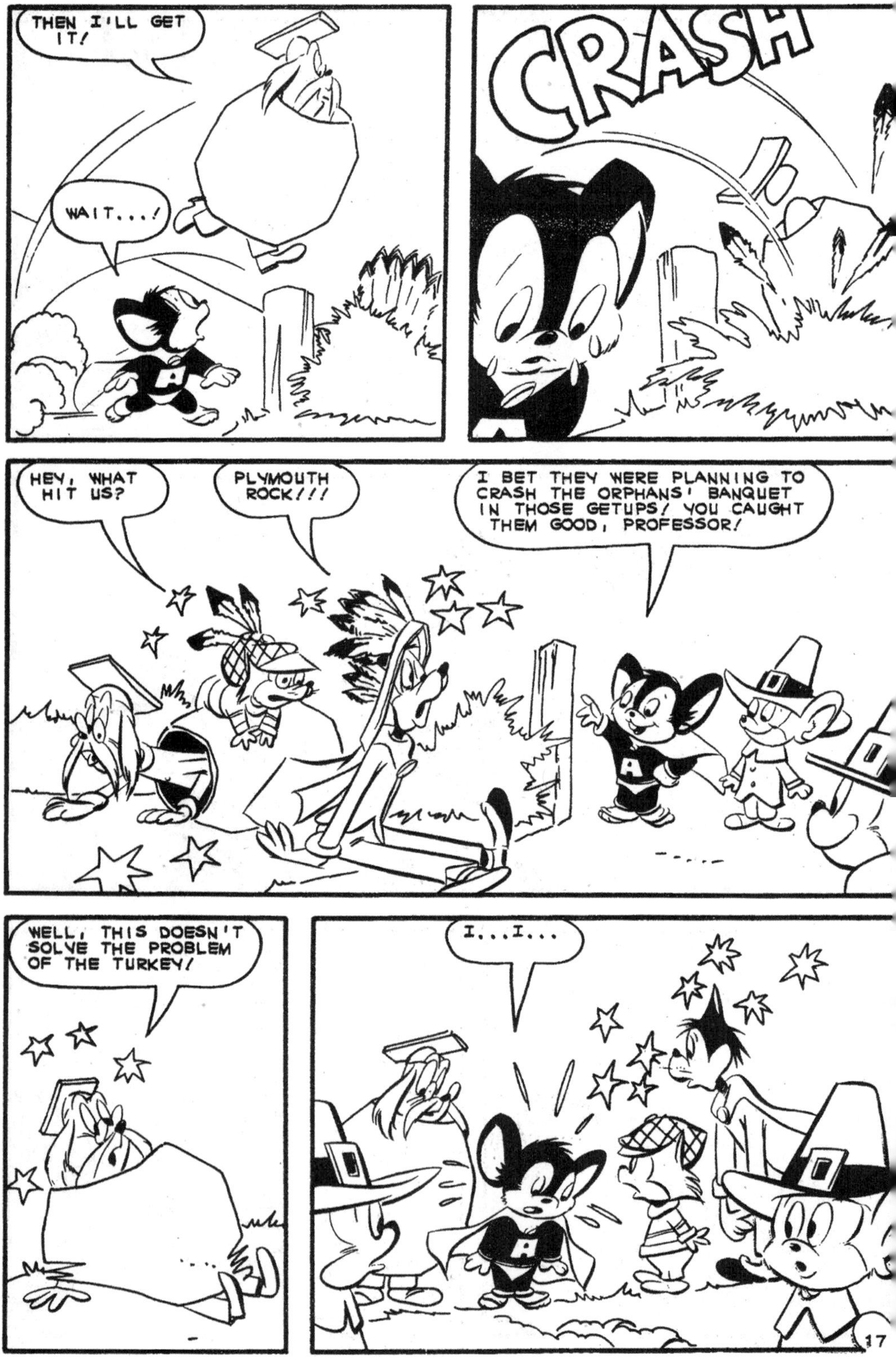
THEN I'LL GET IT!
WAIT...!
CRASH
HEY, WHAT HIT US?
PLYMOUTH ROCK!!!
I BET THEY WERE PLANNING TO CRASH THE ORPHANS' BANQUET IN THOSE GETUPS! YOU CAUGHT THEM GOOD, PROFESSOR!
WELL, THIS DOESN'T SOLVE THE PROBLEM OF THE TURKEY!
I...I...

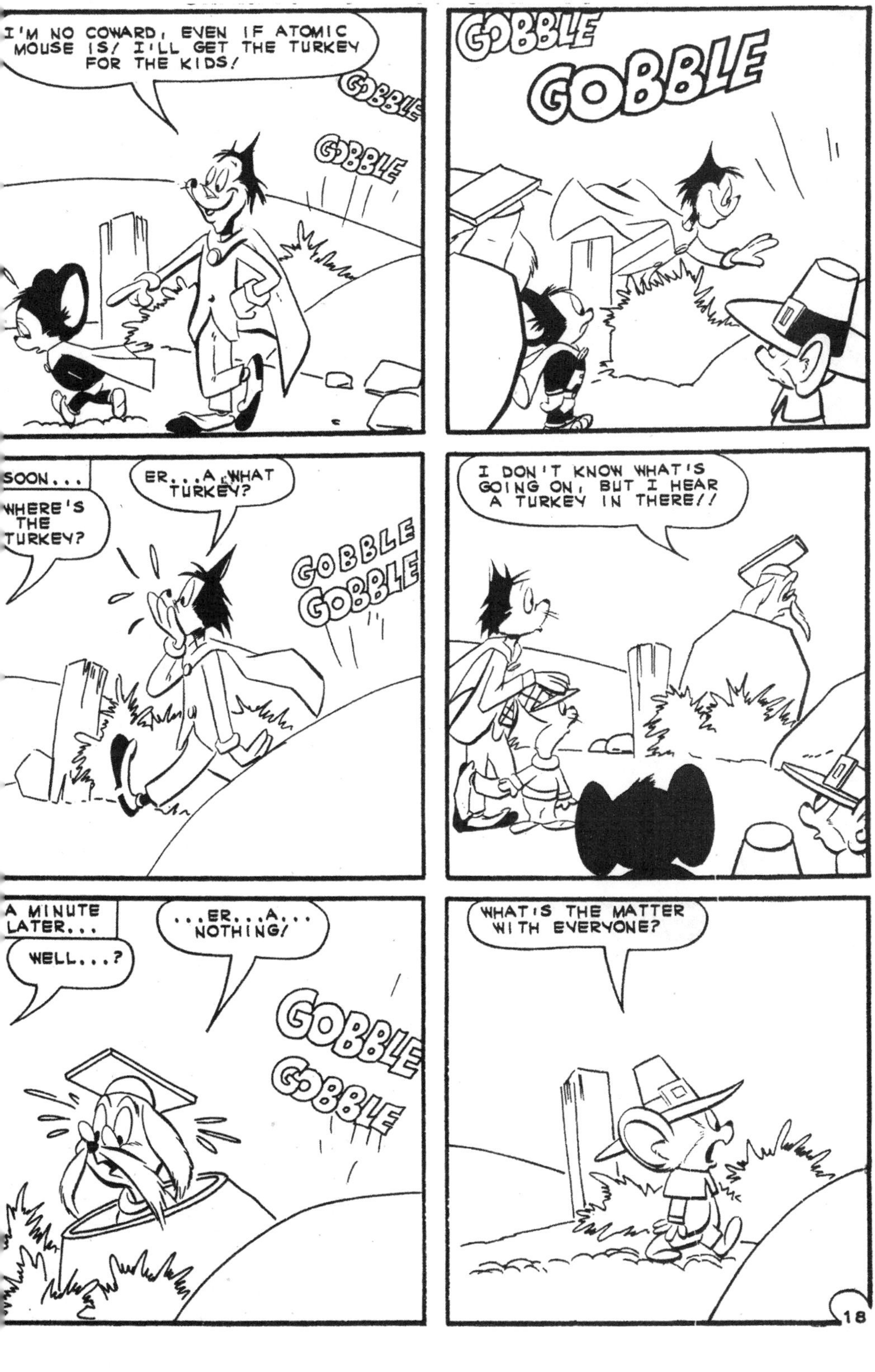
I'M NO COWARD, EVEN IF ATOMIC MOUSE IS! I'LL GET THE TURKEY FOR THE KIDS!
GOBBLE
GOBBLE
GOBBLE
GOBBLE
SOON...
WHERE'S THE TURKEY?
ER...A WHAT TURKEY?
GOBBLE
GOBBLE
I DON'T KNOW WHAT'S GOING ON, BUT I HEAR A TURKEY IN THERE!!
A MINUTE LATER...
WELL...?
...ER...A... NOTHING!
GOBBLE
GOBBLE
WHAT'S THE MATTER WITH EVERYONE?

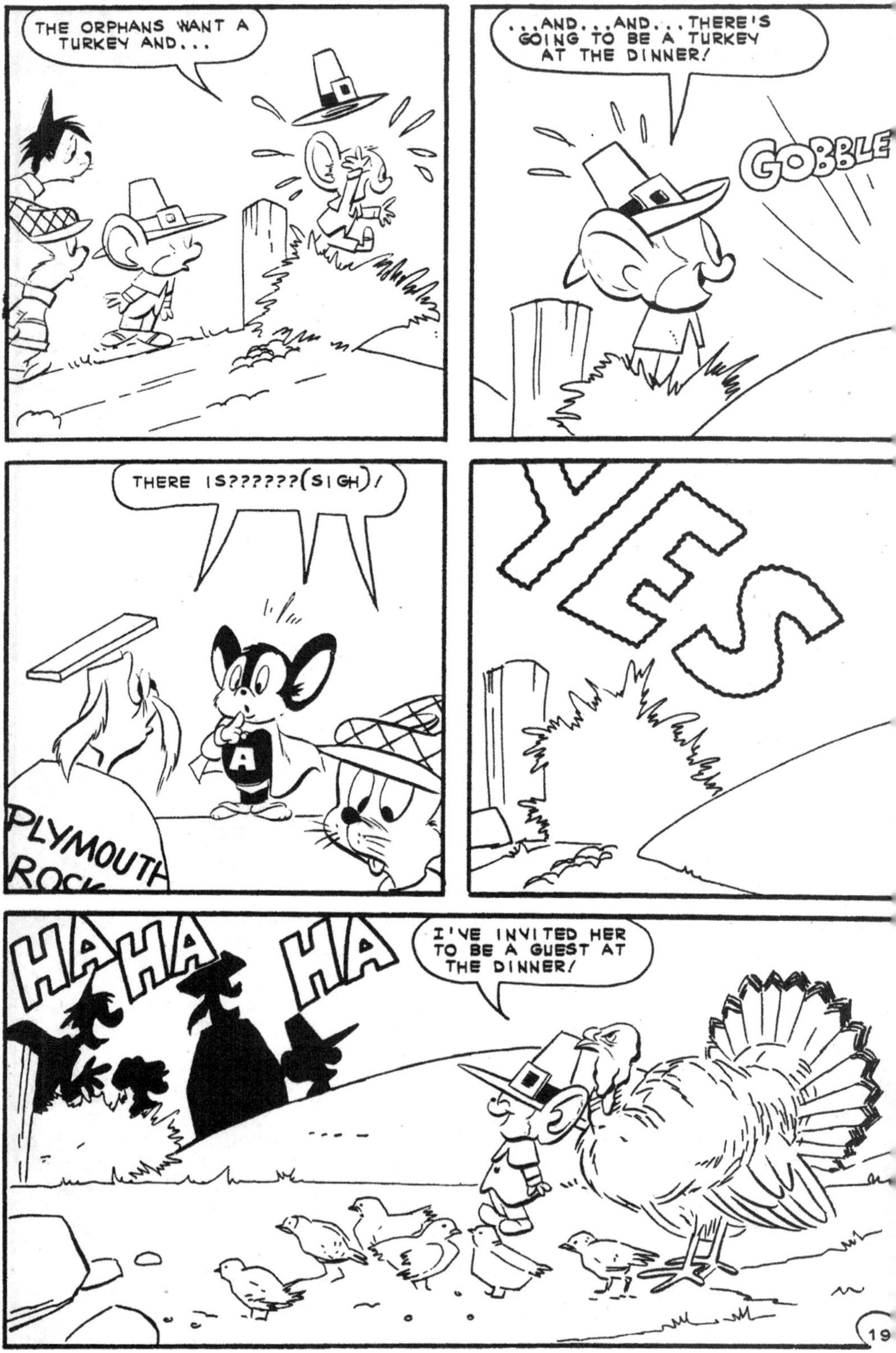
THE ORPHANS WANT A TURKEY AND...
...AND...AND...THERE'S GOING TO BE A TURKEY AT THE DINNER!
GOBBLE
THERE IS??????(SIGH)!
PLYMOUTH ROCK
YES
HA HA HA
I'VE INVITED HER TO BE A GUEST AT THE DINNER!

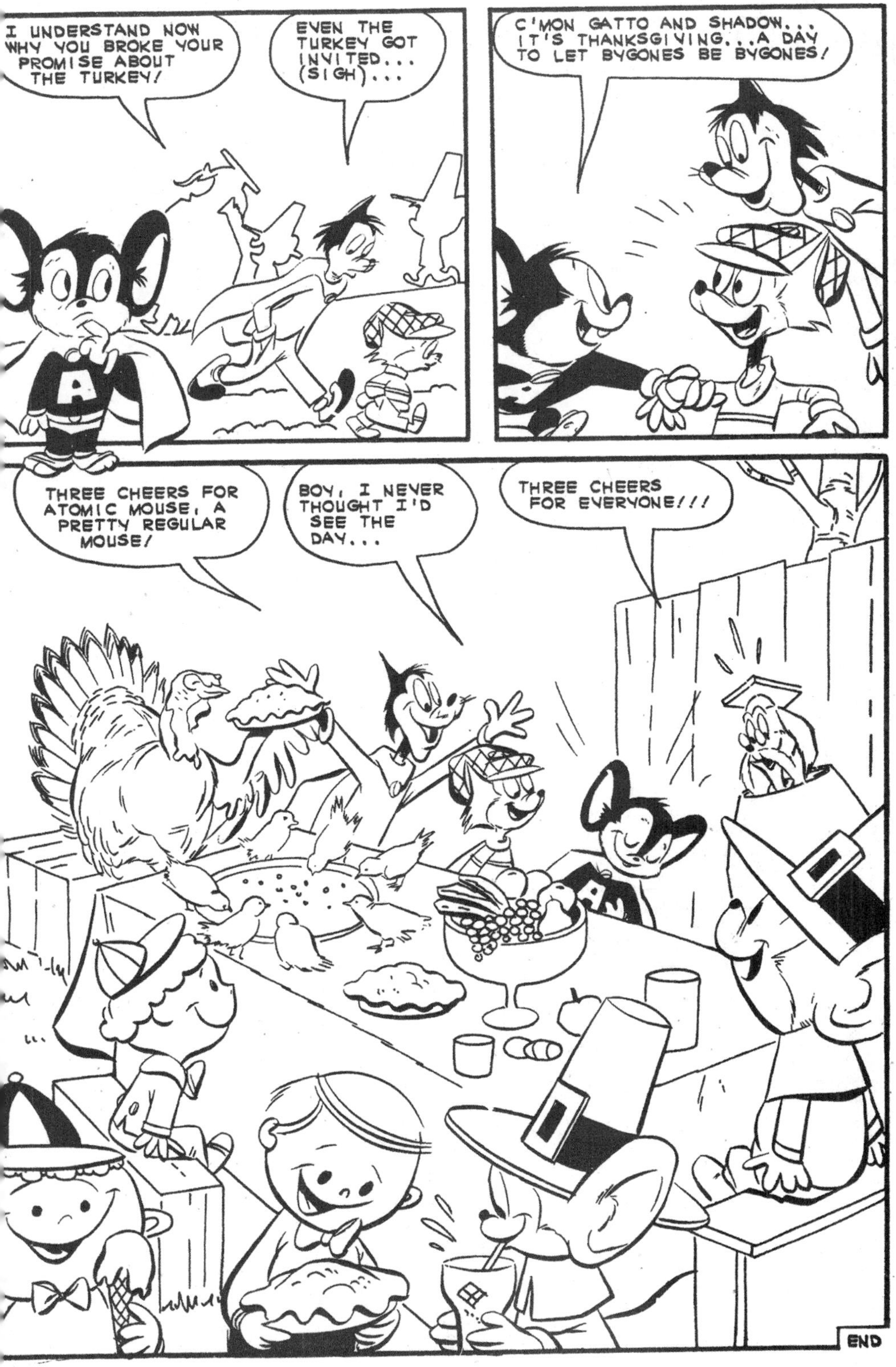

I UNDERSTAND NOW WHY YOU BROKE YOUR PROMISE ABOUT THE TURKEY!
EVEN THE TURKEY GOT INVITED... (SIGH)...
C'MON GATTO AND SHADOW... IT'S THANKSGIVING...A DAY TO LET BYGONES BE BYGONES!
THREE CHEERS FOR ATOMIC MOUSE, A PRETTY REGULAR MOUSE!
BOY, I NEVER THOUGHT I'D SEE THE DAY...
THREE CHEERS FOR EVERYONE!!!
END

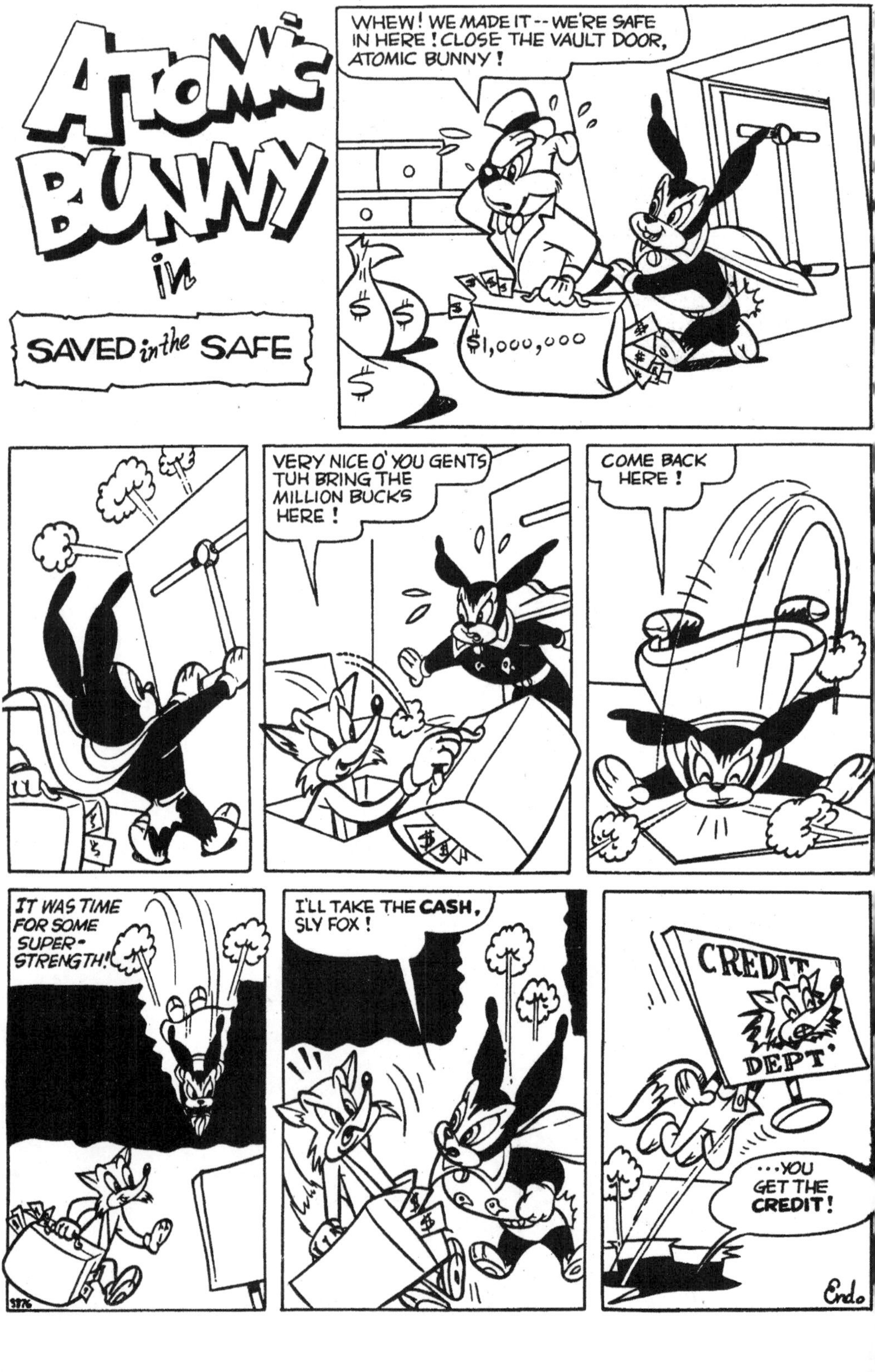
ATOMIC BUNNY
in
SAVED in the SAFE
WHEW! WE MADE IT -- WE'RE SAFE IN HERE! CLOSE THE VAULT DOOR, ATOMIC BUNNY!
$1,000,000
VERY NICE O' YOU GENTS TUH BRING THE MILLION BUCKS HERE!
COME BACK HERE!
IT WAS TIME FOR SOME SUPER-STRENGTH!
I'LL TAKE THE CASH, SLY FOX!
CREDIT DEPT
...YOU GET THE CREDIT!
Endo

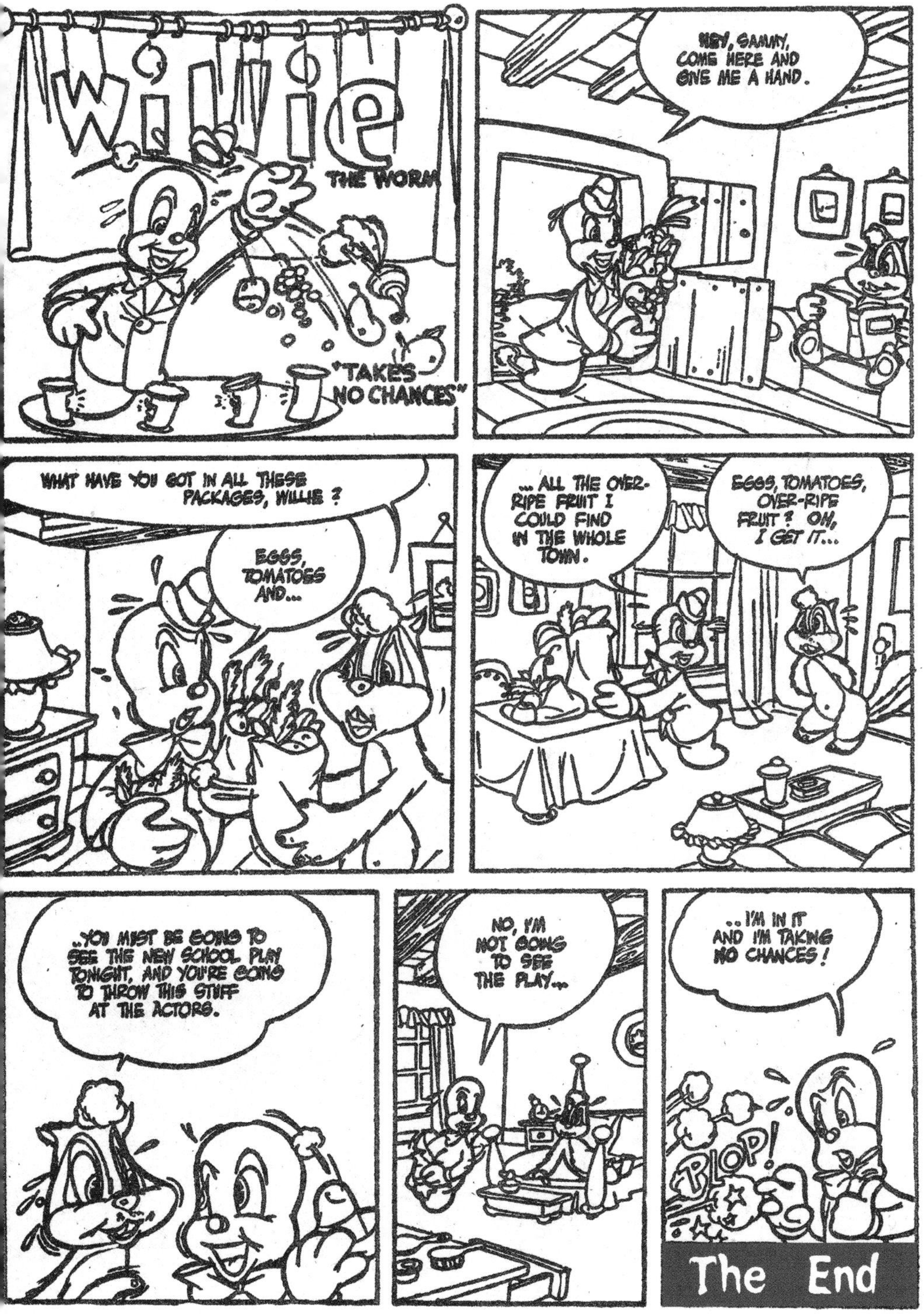
Willie THE WORM
"TAKES NO CHANCES"
HEY, SAMMY, COME HERE AND GIVE ME A HAND.
WHAT HAVE YOU GOT IN ALL THESE PACKAGES, WILLIE ?
EGGS, TOMATOES AND...
... ALL THE OVER-RIPE FRUIT I COULD FIND IN THE WHOLE TOWN.
EGGS, TOMATOES, OVER-RIPE FRUIT ? OH, I GET IT...
..YOU MUST BE GOING TO SEE THE NEW SCHOOL PLAY TONIGHT, AND YOU'RE GOING TO THROW THIS STUFF AT THE ACTORS.
NO, I'M NOT GOING TO SEE THE PLAY...
..I'M IN IT AND I'M TAKING NO CHANCES !
PLOP!
The End

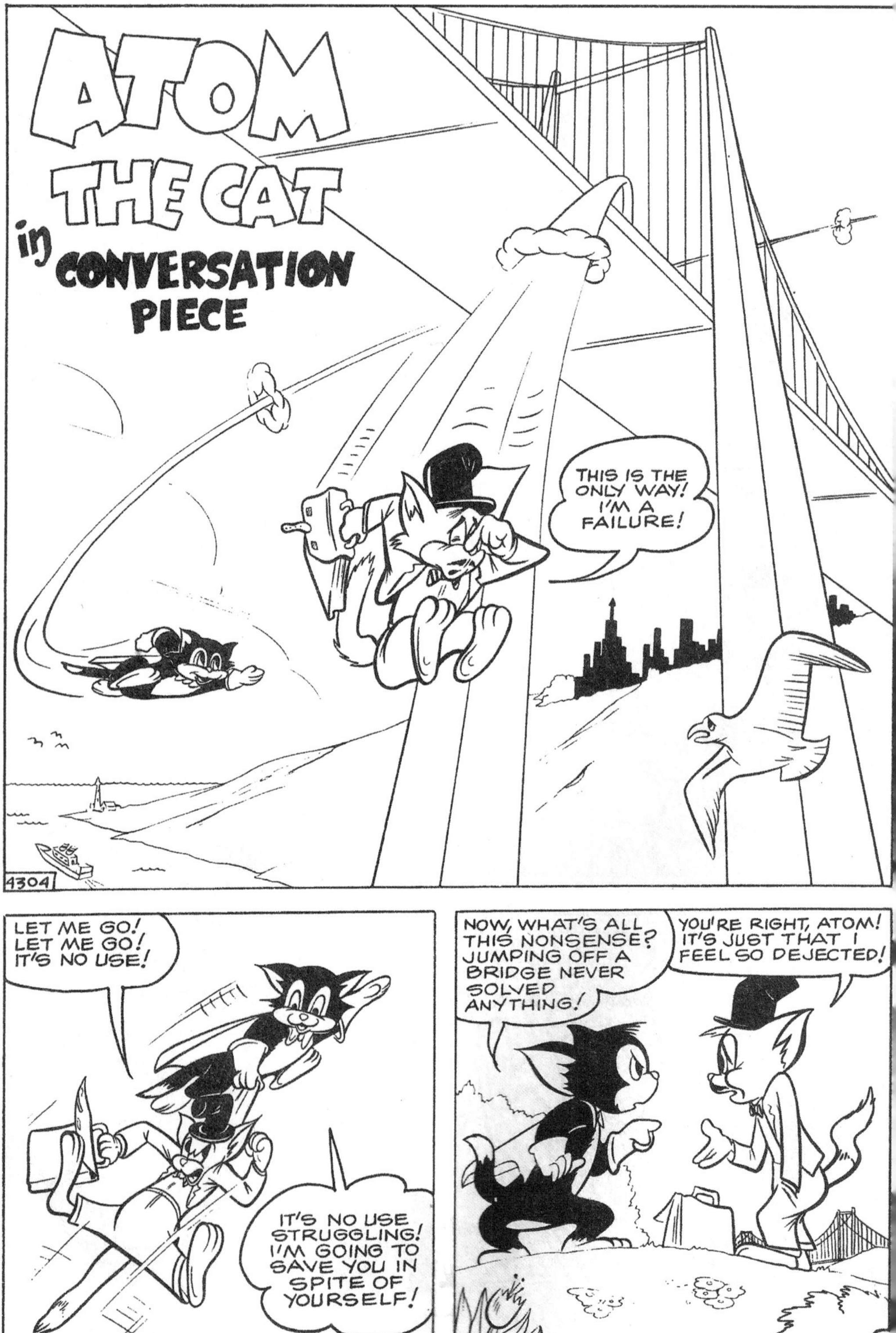
ATOM THE CAT
in CONVERSATION PIECE
THIS IS THE ONLY WAY! I'M A FAILURE!
4304
LET ME GO! LET ME GO! IT'S NO USE!
IT'S NO USE STRUGGLING! I'M GOING TO SAVE YOU IN SPITE OF YOURSELF!
NOW, WHAT'S ALL THIS NONSENSE? JUMPING OFF A BRIDGE NEVER SOLVED ANYTHING!
YOU'RE RIGHT, ATOM! IT'S JUST THAT I FEEL SO DEJECTED!
1

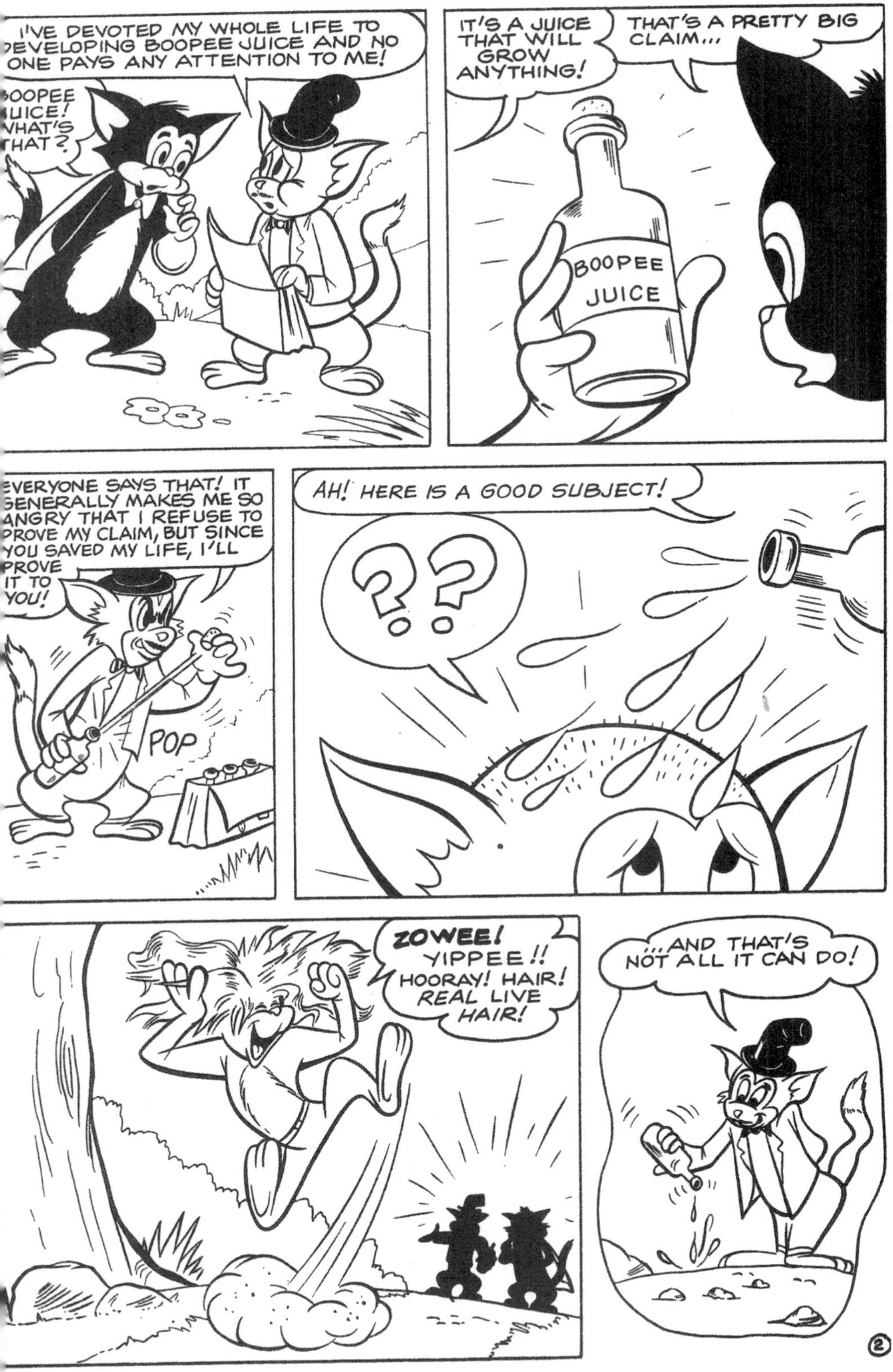
I'VE DEVOTED MY WHOLE LIFE TO DEVELOPING BOOPEE JUICE AND NO ONE PAYS ANY ATTENTION TO ME!
BOOPEE JUICE! WHAT'S THAT?
IT'S A JUICE THAT WILL GROW ANYTHING!
THAT'S A PRETTY BIG CLAIM...
BOOPEE JUICE
EVERYONE SAYS THAT! IT GENERALLY MAKES ME SO ANGRY THAT I REFUSE TO PROVE MY CLAIM, BUT SINCE YOU SAVED MY LIFE, I'LL PROVE IT TO YOU!
POP
AH! HERE IS A GOOD SUBJECT!
??
ZOWEE! YIPPEE!! HOORAY! HAIR! REAL LIVE HAIR!
...AND THAT'S NOT ALL IT CAN DO!

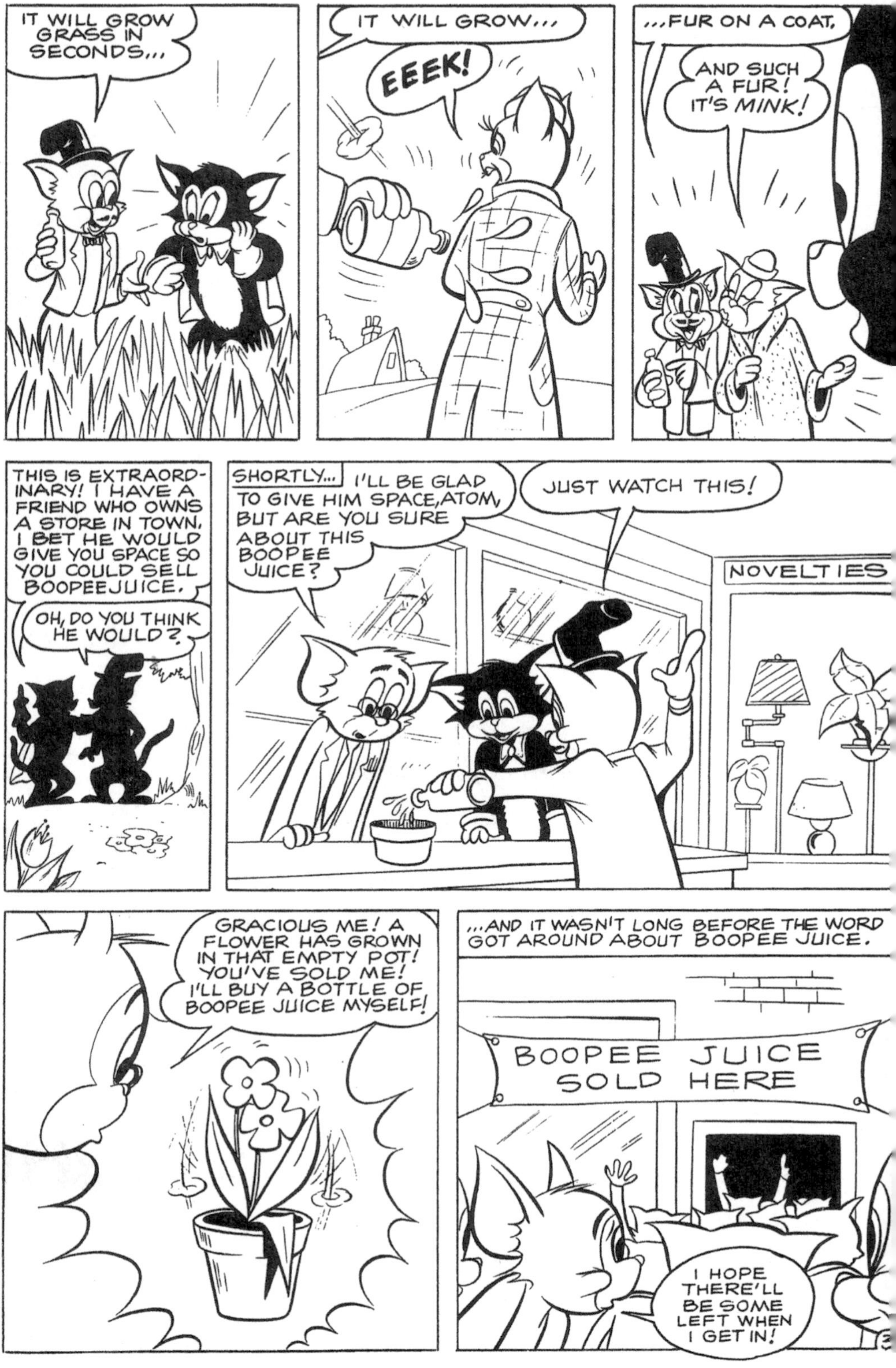
IT WILL GROW GRASS IN SECONDS,,,
IT WILL GROW,,,
EEEK!
,,,FUR ON A COAT,
AND SUCH A FUR! IT'S MINK!
THIS IS EXTRAORDINARY! I HAVE A FRIEND WHO OWNS A STORE IN TOWN, I BET HE WOULD GIVE YOU SPACE SO YOU COULD SELL BOOPEEJUICE,
OH, DO YOU THINK HE WOULD?
SHORTLY...
I'LL BE GLAD TO GIVE HIM SPACE, ATOM, BUT ARE YOU SURE ABOUT THIS BOOPEE JUICE?
JUST WATCH THIS!
NOVELTIES
GRACIOUS ME! A FLOWER HAS GROWN IN THAT EMPTY POT! YOU'VE SOLD ME! I'LL BUY A BOTTLE OF BOOPEE JUICE MYSELF!
...AND IT WASN'T LONG BEFORE THE WORD GOT AROUND ABOUT BOOPEE JUICE.
BOOPEE JUICE SOLD HERE
I HOPE THERE'LL BE SOME LEFT WHEN I GET IN!
3

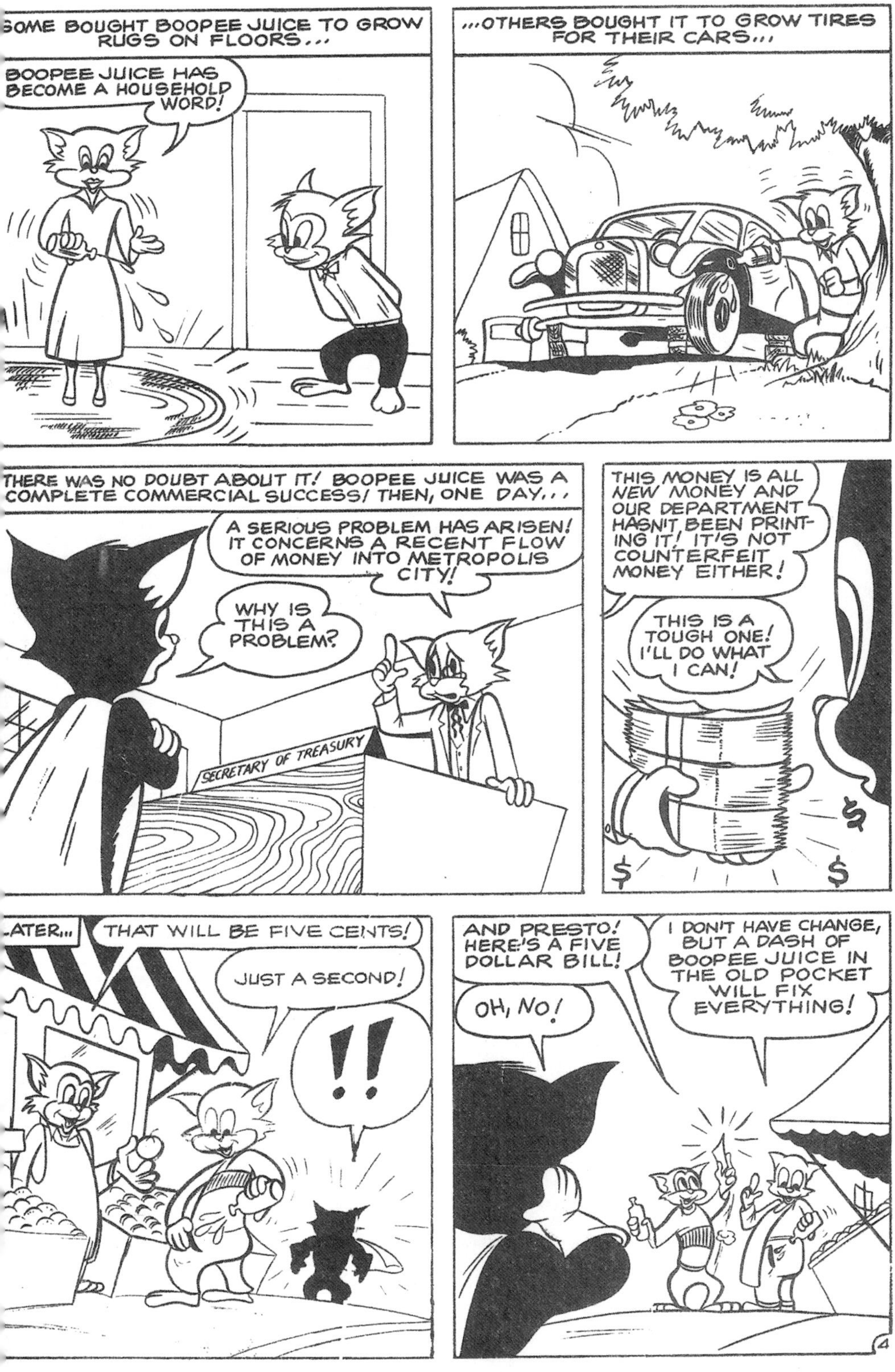
SOME BOUGHT BOOPEE JUICE TO GROW RUGS ON FLOORS...
BOOPEE JUICE HAS BECOME A HOUSEHOLD WORD!
...OTHERS BOUGHT IT TO GROW TIRES FOR THEIR CARS...
THERE WAS NO DOUBT ABOUT IT! BOOPEE JUICE WAS A COMPLETE COMMERCIAL SUCCESS! THEN, ONE DAY...
A SERIOUS PROBLEM HAS ARISEN! IT CONCERNS A RECENT FLOW OF MONEY INTO METROPOLIS CITY!
WHY IS THIS A PROBLEM?
SECRETARY OF TREASURY
THIS MONEY IS ALL NEW MONEY AND OUR DEPARTMENT HASN'T BEEN PRINTING IT! IT'S NOT COUNTERFEIT MONEY EITHER!
THIS IS A TOUGH ONE! I'LL DO WHAT I CAN!
$
$
$
LATER...
THAT WILL BE FIVE CENTS!
JUST A SECOND!
!!
AND PRESTO! HERE'S A FIVE DOLLAR BILL!
I DON'T HAVE CHANGE, BUT A DASH OF BOOPEE JUICE IN THE OLD POCKET WILL FIX EVERYTHING!
OH, NO!

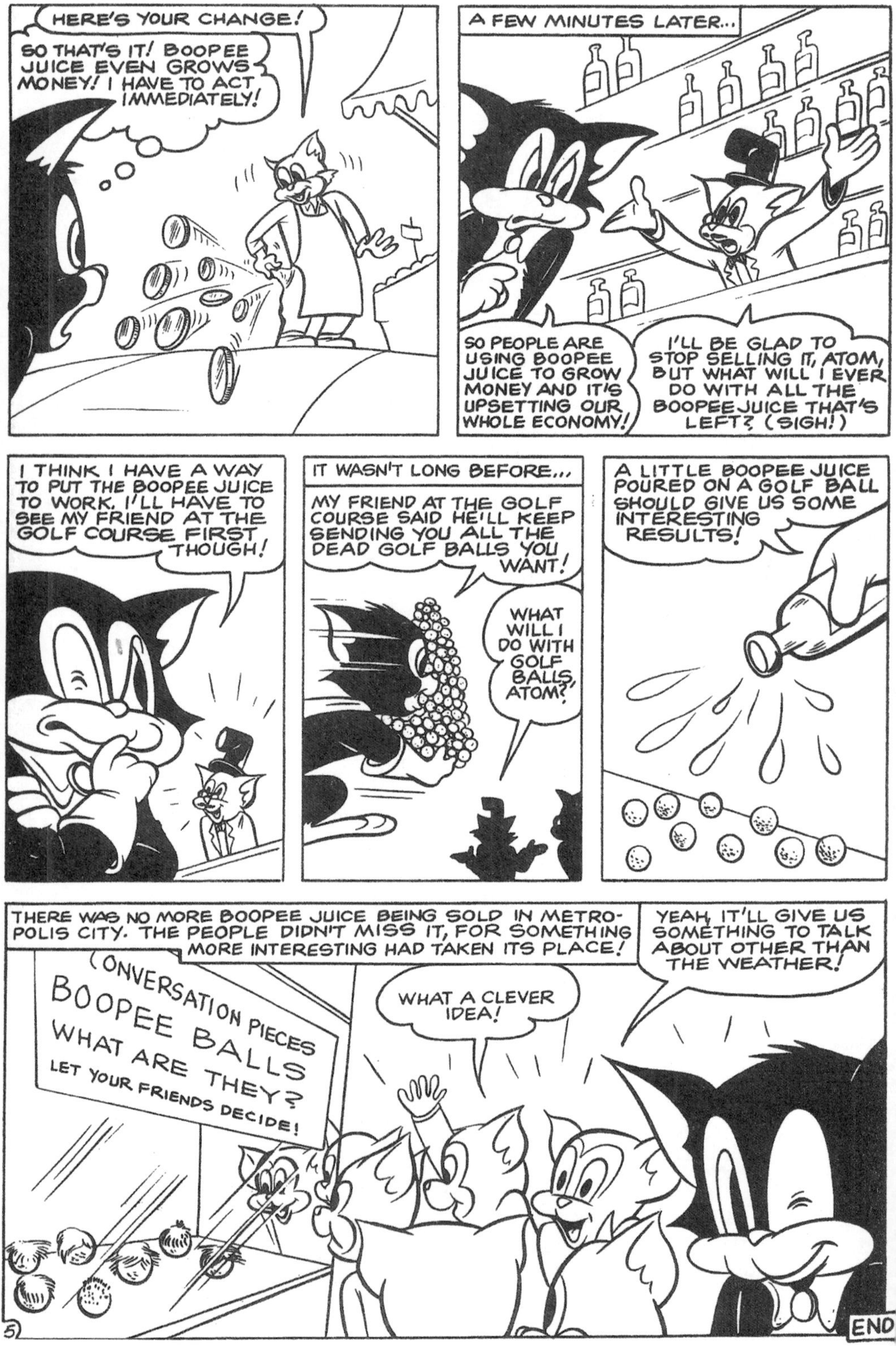
HERE'S YOUR CHANGE!
SO THAT'S IT! BOOPEE JUICE EVEN GROWS MONEY! I HAVE TO ACT IMMEDIATELY!
A FEW MINUTES LATER...
SO PEOPLE ARE USING BOOPEE JUICE TO GROW MONEY AND IT'S UPSETTING OUR WHOLE ECONOMY!
I'LL BE GLAD TO STOP SELLING IT, ATOM, BUT WHAT WILL I EVER DO WITH ALL THE BOOPEE JUICE THAT'S LEFT? (SIGH!)
I THINK I HAVE A WAY TO PUT THE BOOPEE JUICE TO WORK. I'LL HAVE TO SEE MY FRIEND AT THE GOLF COURSE FIRST, THOUGH!
IT WASN'T LONG BEFORE...
MY FRIEND AT THE GOLF COURSE SAID HE'LL KEEP SENDING YOU ALL THE DEAD GOLF BALLS YOU WANT!
WHAT WILL I DO WITH GOLF BALLS, ATOM?
A LITTLE BOOPEE JUICE POURED ON A GOLF BALL SHOULD GIVE US SOME INTERESTING RESULTS!
THERE WAS NO MORE BOOPEE JUICE BEING SOLD IN METROPOLIS CITY. THE PEOPLE DIDN'T MISS IT, FOR SOMETHING MORE INTERESTING HAD TAKEN ITS PLACE!
YEAH, IT'LL GIVE US SOMETHING TO TALK ABOUT OTHER THAN THE WEATHER!
CONVERSATION PIECES
BOOPEE BALLS
WHAT ARE THEY?
LET YOUR FRIENDS DECIDE!
WHAT A CLEVER IDEA!
5
END

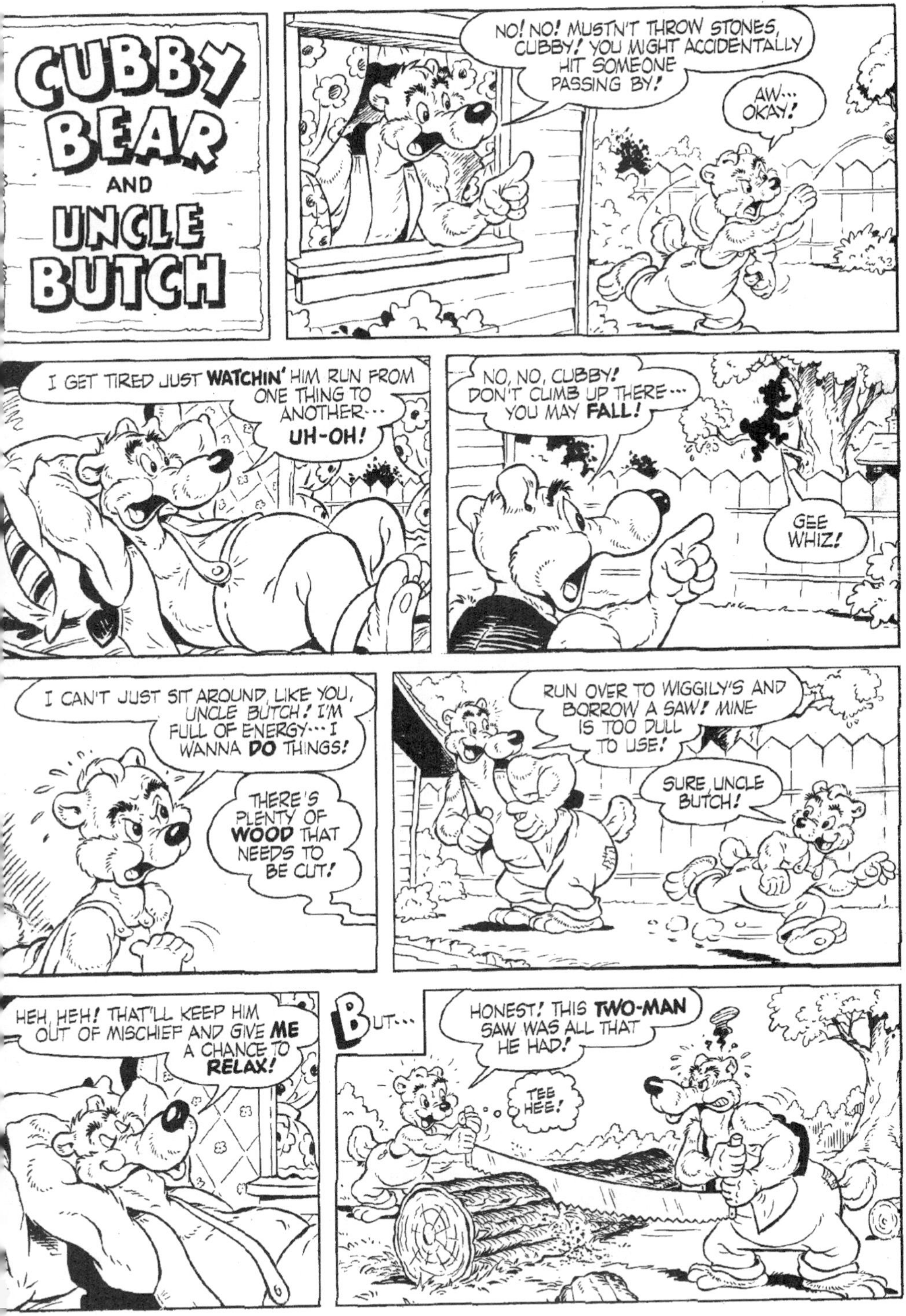

CUBBY BEAR AND UNCLE BUTCH
NO! NO! MUSTN'T THROW STONES, CUBBY! YOU MIGHT ACCIDENTALLY HIT SOMEONE PASSING BY!
AW... OKAY!
I GET TIRED JUST WATCHIN' HIM RUN FROM ONE THING TO ANOTHER... UH-OH!
NO, NO, CUBBY! DON'T CLIMB UP THERE... YOU MAY FALL!
GEE WHIZ!
I CAN'T JUST SIT AROUND LIKE YOU, UNCLE BUTCH! I'M FULL OF ENERGY... I WANNA DO THINGS!
THERE'S PLENTY OF WOOD THAT NEEDS TO BE CUT!
RUN OVER TO WIGGILY'S AND BORROW A SAW! MINE IS TOO DULL TO USE!
SURE, UNCLE BUTCH!
HEH, HEH! THAT'LL KEEP HIM OUT OF MISCHIEF AND GIVE ME A CHANCE TO RELAX!
BUT...
HONEST! THIS TWO-MAN SAW WAS ALL THAT HE HAD!
TEE HEE!

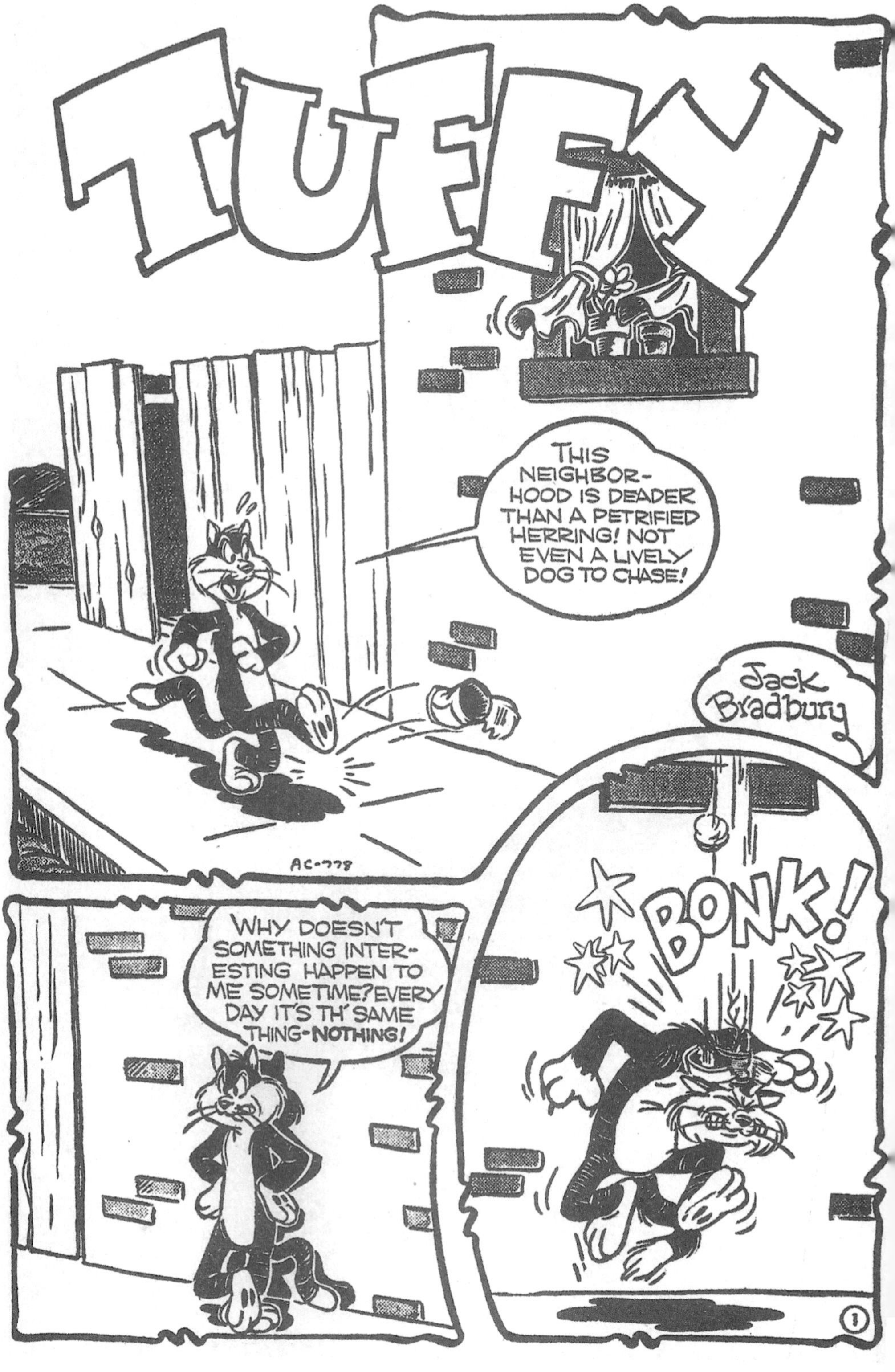
TUFFY
THIS NEIGHBOR-HOOD IS DEADER THAN A PETRIFIED HERRING! NOT EVEN A LIVELY DOG TO CHASE!
Jack Bradbury
AC-778
WHY DOESN'T SOMETHING INTER-ESTING HAPPEN TO ME SOMETIME? EVERY DAY IT'S TH' SAME THING-NOTHING!
BONK!
1

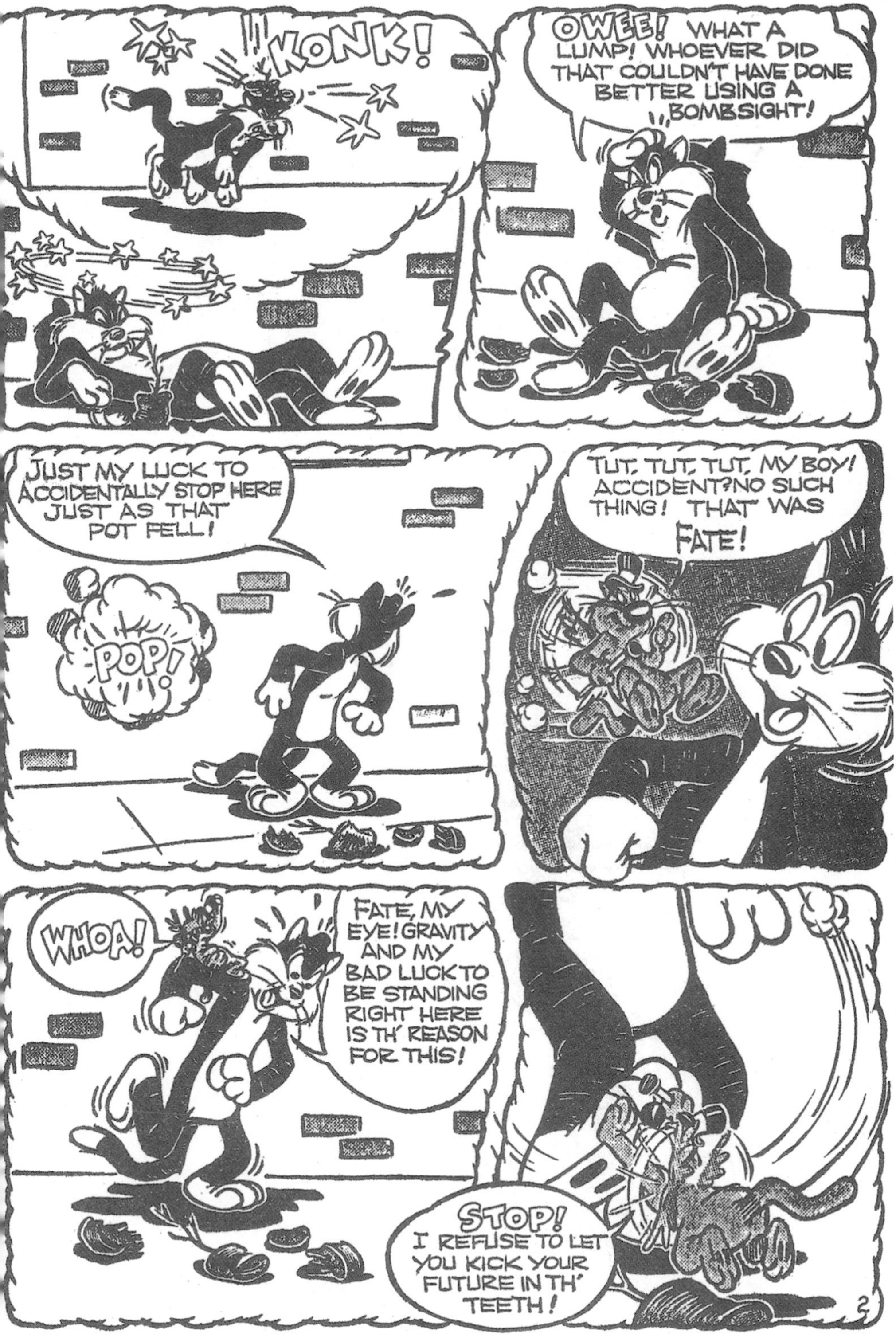
KONK!
OWEE! WHAT A LUMP! WHOEVER DID THAT COULDN'T HAVE DONE BETTER USING A BOMBSIGHT!
JUST MY LUCK TO ACCIDENTALLY STOP HERE JUST AS THAT POT FELL!
POP!
TUT, TUT, TUT, MY BOY! ACCIDENT? NO SUCH THING! THAT WAS FATE!
WHOA!
FATE, MY EYE! GRAVITY AND MY BAD LUCK TO BE STANDING RIGHT HERE IS TH' REASON FOR THIS!
STOP! I REFUSE TO LET YOU KICK YOUR FUTURE IN TH' TEETH!

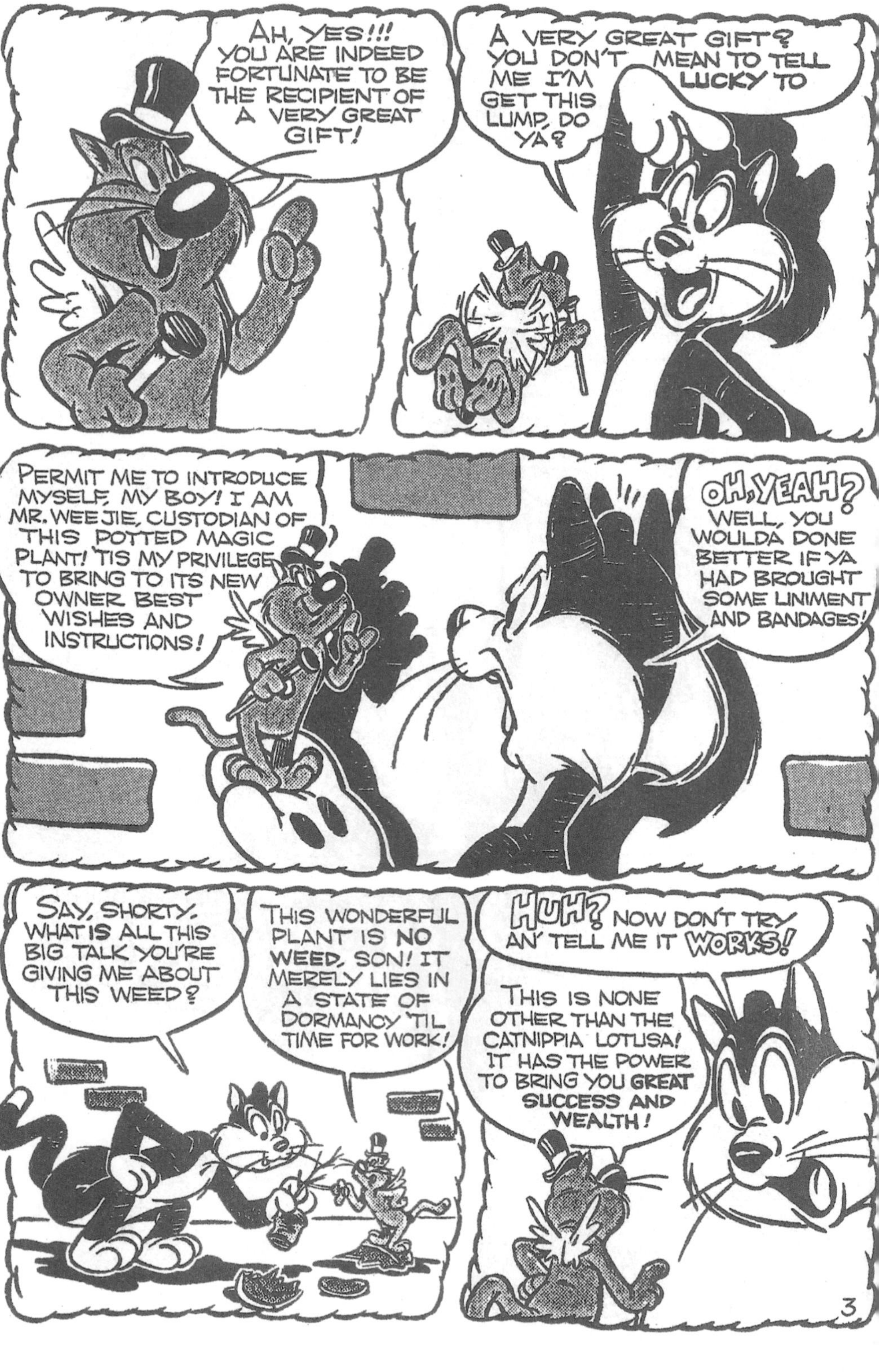

AH, YES!!! YOU ARE INDEED FORTUNATE TO BE THE RECIPIENT OF A VERY GREAT GIFT!
A VERY GREAT GIFT? YOU DON'T MEAN TO TELL ME I'M LUCKY TO GET THIS LUMP, DO YA?
PERMIT ME TO INTRODUCE MYSELF, MY BOY! I AM MR. WEE JIE, CUSTODIAN OF THIS POTTED MAGIC PLANT! 'TIS MY PRIVILEGE TO BRING TO ITS NEW OWNER BEST WISHES AND INSTRUCTIONS!
OH, YEAH? WELL, YOU WOULDA DONE BETTER IF YA HAD BROUGHT SOME LINIMENT AND BANDAGES!
SAY, SHORTY. WHAT IS ALL THIS BIG TALK YOU'RE GIVING ME ABOUT THIS WEED?
THIS WONDERFUL PLANT IS NO WEED, SON! IT MERELY LIES IN A STATE OF DORMANCY 'TIL TIME FOR WORK!
HUH? NOW DON'T TRY AN' TELL ME IT WORKS!
THIS IS NONE OTHER THAN THE CATNIPPIA LOTUSA! IT HAS THE POWER TO BRING YOU GREAT SUCCESS AND WEALTH!

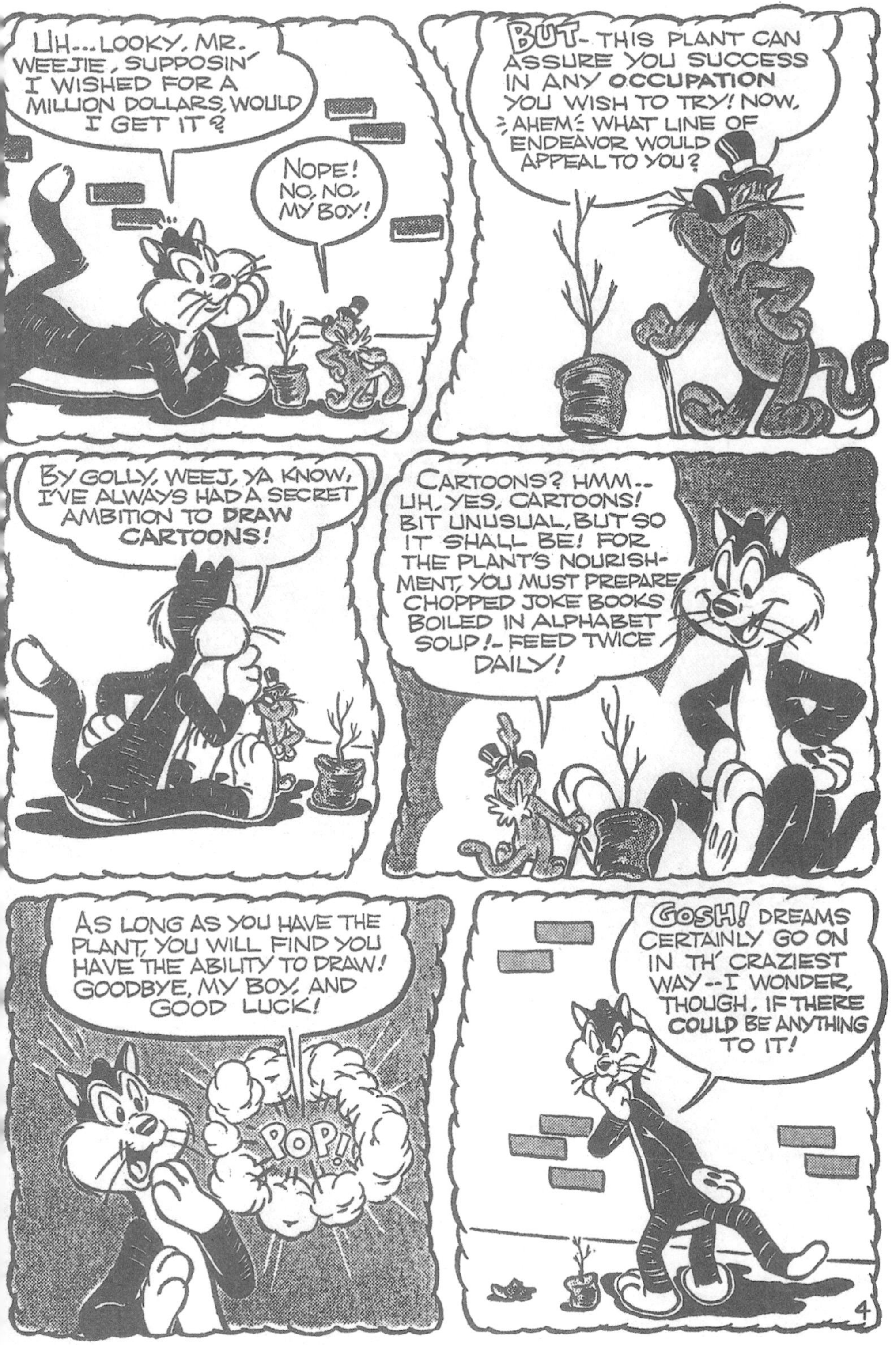
UH...LOOKY, MR. WEEJIE, SUPPOSIN' I WISHED FOR A MILLION DOLLARS, WOULD I GET IT?
NOPE! NO, NO, MY BOY!
BUT- THIS PLANT CAN ASSURE YOU SUCCESS IN ANY OCCUPATION YOU WISH TO TRY! NOW, AHEM WHAT LINE OF ENDEAVOR WOULD APPEAL TO YOU?
BY GOLLY, WEEJ, YA KNOW, I'VE ALWAYS HAD A SECRET AMBITION TO DRAW CARTOONS!
CARTOONS? HMM.. UH, YES, CARTOONS! BIT UNUSUAL, BUT SO IT SHALL BE! FOR THE PLANT'S NOURISHMENT, YOU MUST PREPARE CHOPPED JOKE BOOKS BOILED IN ALPHABET SOUP!- FEED TWICE DAILY!
AS LONG AS YOU HAVE THE PLANT, YOU WILL FIND YOU HAVE THE ABILITY TO DRAW! GOODBYE, MY BOY, AND GOOD LUCK!
POP!
GOSH! DREAMS CERTAINLY GO ON IN TH' CRAZIEST WAY--I WONDER, THOUGH, IF THERE COULD BE ANYTHING TO IT!
4

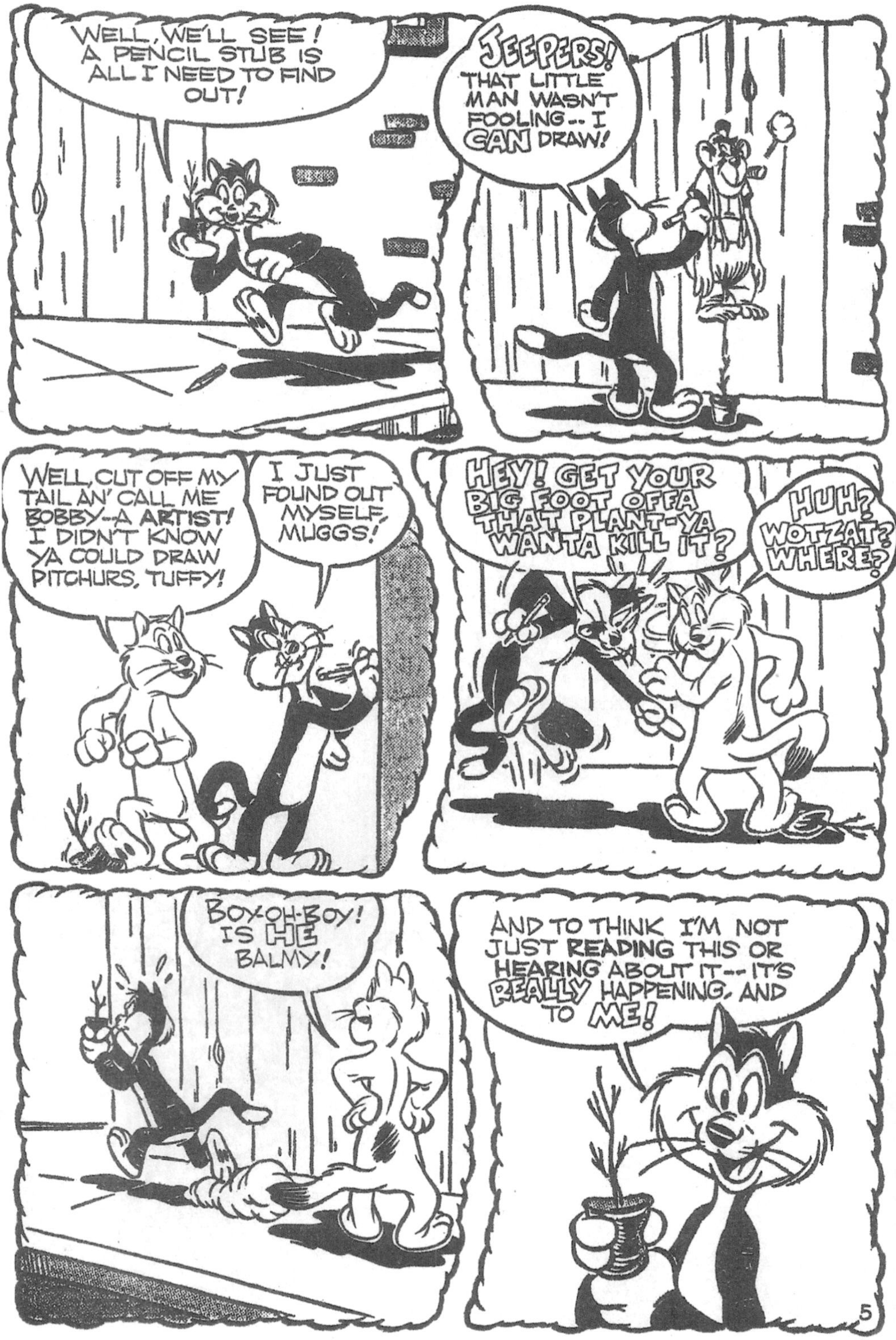
WELL, WE'LL SEE! A PENCIL STUB IS ALL I NEED TO FIND OUT!
JEEPERS! THAT LITTLE MAN WASN'T FOOLING-- I CAN DRAW!
WELL, CUT OFF MY TAIL AN' CALL ME BOBBY--A ARTIST! I DIDN'T KNOW YA COULD DRAW PITCHURS, TUFFY!
I JUST FOUND OUT MYSELF, MUGGS!
HEY! GET YOUR BIG FOOT OFFA THAT PLANT-YA WANTA KILL IT?
HUH? WOTZAT? WHERE?
BOY-OH-BOY! IS HE BALMY!
AND TO THINK I'M NOT JUST READING THIS OR HEARING ABOUT IT-- IT'S REALLY HAPPENING, AND TO ME!

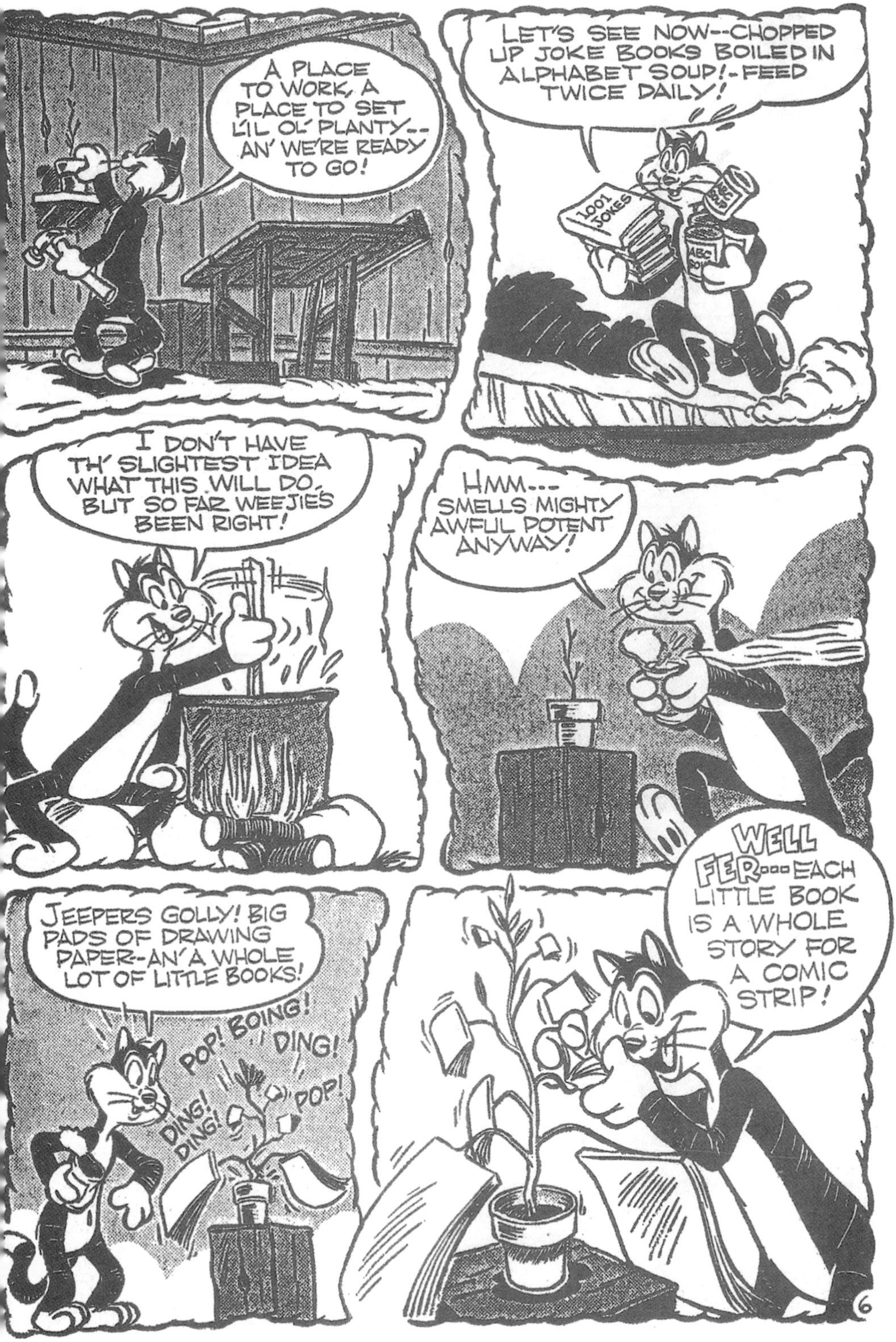
A PLACE TO WORK, A PLACE TO SET L'IL OL' PLANTY-- AN' WE'RE READY TO GO!
LET'S SEE NOW--CHOPPED UP JOKE BOOKS BOILED IN ALPHABET SOUP!-FEED TWICE DAILY!
1001 JOKES
ABC SOUP
I DON'T HAVE TH' SLIGHTEST IDEA WHAT THIS WILL DO, BUT SO FAR WEEJIE'S BEEN RIGHT!
HMM... SMELLS MIGHTY AWFUL POTENT ANYWAY!
JEEPERS GOLLY! BIG PADS OF DRAWING PAPER-AN' A WHOLE LOT OF LITTLE BOOKS!
POP! BOING! DING!
DING! DING! POP!
WELL FER... EACH LITTLE BOOK IS A WHOLE STORY FOR A COMIC STRIP!
6

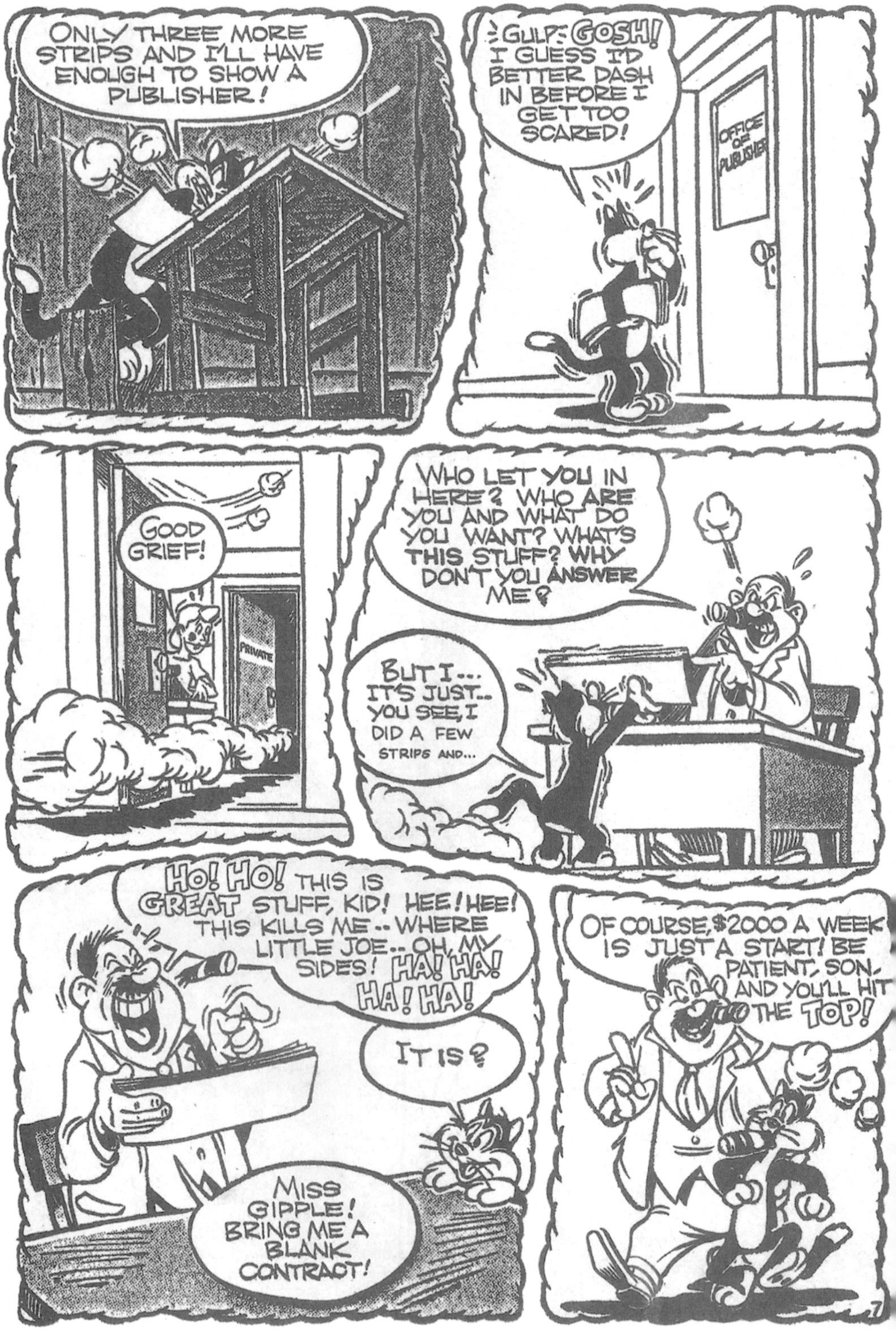
ONLY THREE MORE STRIPS AND I'LL HAVE ENOUGH TO SHOW A PUBLISHER!
GULP! GOSH! I GUESS I'D BETTER DASH IN BEFORE I GET TOO SCARED!
OFFICE OF PUBLISHER
GOOD GRIEF!
PRIVATE
WHO LET YOU IN HERE? WHO ARE YOU AND WHAT DO YOU WANT? WHAT'S THIS STUFF? WHY DON'T YOU ANSWER ME?
BUT I... IT'S JUST.. YOU SEE, I DID A FEW STRIPS AND...
HO! HO! THIS IS GREAT STUFF, KID! HEE! HEE! THIS KILLS ME -- WHERE LITTLE JOE.. OH, MY SIDES! HA! HA! HA! HA!
IT IS?
MISS GIPPLE! BRING ME A BLANK CONTRACT!
OF COURSE, $2000 A WEEK IS JUST A START! BE PATIENT, SON, AND YOU'LL HIT THE TOP!

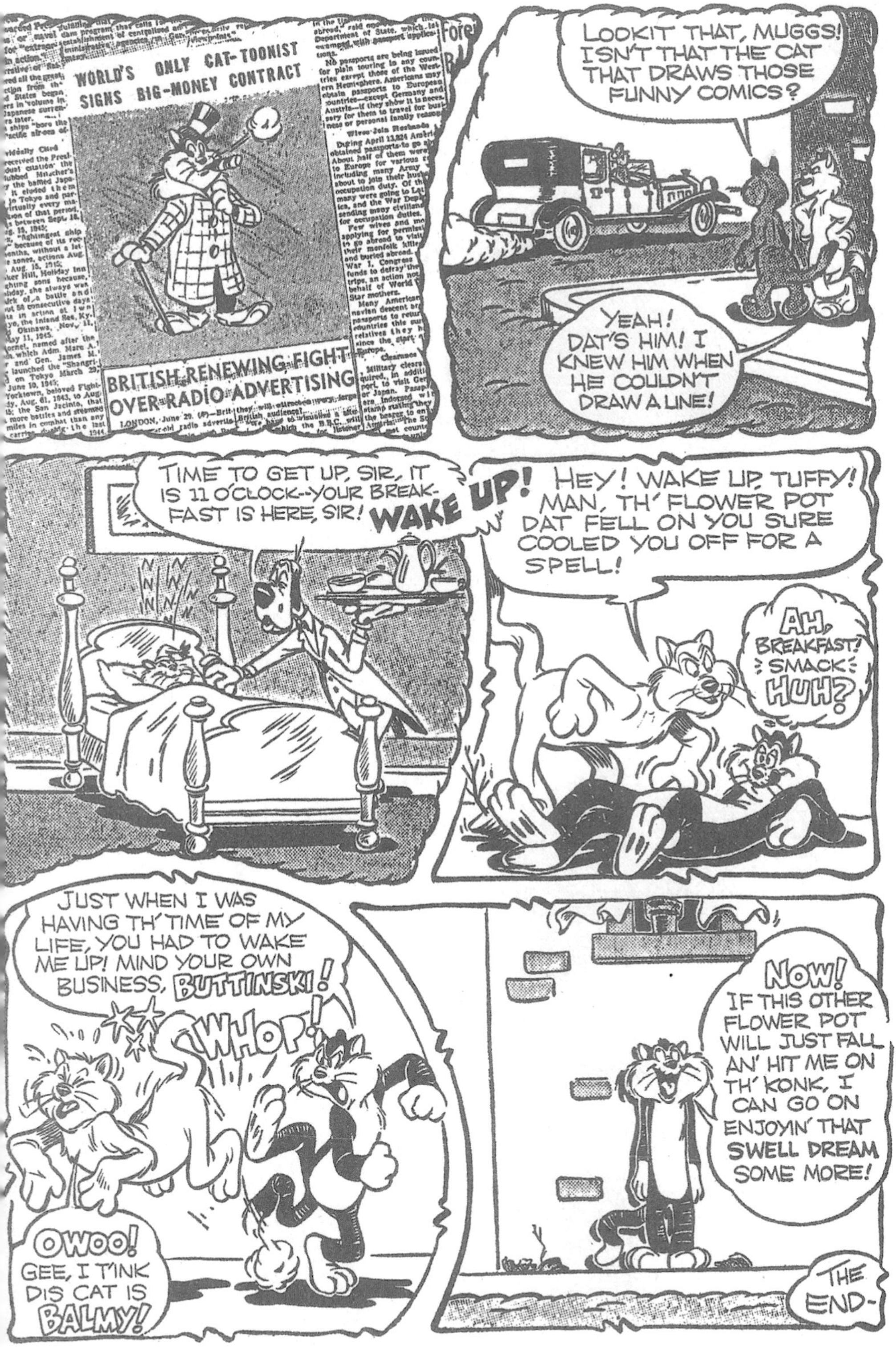

WORLD'S ONLY CAT-TOONIST SIGNS BIG-MONEY CONTRACT
BRITISH RENEWING FIGHT OVER RADIO ADVERTISING
LOOKIT THAT, MUGGS! ISN'T THAT THE CAT THAT DRAWS THOSE FUNNY COMICS?
YEAH! DAT'S HIM! I KNEW HIM WHEN HE COULDN'T DRAW A LINE!
TIME TO GET UP, SIR, IT IS 11 O'CLOCK--YOUR BREAK-FAST IS HERE, SIR!
WAKE UP!
HEY! WAKE UP, TUFFY! MAN, TH' FLOWER POT DAT FELL ON YOU SURE COOLED YOU OFF FOR A SPELL!
AH, BREAKFAST! SMACK HUH?
JUST WHEN I WAS HAVING TH' TIME OF MY LIFE, YOU HAD TO WAKE ME UP! MIND YOUR OWN BUSINESS, BUTTINSKI!
SWHOP!
OWOO! GEE, I T'INK DIS CAT IS BALMY!
NOW! IF THIS OTHER FLOWER POT WILL JUST FALL AN' HIT ME ON TH' KONK, I CAN GO ON ENJOYIN' THAT SWELL DREAM SOME MORE!
THE END-

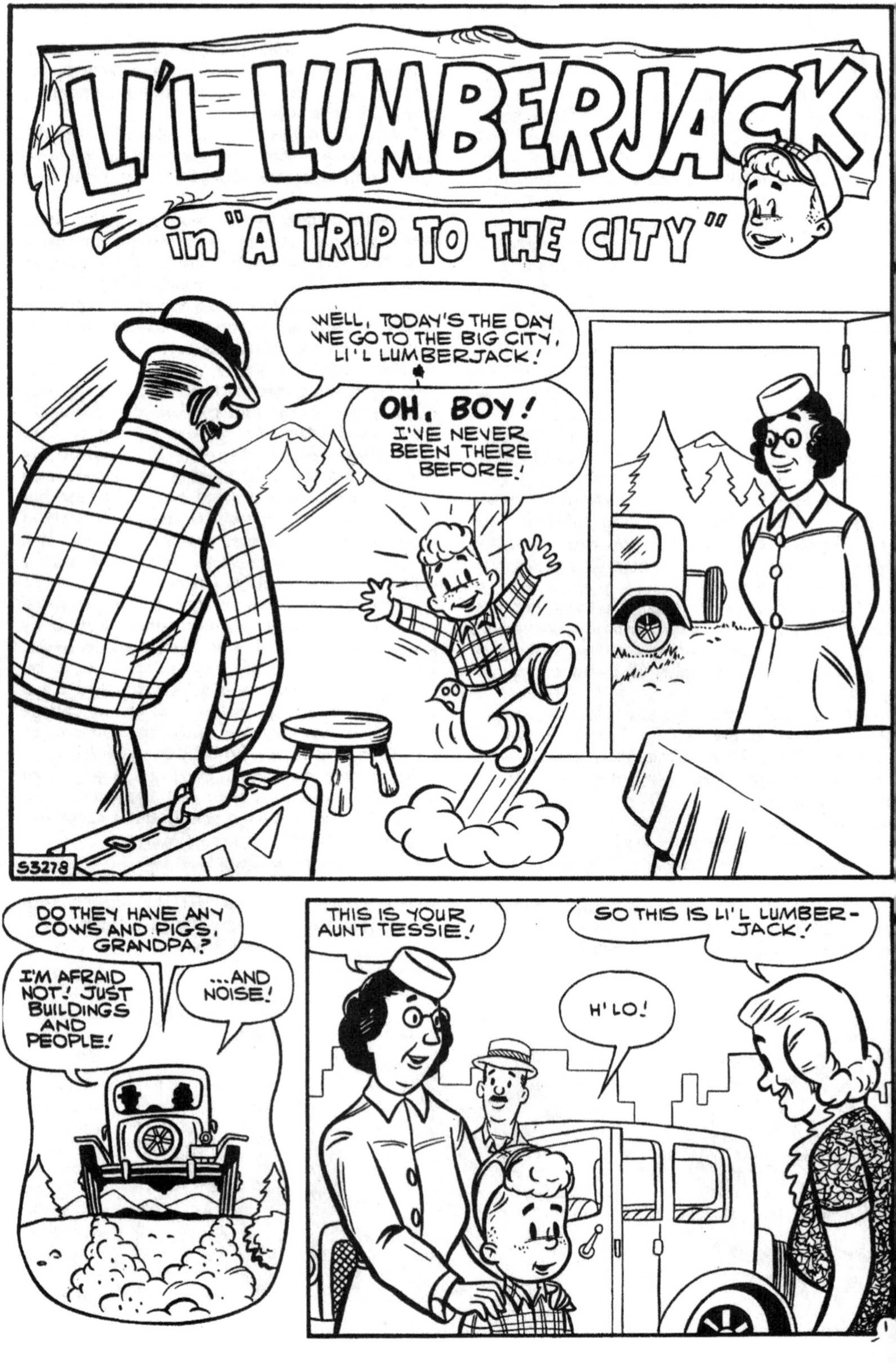
LI'L LUMBERJACK
in "A TRIP TO THE CITY"
WELL, TODAY'S THE DAY WE GO TO THE BIG CITY, LI'L LUMBERJACK!
OH, BOY! I'VE NEVER BEEN THERE BEFORE!
S3278
DO THEY HAVE ANY COWS AND PIGS, GRANDPA?
I'M AFRAID NOT! JUST BUILDINGS AND PEOPLE!
...AND NOISE!
THIS IS YOUR AUNT TESSIE!
SO THIS IS LI'L LUMBER-JACK!
H'LO!

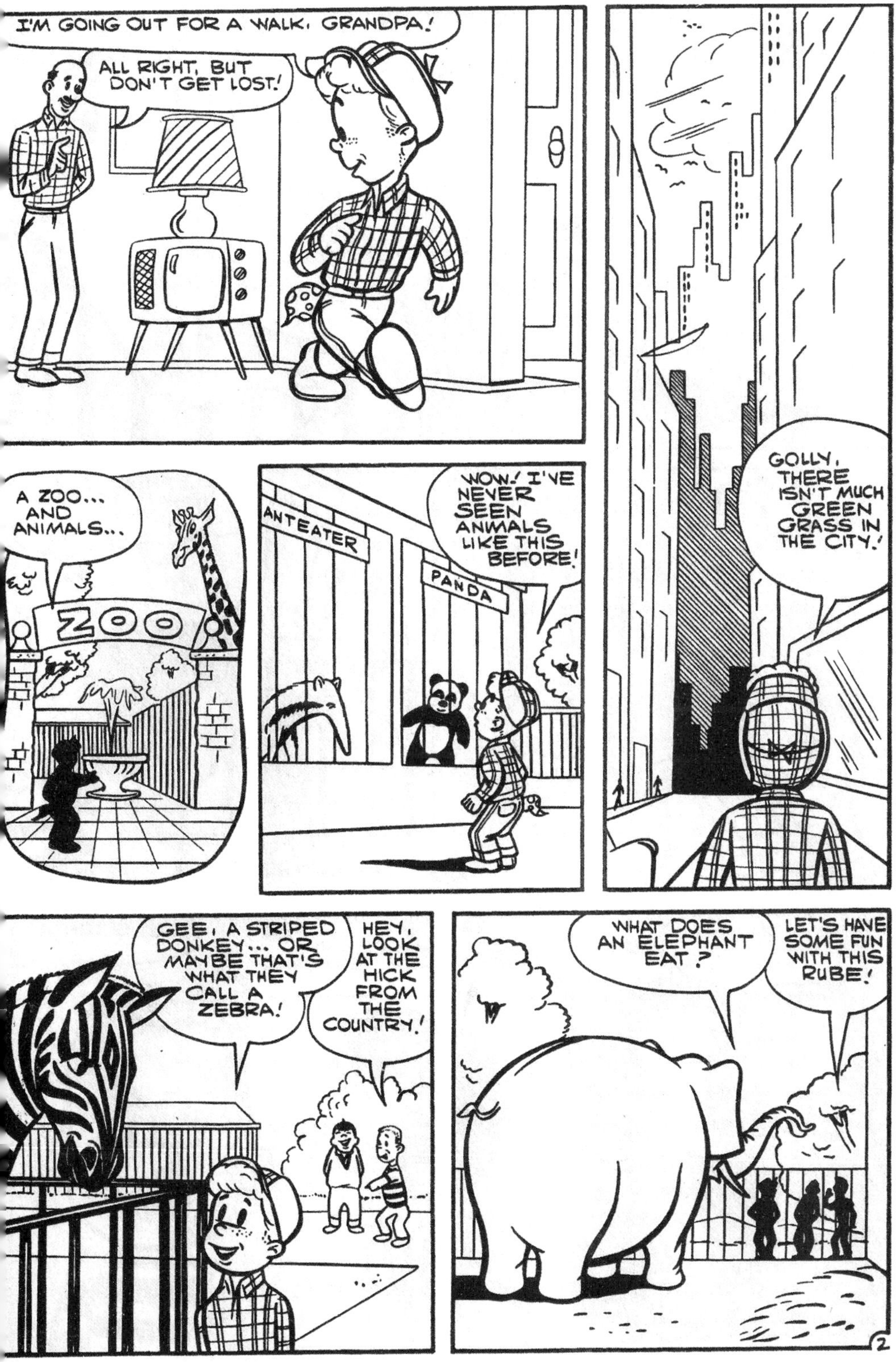
I'M GOING OUT FOR A WALK, GRANDPA!
ALL RIGHT, BUT DON'T GET LOST!
GOLLY, THERE ISN'T MUCH GREEN GRASS IN THE CITY!
A ZOO... AND ANIMALS...
ZOO
ANTEATER
PANDA
WOW! I'VE NEVER SEEN ANIMALS LIKE THIS BEFORE!
GEE, A STRIPED DONKEY... OR MAYBE THAT'S WHAT THEY CALL A ZEBRA!
HEY, LOOK AT THE HICK FROM THE COUNTRY!
WHAT DOES AN ELEPHANT EAT?
LET'S HAVE SOME FUN WITH THIS RUBE!

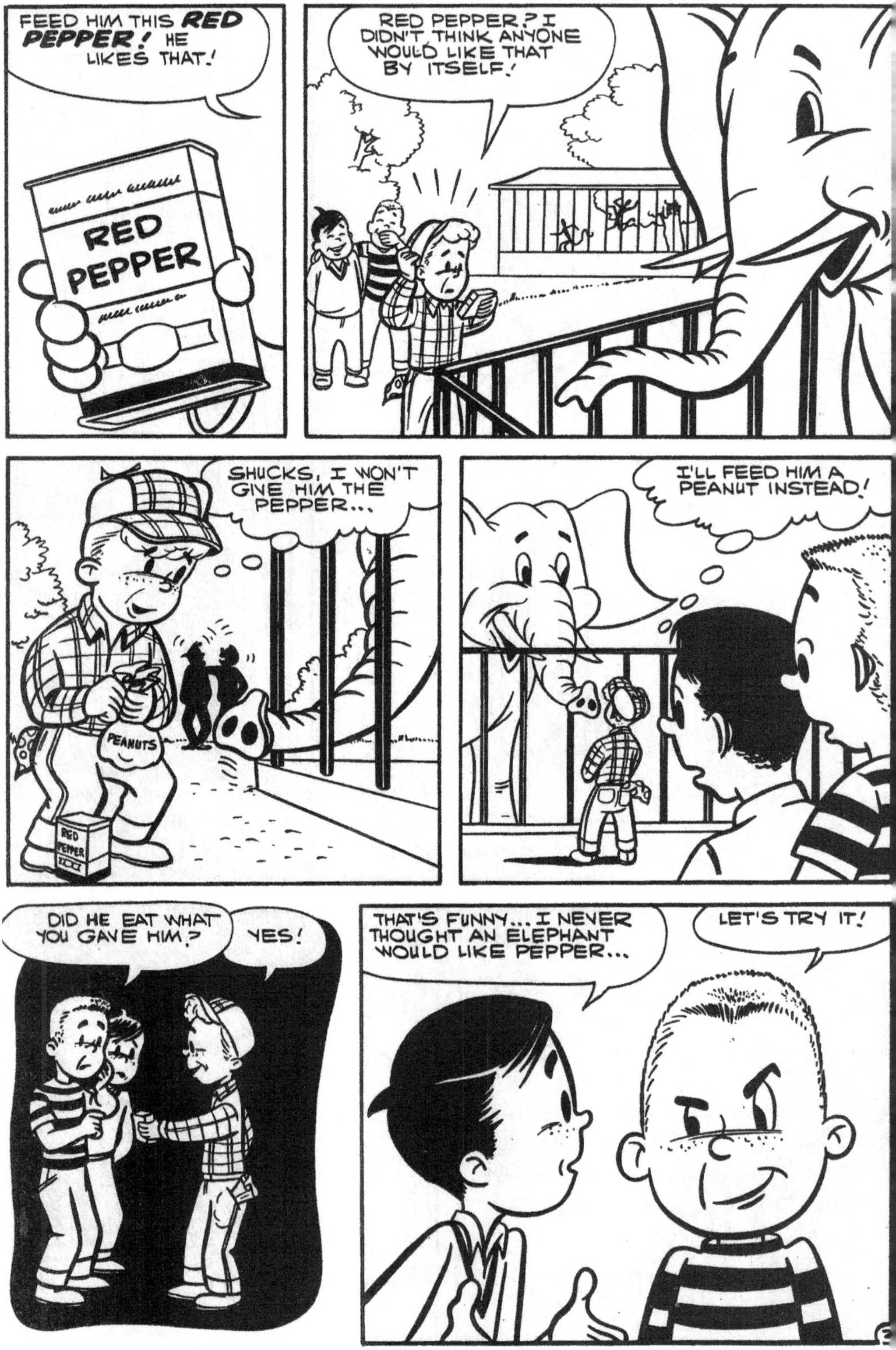
FEED HIM THIS RED PEPPER! HE LIKES THAT!
RED PEPPER
RED PEPPER? I DIDN'T THINK ANYONE WOULD LIKE THAT BY ITSELF!
SHUCKS, I WON'T GIVE HIM THE PEPPER...
PEANUTS
RED PEPPER
I'LL FEED HIM A PEANUT INSTEAD!
DID HE EAT WHAT YOU GAVE HIM?
YES!
THAT'S FUNNY... I NEVER THOUGHT AN ELEPHANT WOULD LIKE PEPPER...
LET'S TRY IT!

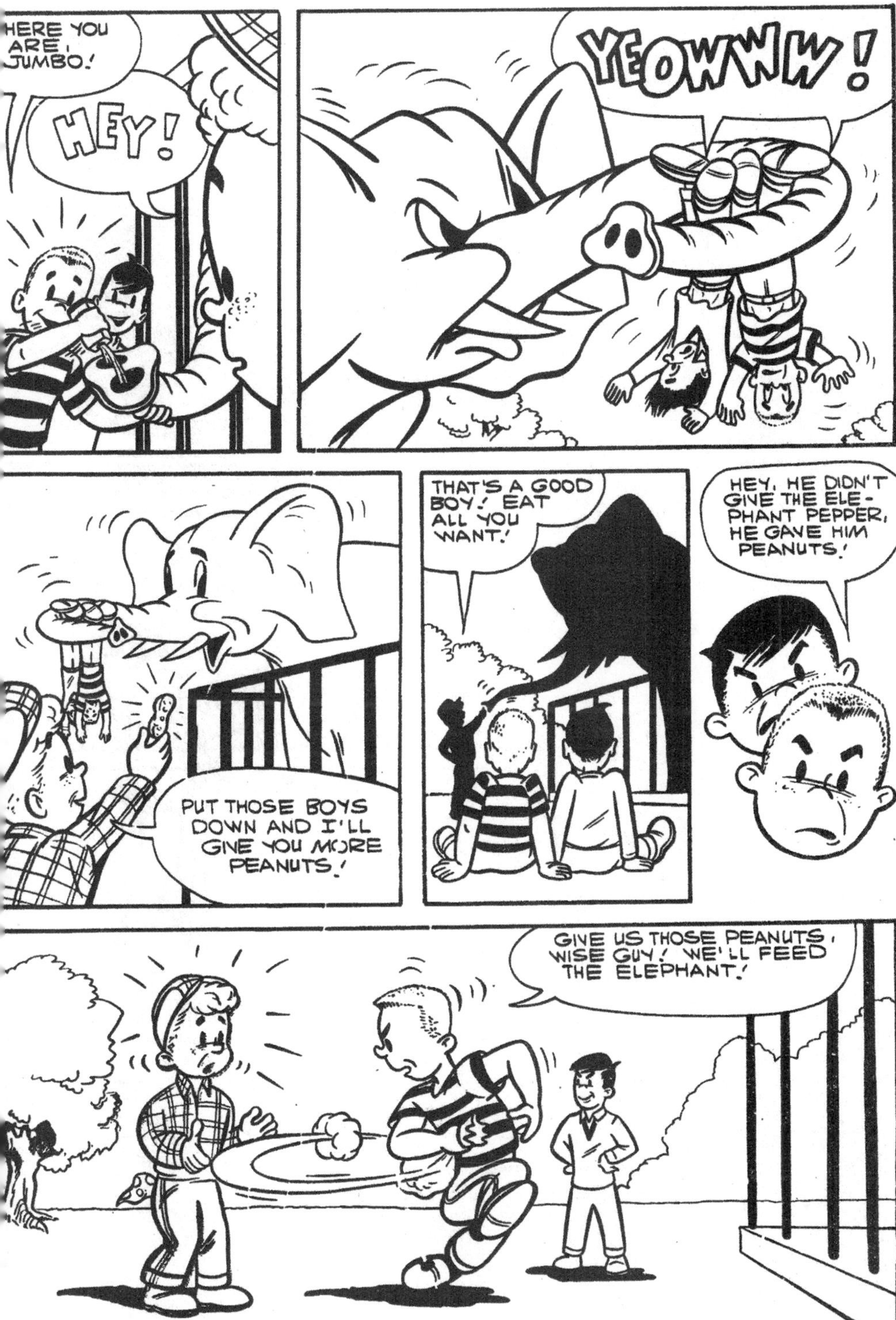

HERE YOU ARE, JUMBO!
HEY!
YEOWWWW!
THAT'S A GOOD BOY! EAT ALL YOU WANT!
HEY, HE DIDN'T GIVE THE ELE-PHANT PEPPER, HE GAVE HIM PEANUTS!
PUT THOSE BOYS DOWN AND I'LL GIVE YOU MORE PEANUTS!
GIVE US THOSE PEANUTS, WISE GUY! WE'LL FEED THE ELEPHANT!

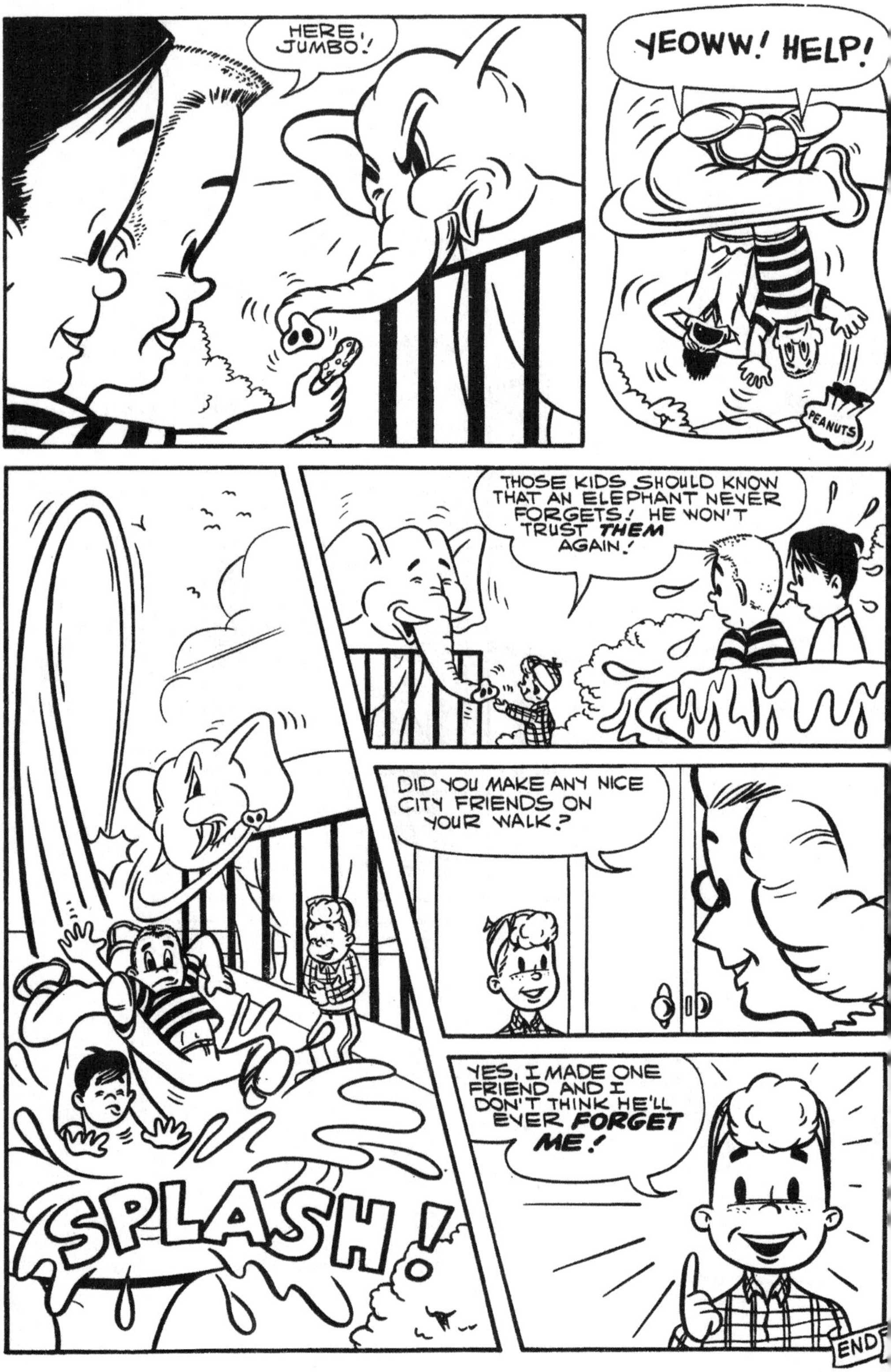
HERE, JUMBO!
YEOWW! HELP!
PEANUTS
SPLASH!
THOSE KIDS SHOULD KNOW THAT AN ELEPHANT NEVER FORGETS! HE WON'T TRUST THEM AGAIN!
DID YOU MAKE ANY NICE CITY FRIENDS ON YOUR WALK?
YES, I MADE ONE FRIEND AND I DON'T THINK HE'LL EVER FORGET ME!
END

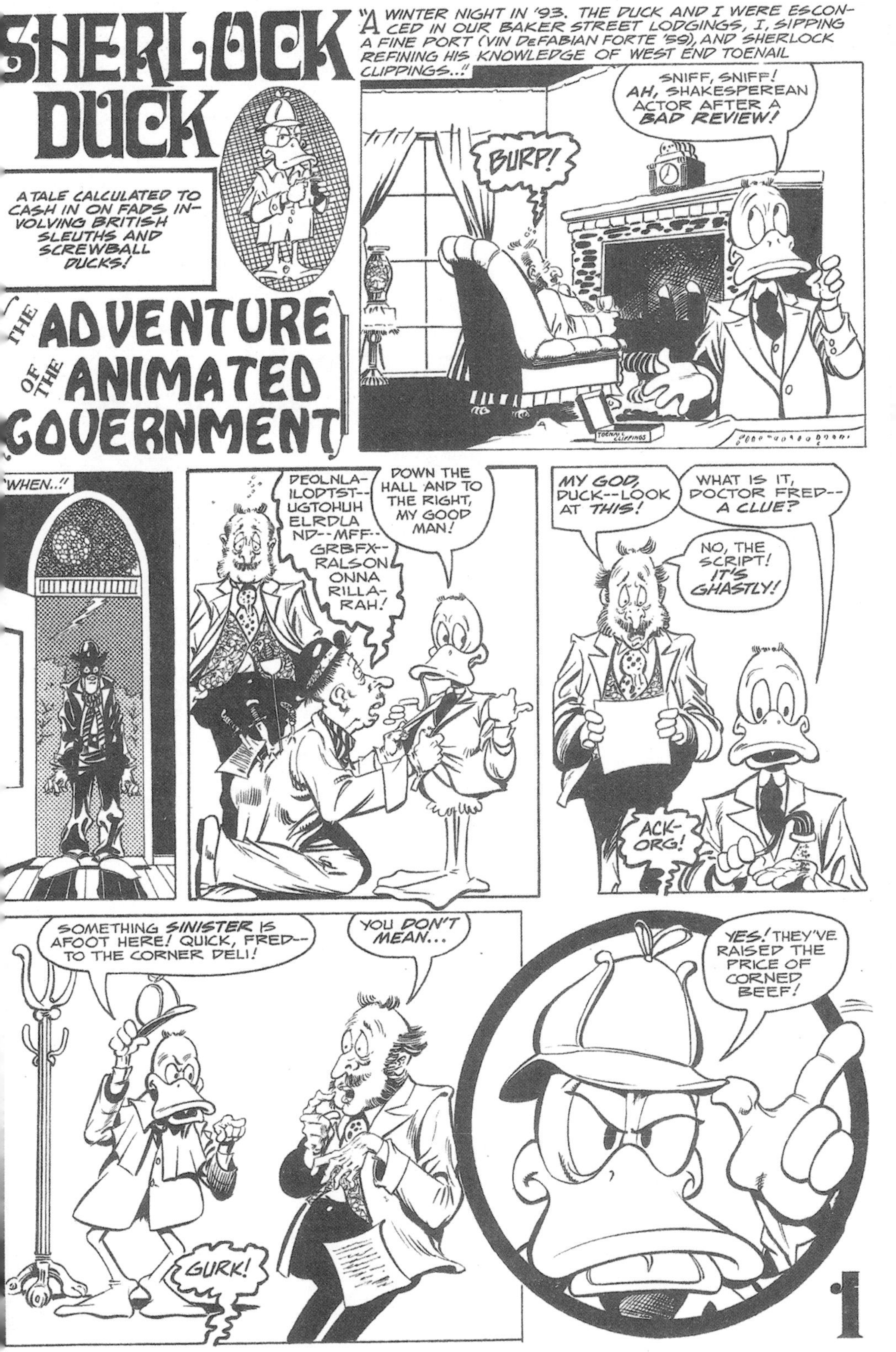
SHERLOCK DUCK
A TALE CALCULATED TO CASH IN ON FADS INVOLVING BRITISH SLEUTHS AND SCREWBALL DUCKS!
THE ADVENTURE OF THE ANIMATED GOVERNMENT
"A WINTER NIGHT IN '93. THE DUCK AND I WERE ESCONCED IN OUR BAKER STREET LODGINGS, I, SIPPING A FINE PORT (VIN DeFABIAN FORTE '59), AND SHERLOCK REFINING HIS KNOWLEDGE OF WEST END TOENAIL CLIPPINGS..!"
SNIFF, SNIFF! AH, SHAKESPEREAN ACTOR AFTER A BAD REVIEW!
BURP!
TOENAIL CLIPPINGS
"WHEN..!"
DEOLNLA-ILODTST--UGTOHUH ELRDLA ND--MFF--GRBFX--RALSON ONNA RILLA-RAH!
DOWN THE HALL AND TO THE RIGHT, MY GOOD MAN!
MY GOD, DUCK--LOOK AT THIS!
WHAT IS IT, DOCTOR FRED--A CLUE?
NO, THE SCRIPT! IT'S GHASTLY!
ACK-ORG!
SOMETHING SINISTER IS AFOOT HERE! QUICK, FRED--TO THE CORNER DELI!
YOU DON'T MEAN...
YES! THEY'VE RAISED THE PRICE OF CORNED BEEF!
GURK!
1

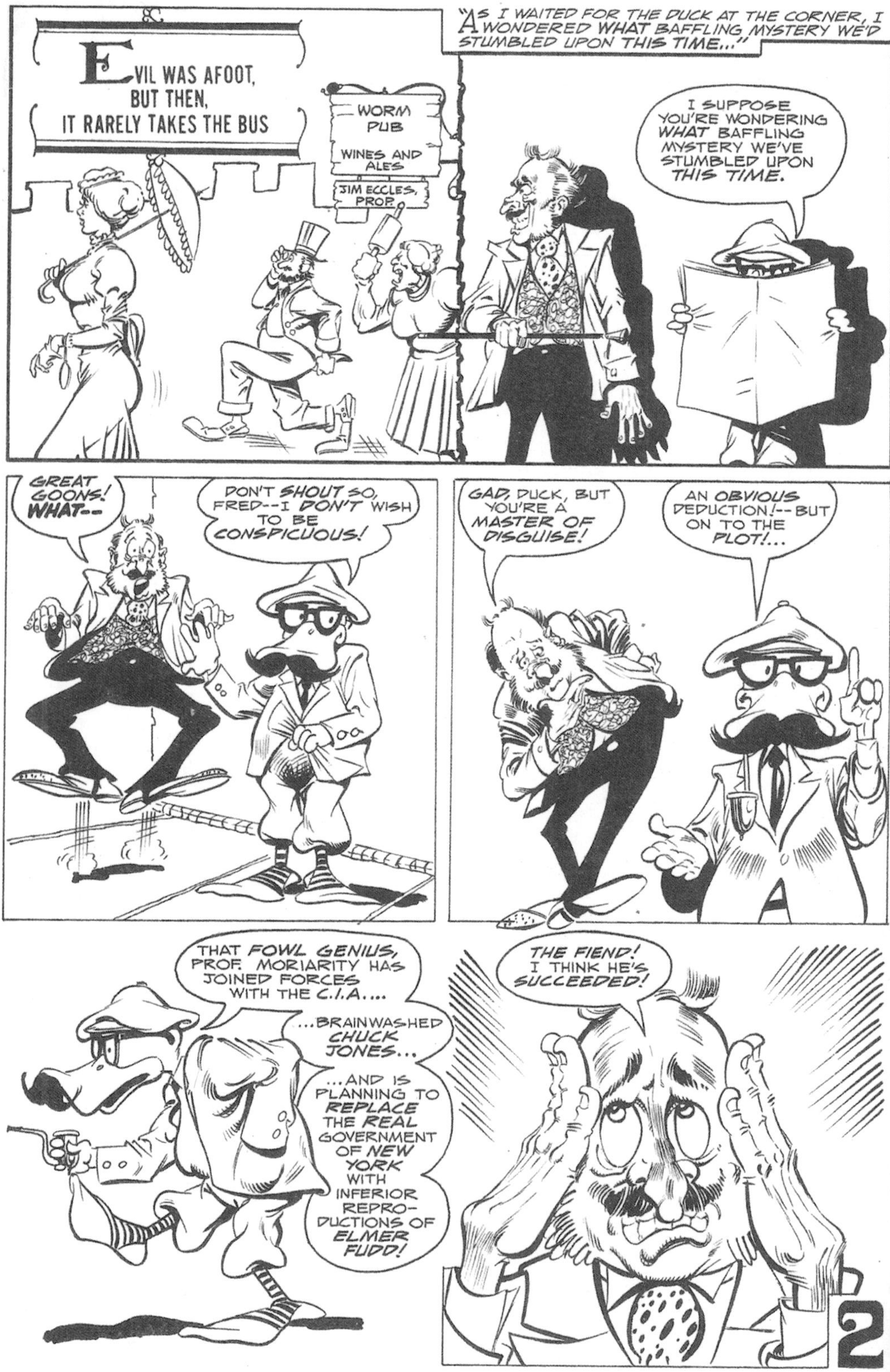
EVIL WAS AFOOT, BUT THEN, IT RARELY TAKES THE BUS
WORM PUB
WINES AND ALES
JIM ECCLES, PROP.
"AS I WAITED FOR THE DUCK AT THE CORNER, I WONDERED WHAT BAFFLING MYSTERY WE'D STUMBLED UPON THIS TIME..."
I SUPPOSE YOU'RE WONDERING WHAT BAFFLING MYSTERY WE'VE STUMBLED UPON THIS TIME.
GREAT GOONS! WHAT--
DON'T SHOUT SO, FRED--I DON'T WISH TO BE CONSPICUOUS!
GAD, DUCK, BUT YOU'RE A MASTER OF DISGUISE!
AN OBVIOUS DEDUCTION!--BUT ON TO THE PLOT!...
THAT FOWL GENIUS, PROF. MORIARITY HAS JOINED FORCES WITH THE C.I.A....
...BRAINWASHED CHUCK JONES...
...AND IS PLANNING TO REPLACE THE REAL GOVERNMENT OF NEW YORK WITH INFERIOR REPRODUCTIONS OF ELMER FUDD!
THE FIEND! I THINK HE'S SUCCEEDED!
2

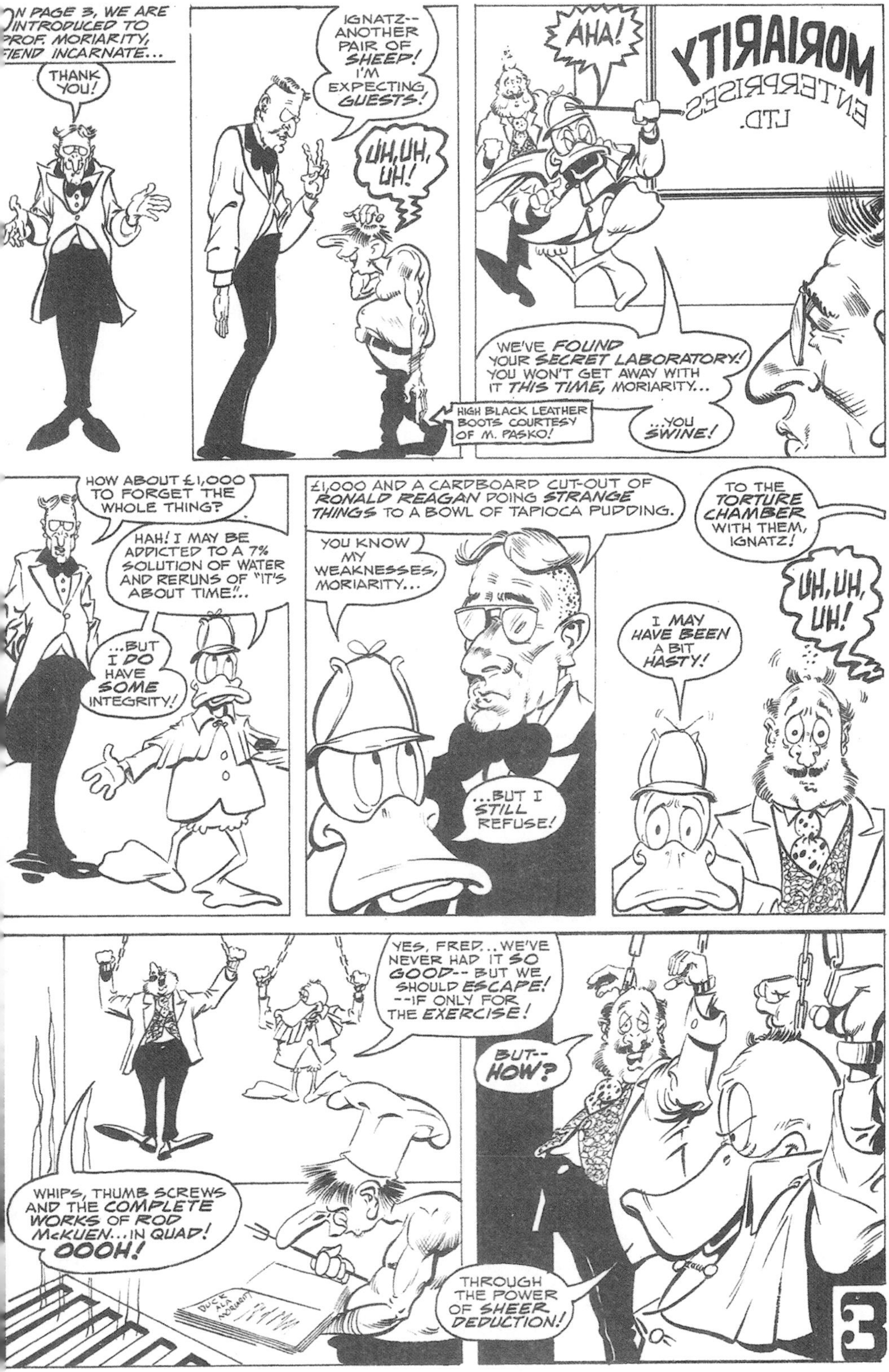
ON PAGE 3, WE ARE INTRODUCED TO PROF. MORIARITY, FIEND INCARNATE...
THANK YOU!
IGNATZ-- ANOTHER PAIR OF SHEEP! I'M EXPECTING GUESTS!
UH, UH, UH!
HIGH BLACK LEATHER BOOTS COURTESY OF M. PASKO!
AHA!
MORIARITY ENTERPRISES LTD.
WE'VE FOUND YOUR SECRET LABORATORY! YOU WON'T GET AWAY WITH IT THIS TIME, MORIARITY...
...YOU SWINE!
HOW ABOUT £1,000 TO FORGET THE WHOLE THING?
HAH! I MAY BE ADDICTED TO A 7% SOLUTION OF WATER AND RERUNS OF "IT'S ABOUT TIME"!...
...BUT I DO HAVE SOME INTEGRITY!
£1,000 AND A CARDBOARD CUT-OUT OF RONALD REAGAN DOING STRANGE THINGS TO A BOWL OF TAPIOCA PUDDING.
YOU KNOW MY WEAKNESSES, MORIARITY...
...BUT I STILL REFUSE!
TO THE TORTURE CHAMBER WITH THEM, IGNATZ!
UH, UH, UH!
I MAY HAVE BEEN A BIT HASTY!
YES, FRED... WE'VE NEVER HAD IT SO GOOD-- BUT WE SHOULD ESCAPE! --IF ONLY FOR THE EXERCISE!
BUT-- HOW?
WHIPS, THUMB SCREWS AND THE COMPLETE WORKS OF ROD McKUEN... IN QUAD! OOOH!
DUCK ALA MORIARITY
THROUGH THE POWER OF SHEER DEDUCTION!
3

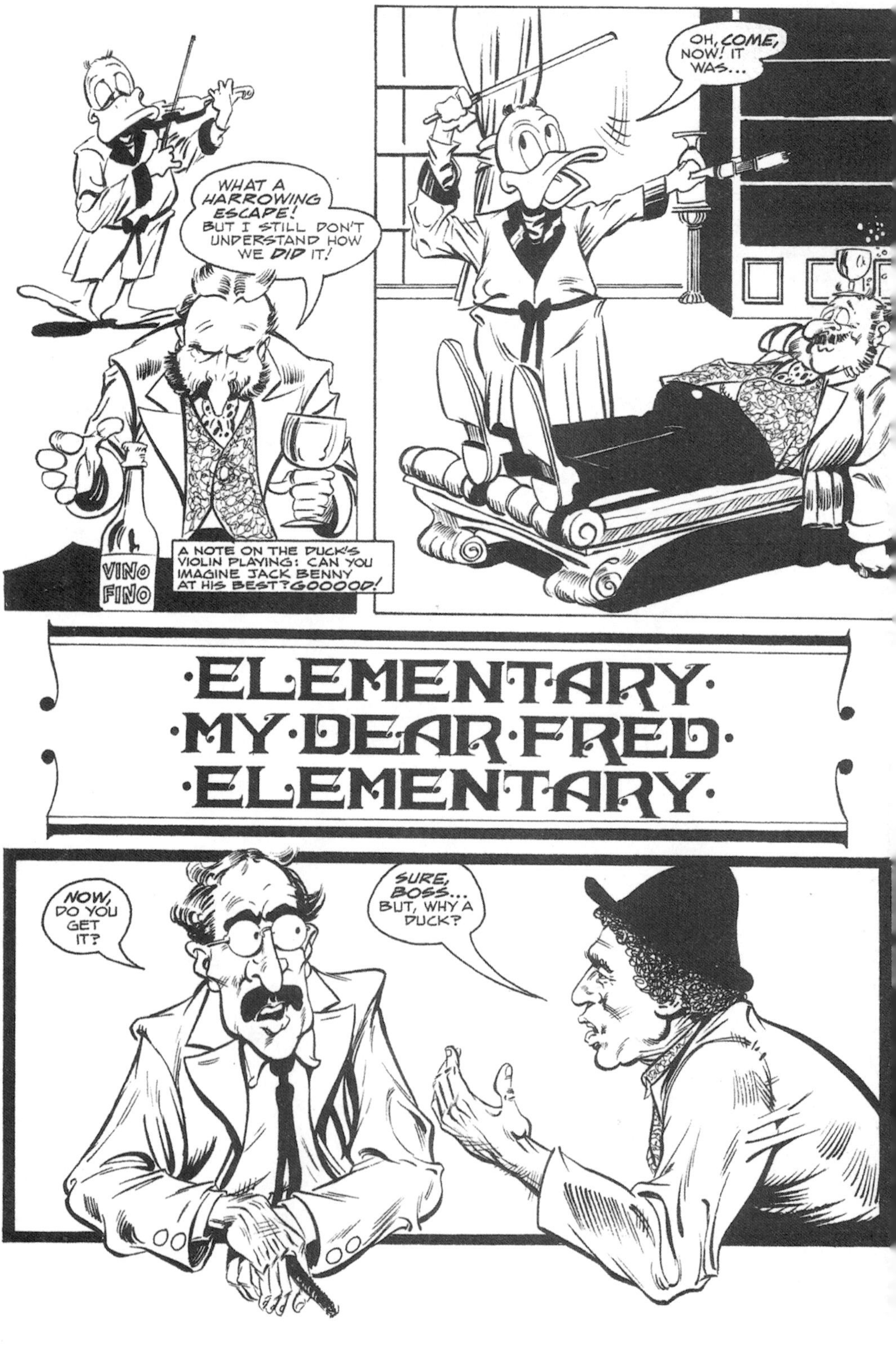
WHAT A HARROWING ESCAPE! BUT I STILL DON'T UNDERSTAND HOW WE DID IT!
VINO FINO
A NOTE ON THE DUCK'S VIOLIN PLAYING: CAN YOU IMAGINE JACK BENNY AT HIS BEST? GOOOOD!
OH, COME, NOW! IT WAS...
·ELEMENTARY· ·MY·DEAR·FRED· ·ELEMENTARY·
NOW, DO YOU GET IT?
SURE, BOSS... BUT, WHY A DUCK?

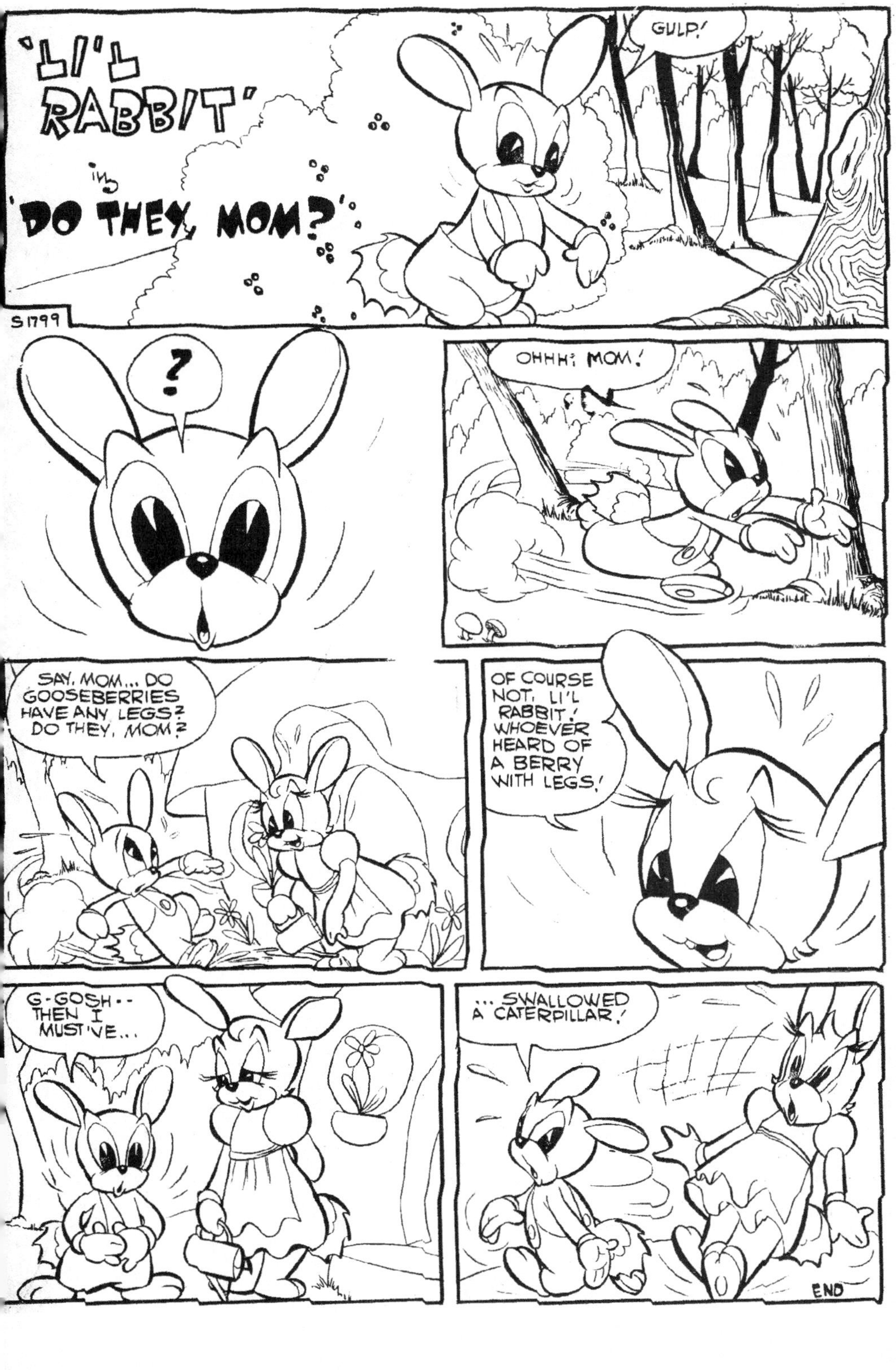

'LI'L RABBIT'
in
'DO THEY, MOM?'
S1799
GULP!
?
OHHH, MOM!
SAY, MOM... DO GOOSEBERRIES HAVE ANY LEGS? DO THEY, MOM?
OF COURSE NOT, LI'L RABBIT! WHOEVER HEARD OF A BERRY WITH LEGS!
G-GOSH.. THEN I MUST'VE...
...SWALLOWED A CATERPILLAR!
END

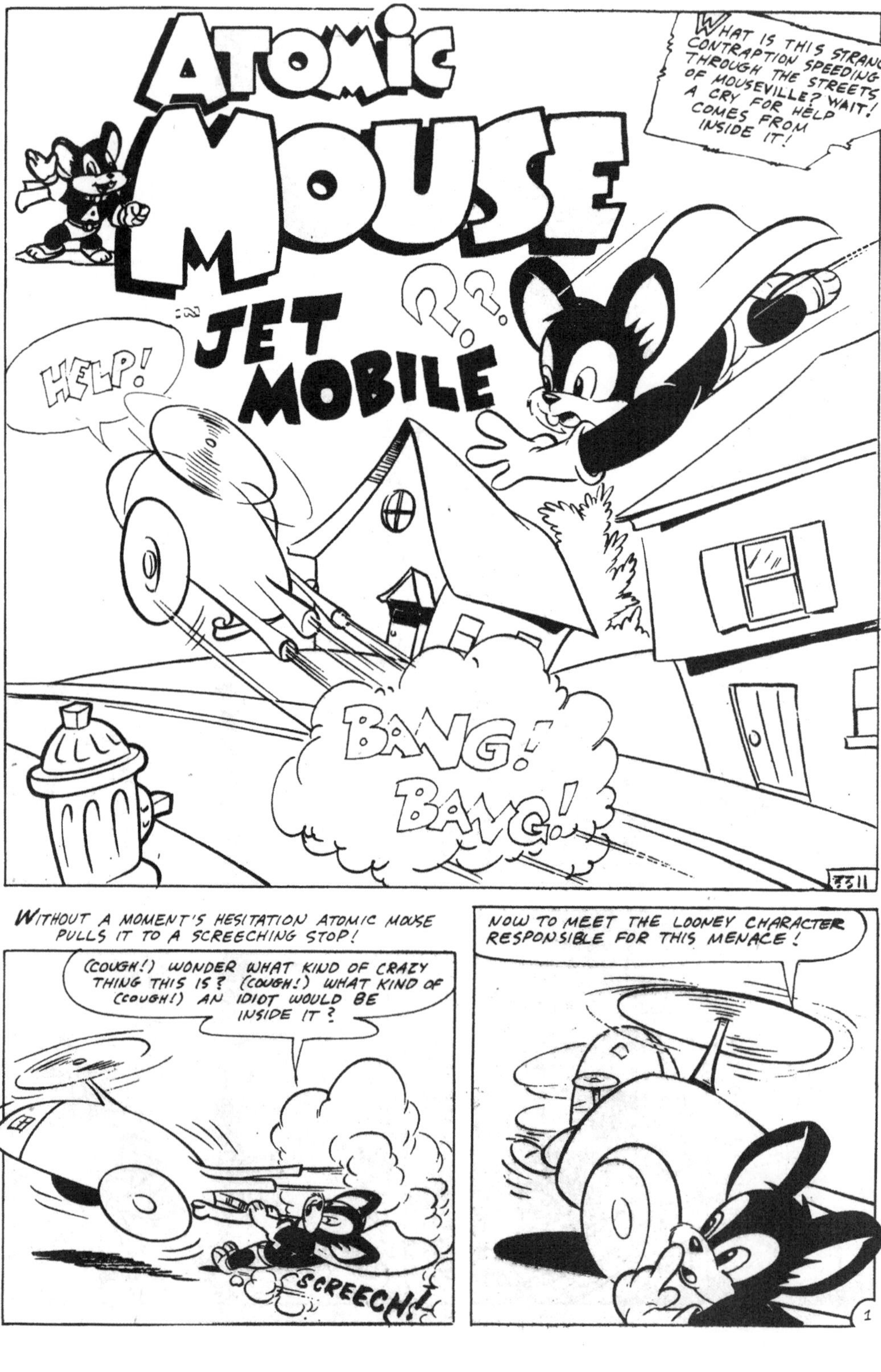
ATOMIC MOUSE
in
JET MOBILE
WHAT IS THIS STRANGE CONTRAPTION SPEEDING THROUGH THE STREETS OF MOUSEVILLE? WAIT! A CRY FOR HELP COMES FROM INSIDE IT!
HELP!
BANG! BANG!
WITHOUT A MOMENT'S HESITATION ATOMIC MOUSE PULLS IT TO A SCREECHING STOP!
(COUGH!) WONDER WHAT KIND OF CRAZY THING THIS IS? (COUGH!) WHAT KIND OF (COUGH!) AN IDIOT WOULD BE INSIDE IT?
SCREECH!
NOW TO MEET THE LOONEY CHARACTER RESPONSIBLE FOR THIS MENACE!

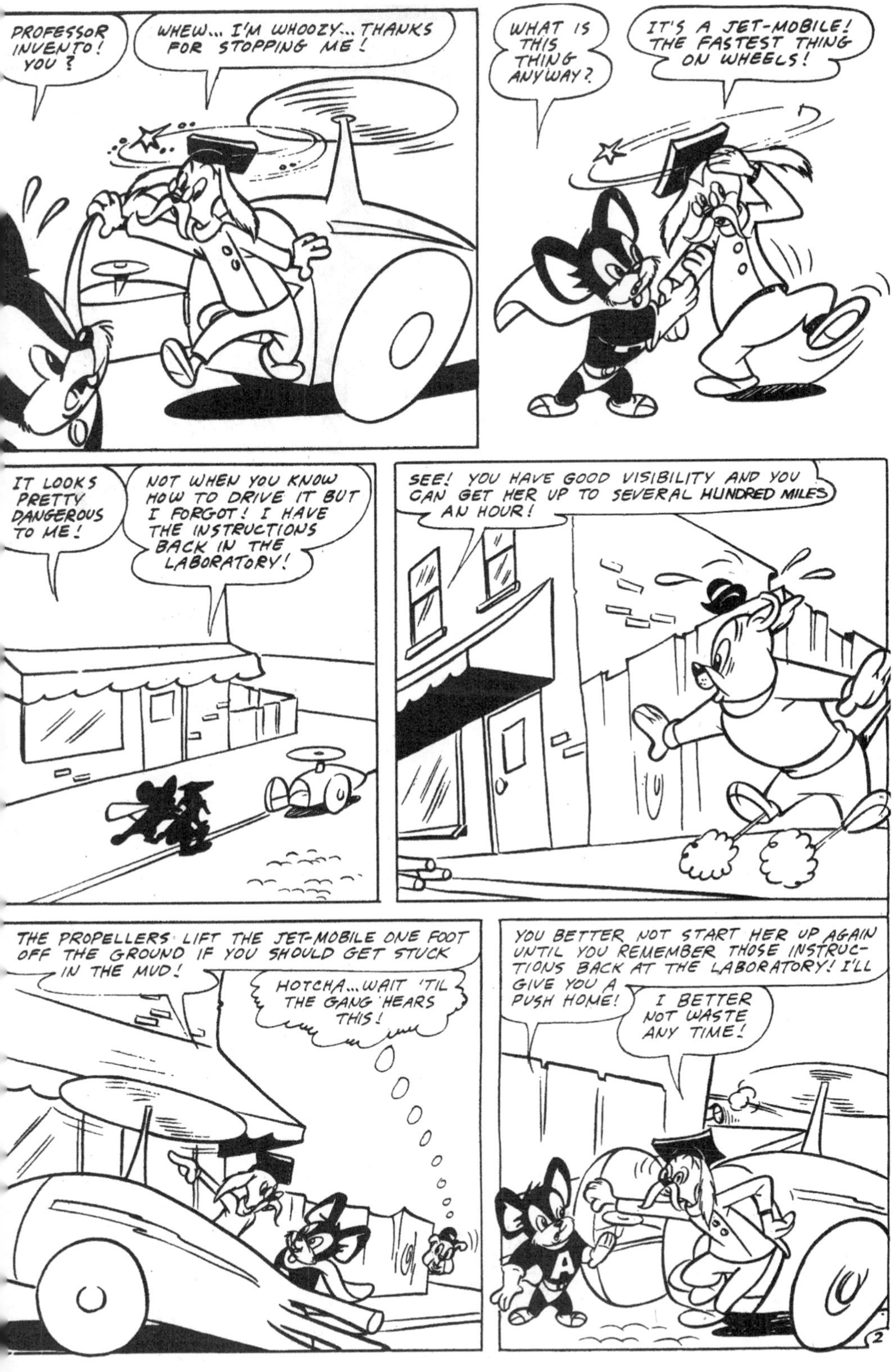
PROFESSOR INVENTO! YOU?
WHEW... I'M WHOOZY... THANKS FOR STOPPING ME!
WHAT IS THIS THING ANYWAY?
IT'S A JET-MOBILE! THE FASTEST THING ON WHEELS!
IT LOOKS PRETTY DANGEROUS TO ME!
NOT WHEN YOU KNOW HOW TO DRIVE IT BUT I FORGOT! I HAVE THE INSTRUCTIONS BACK IN THE LABORATORY!
SEE! YOU HAVE GOOD VISIBILITY AND YOU CAN GET HER UP TO SEVERAL HUNDRED MILES AN HOUR!
THE PROPELLERS LIFT THE JET-MOBILE ONE FOOT OFF THE GROUND IF YOU SHOULD GET STUCK IN THE MUD!
HOTCHA... WAIT 'TIL THE GANG HEARS THIS!
YOU BETTER NOT START HER UP AGAIN UNTIL YOU REMEMBER THOSE INSTRUCTIONS BACK AT THE LABORATORY! I'LL GIVE YOU A PUSH HOME!
I BETTER NOT WASTE ANY TIME!
2

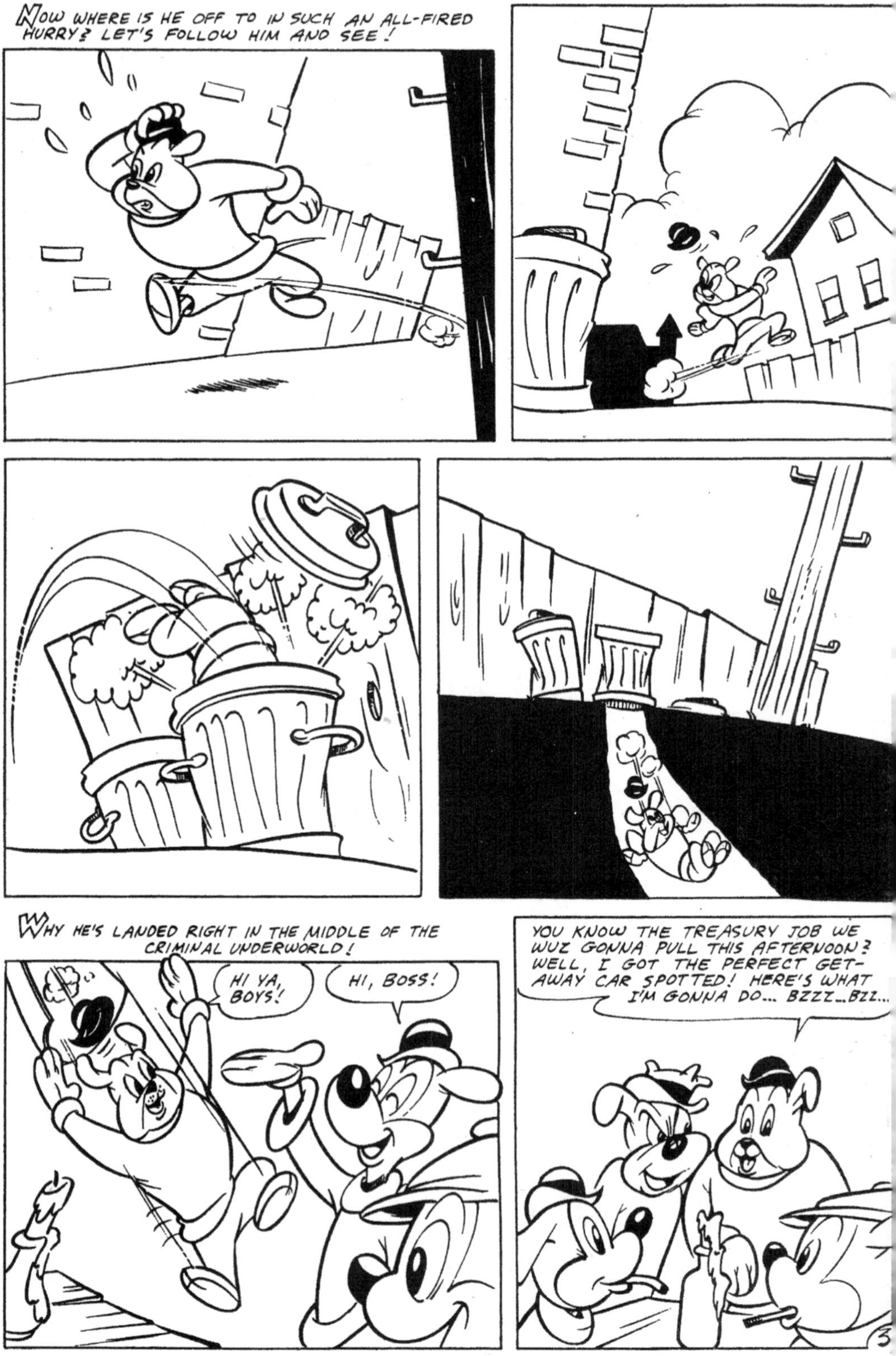
NOW WHERE IS HE OFF TO IN SUCH AN ALL-FIRED HURRY? LET'S FOLLOW HIM AND SEE!
WHY HE'S LANDED RIGHT IN THE MIDDLE OF THE CRIMINAL UNDERWORLD!
HI YA, BOYS!
HI, BOSS!
YOU KNOW THE TREASURY JOB WE WUZ GONNA PULL THIS AFTERNOON? WELL, I GOT THE PERFECT GET-AWAY CAR SPOTTED! HERE'S WHAT I'M GONNA DO... BZZZ...BZZ...
3

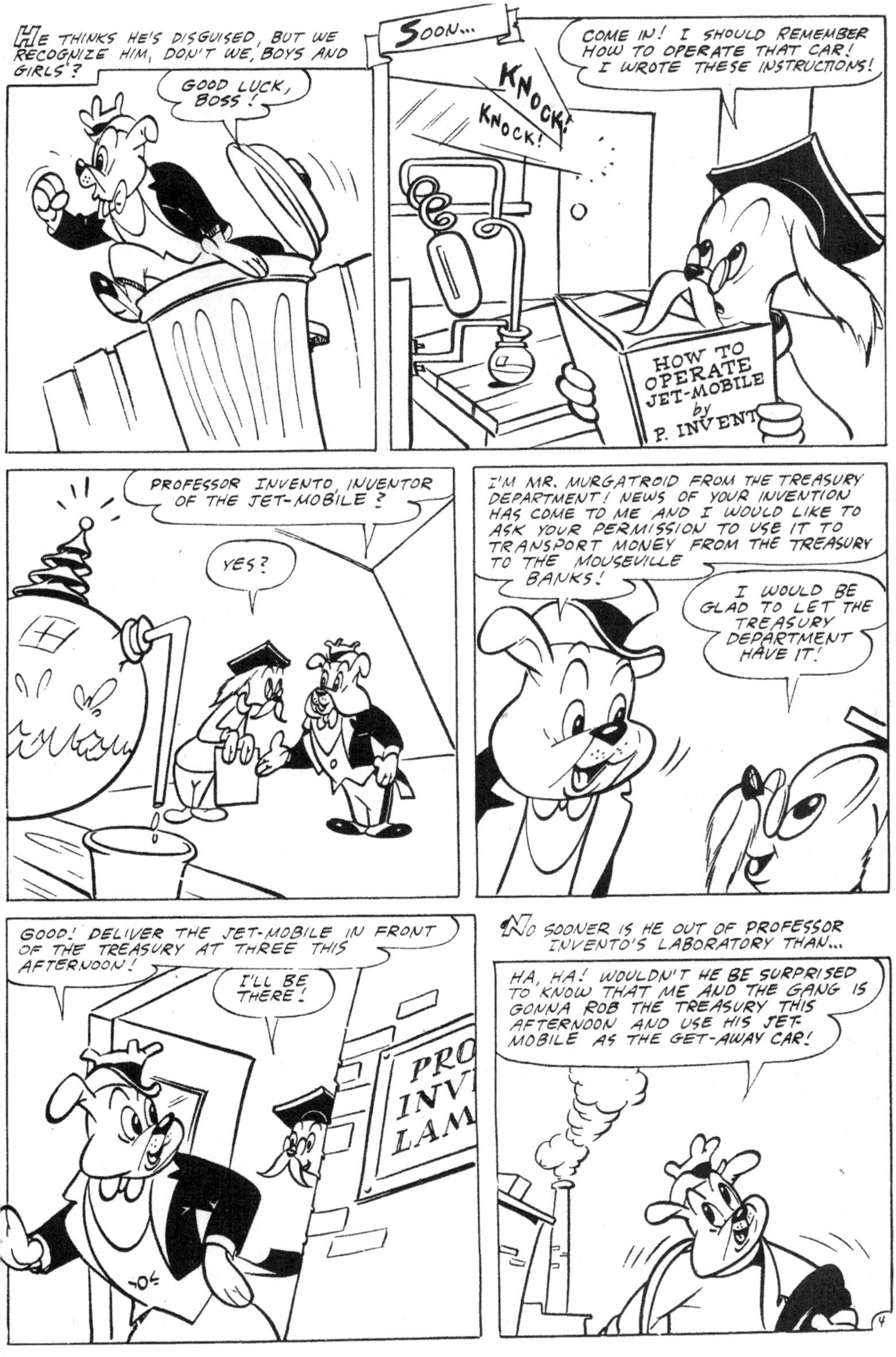
HE THINKS HE'S DISGUISED, BUT WE RECOGNIZE HIM, DON'T WE, BOYS AND GIRLS?
GOOD LUCK, BOSS!
SOON...
KNOCK!
KNOCK!
COME IN! I SHOULD REMEMBER HOW TO OPERATE THAT CAR! I WROTE THESE INSTRUCTIONS!
HOW TO OPERATE JET-MOBILE by P. INVENT
PROFESSOR INVENTO, INVENTOR OF THE JET-MOBILE?
YES?
I'M MR. MURGATROID FROM THE TREASURY DEPARTMENT! NEWS OF YOUR INVENTION HAS COME TO ME AND I WOULD LIKE TO ASK YOUR PERMISSION TO USE IT TO TRANSPORT MONEY FROM THE TREASURY TO THE MOUSEVILLE BANKS!
I WOULD BE GLAD TO LET THE TREASURY DEPARTMENT HAVE IT!
GOOD! DELIVER THE JET-MOBILE IN FRONT OF THE TREASURY AT THREE THIS AFTERNOON!
I'LL BE THERE!
NO SOONER IS HE OUT OF PROFESSOR INVENTO'S LABORATORY THAN...
HA, HA! WOULDN'T HE BE SURPRISED TO KNOW THAT ME AND THE GANG IS GONNA ROB THE TREASURY THIS AFTERNOON AND USE HIS JET-MOBILE AS THE GET-AWAY CAR!

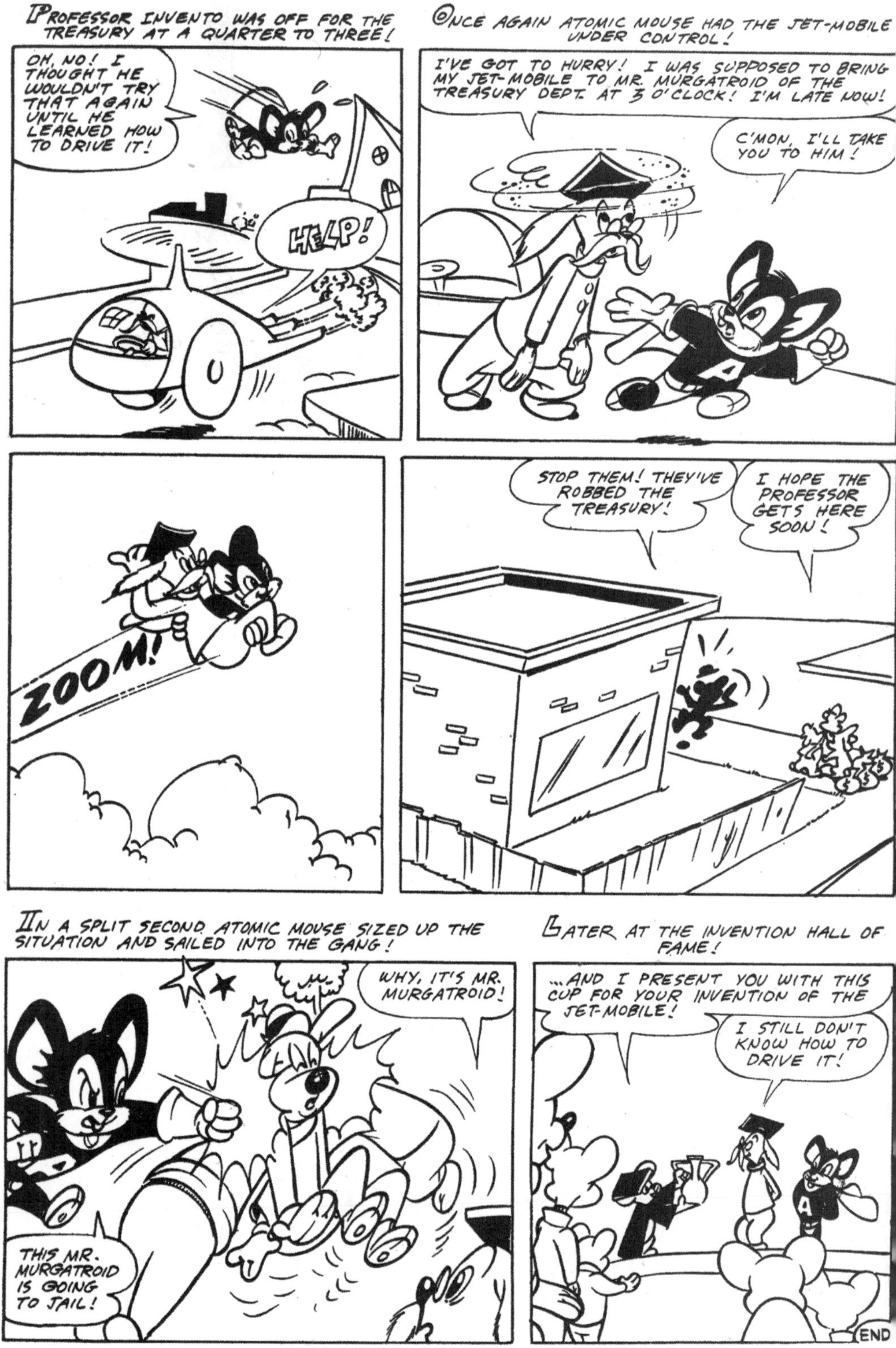
PROFESSOR INVENTO WAS OFF FOR THE TREASURY AT A QUARTER TO THREE!
OH, NO! I THOUGHT HE WOULDN'T TRY THAT AGAIN UNTIL HE LEARNED HOW TO DRIVE IT!
HELP!
ONCE AGAIN ATOMIC MOUSE HAD THE JET-MOBILE UNDER CONTROL!
I'VE GOT TO HURRY! I WAS SUPPOSED TO BRING MY JET-MOBILE TO MR. MURGATROID OF THE TREASURY DEPT. AT 3 O'CLOCK! I'M LATE NOW!
C'MON, I'LL TAKE YOU TO HIM!
ZOOM!
STOP THEM! THEY'VE ROBBED THE TREASURY!
I HOPE THE PROFESSOR GETS HERE SOON!
IN A SPLIT SECOND ATOMIC MOUSE SIZED UP THE SITUATION AND SAILED INTO THE GANG!
WHY, IT'S MR. MURGATROID!
THIS MR. MURGATROID IS GOING TO JAIL!
LATER AT THE INVENTION HALL OF FAME!
...AND I PRESENT YOU WITH THIS CUP FOR YOUR INVENTION OF THE JET-MOBILE!
I STILL DON'T KNOW HOW TO DRIVE IT!
END

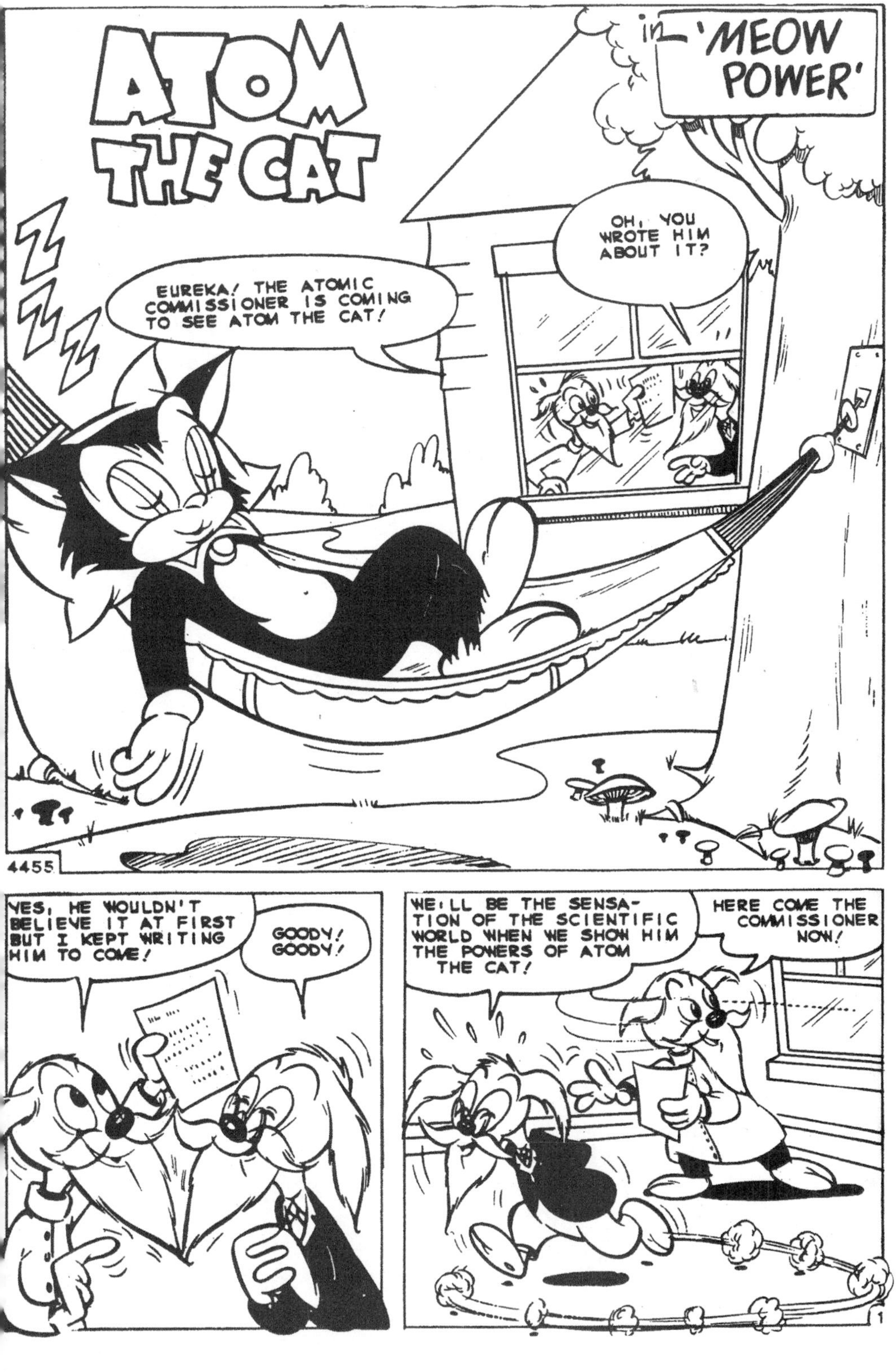
ATOM THE CAT
in 'MEOW POWER'
EUREKA! THE ATOMIC COMMISSIONER IS COMING TO SEE ATOM THE CAT!
OH, YOU WROTE HIM ABOUT IT?
4455
YES, HE WOULDN'T BELIEVE IT AT FIRST BUT I KEPT WRITING HIM TO COME!
GOODY! GOODY!
WE'LL BE THE SENSATION OF THE SCIENTIFIC WORLD WHEN WE SHOW HIM THE POWERS OF ATOM THE CAT!
HERE COME THE COMMISSIONER NOW!
1

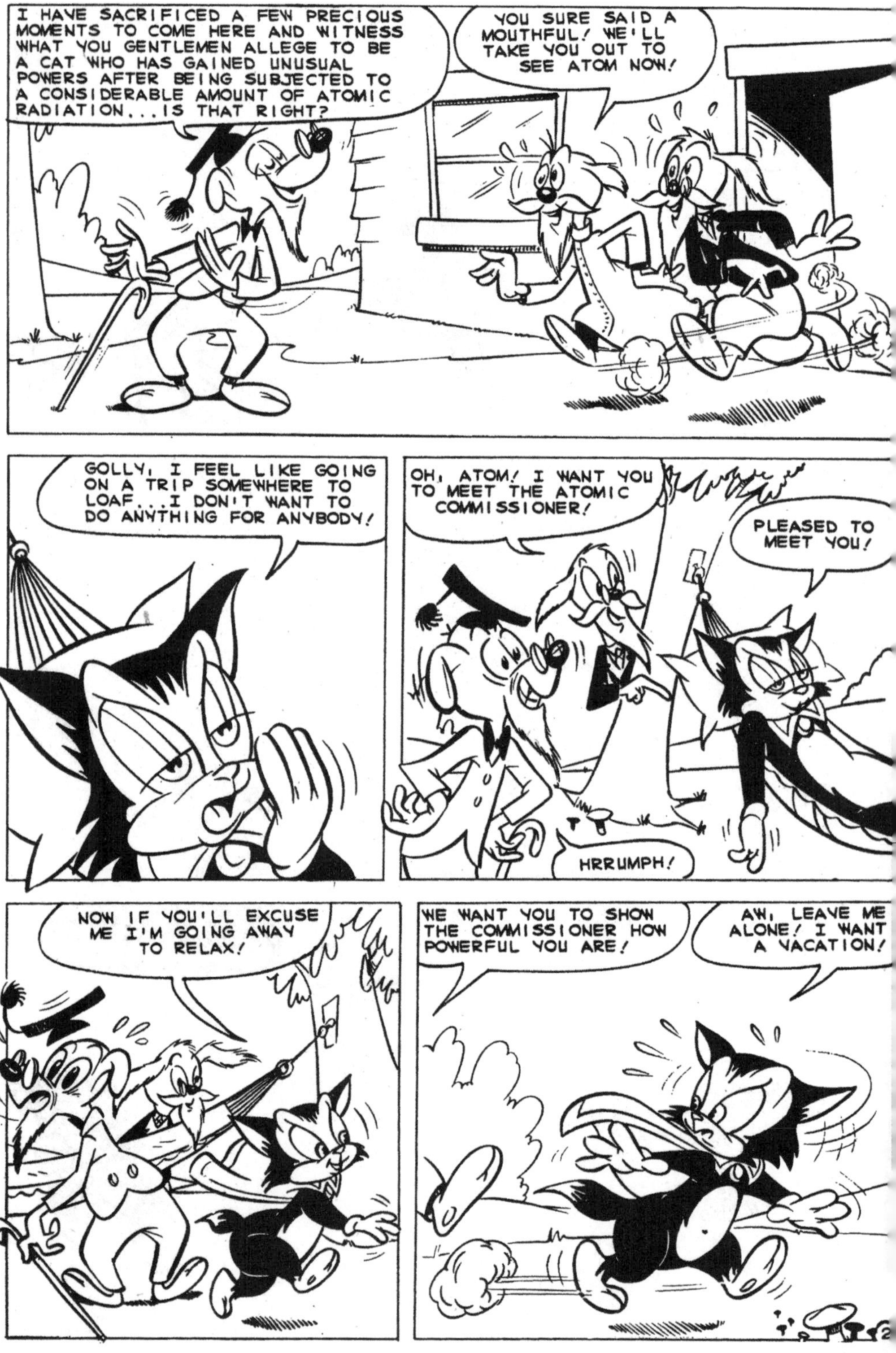
I HAVE SACRIFICED A FEW PRECIOUS MOMENTS TO COME HERE AND WITNESS WHAT YOU GENTLEMEN ALLEGE TO BE A CAT WHO HAS GAINED UNUSUAL POWERS AFTER BEING SUBJECTED TO A CONSIDERABLE AMOUNT OF ATOMIC RADIATION...IS THAT RIGHT?
YOU SURE SAID A MOUTHFUL! WE'LL TAKE YOU OUT TO SEE ATOM NOW!
GOLLY, I FEEL LIKE GOING ON A TRIP SOMEWHERE TO LOAF...I DON'T WANT TO DO ANYTHING FOR ANYBODY!
OH, ATOM! I WANT YOU TO MEET THE ATOMIC COMMISSIONER!
PLEASED TO MEET YOU!
HRRUMPH!
NOW IF YOU'LL EXCUSE ME I'M GOING AWAY TO RELAX!
WE WANT YOU TO SHOW THE COMMISSIONER HOW POWERFUL YOU ARE!
AW, LEAVE ME ALONE! I WANT A VACATION!

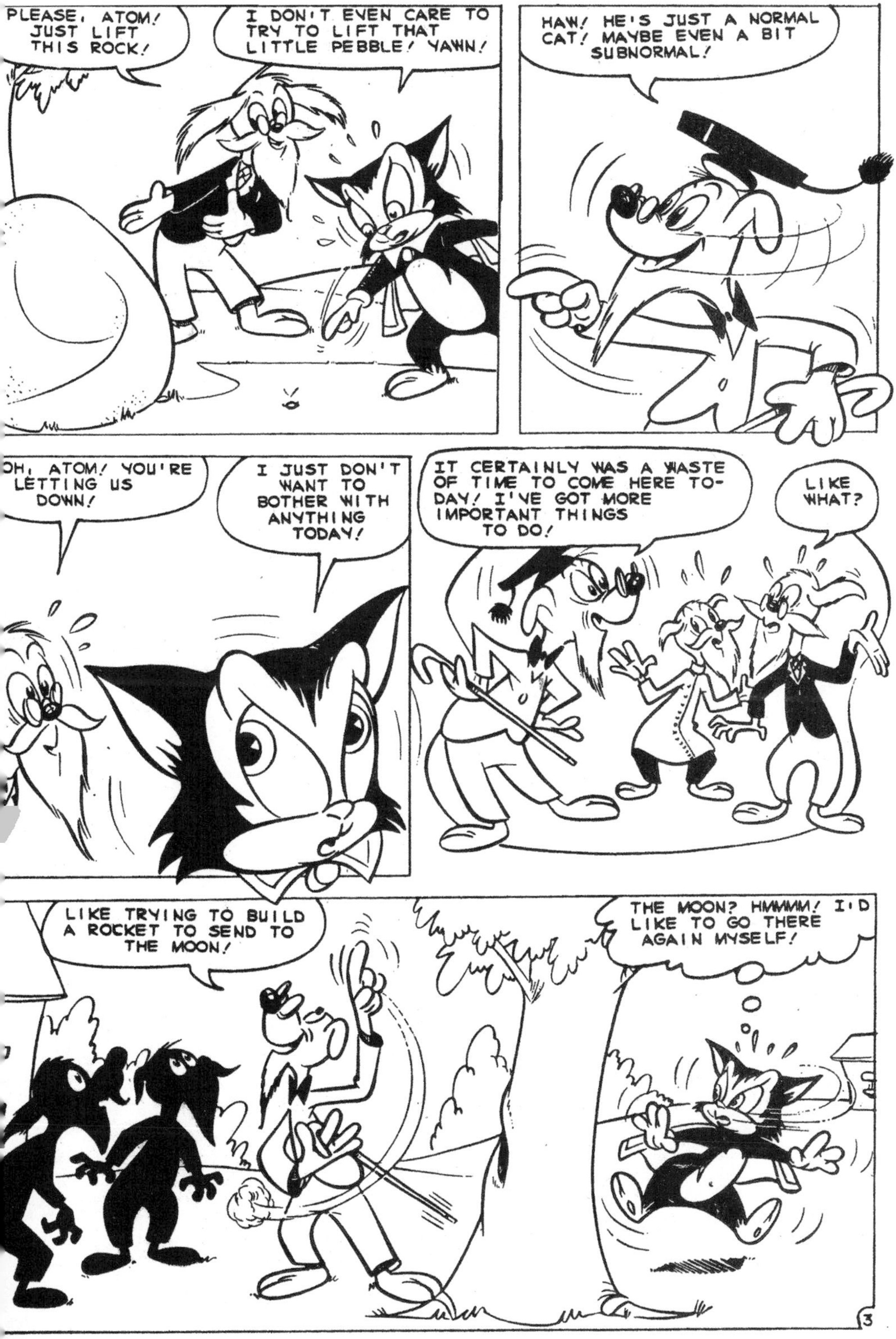
PLEASE, ATOM! JUST LIFT THIS ROCK!
I DON'T EVEN CARE TO TRY TO LIFT THAT LITTLE PEBBLE! YAWN!
HAW! HE'S JUST A NORMAL CAT! MAYBE EVEN A BIT SUBNORMAL!
OH, ATOM! YOU'RE LETTING US DOWN!
I JUST DON'T WANT TO BOTHER WITH ANYTHING TODAY!
IT CERTAINLY WAS A WASTE OF TIME TO COME HERE TO-DAY! I'VE GOT MORE IMPORTANT THINGS TO DO!
LIKE WHAT?
LIKE TRYING TO BUILD A ROCKET TO SEND TO THE MOON!
THE MOON? HMMMM! I'D LIKE TO GO THERE AGAIN MYSELF!

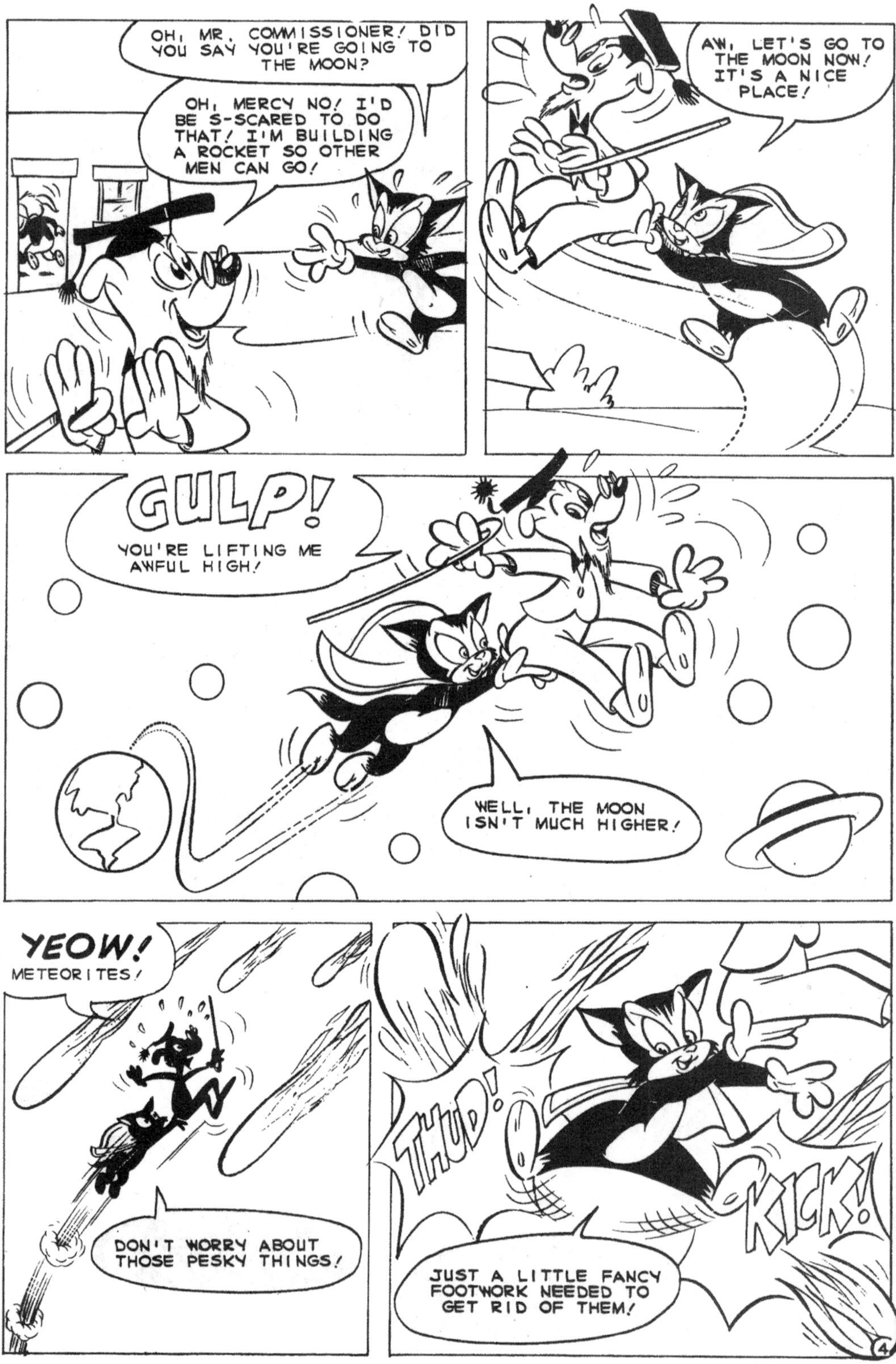
OH, MR. COMMISSIONER! DID YOU SAY YOU'RE GOING TO THE MOON?
OH, MERCY NO! I'D BE S-SCARED TO DO THAT! I'M BUILDING A ROCKET SO OTHER MEN CAN GO!
AW, LET'S GO TO THE MOON NOW! IT'S A NICE PLACE!
GULP! YOU'RE LIFTING ME AWFUL HIGH!
WELL, THE MOON ISN'T MUCH HIGHER!
YEOW! METEORITES!
DON'T WORRY ABOUT THOSE PESKY THINGS!
THUD!
KICK!
JUST A LITTLE FANCY FOOTWORK NEEDED TO GET RID OF THEM!

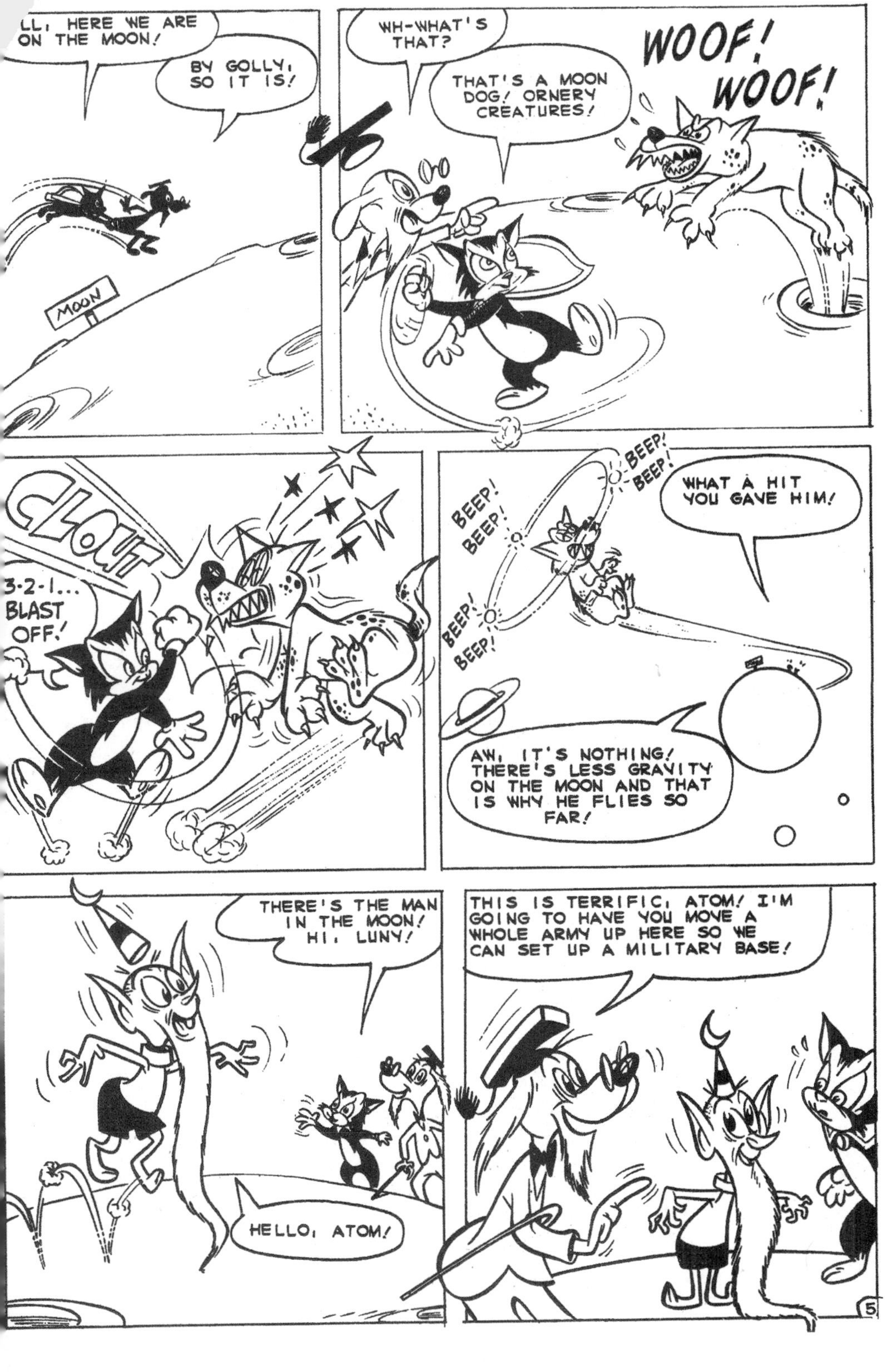
LL, HERE WE ARE ON THE MOON!
BY GOLLY, SO IT IS!
MOON
WH-WHAT'S THAT?
THAT'S A MOON DOG! ORNERY CREATURES!
WOOF! WOOF!
CLOUT
3-2-1... BLAST OFF!
BEEP! BEEP!
BEEP! BEEP!
BEEP! BEEP!
WHAT A HIT YOU GAVE HIM!
AW, IT'S NOTHING! THERE'S LESS GRAVITY ON THE MOON AND THAT IS WHY HE FLIES SO FAR!
THERE'S THE MAN IN THE MOON! HI, LUNY!
HELLO, ATOM!
THIS IS TERRIFIC, ATOM! I'M GOING TO HAVE YOU MOVE A WHOLE ARMY UP HERE SO WE CAN SET UP A MILITARY BASE!

AMERICAN CIRCLE CORP.

"BLACK CAT" SURVIVAL KNIFE. World famous lock blade 506 survival knife. Opens instantly to an 8" position and lock automatically. Its razor sharp cutlery steel makes it just right for any emergency.
☐ No. 668 $1.25

TRICK DECK is the champion of all decks! Backs are marked for reading and deck is also secretly gimmicked for selecting any card instantly. Looks like regular deck. You can even play an honest game of cards. Amaze your friends. Full set of instructions plus suggestions for over 20 tricks.
☐ No. 107 $1.98

RAZZ

WHOOPIE CUSHION. Simply place it on someone's chair or couch. When your favorite victim sits down—watch the fun and whoopie begin! Strange sound effects, better imagined than described, will fill the air much to their embarrassment.
☐ No. 108 $1.00

HOT SEAT. Funniest gag ever! It's like a miniature electric chair. Just place it on your favorite victim's seat or in his pocket. In a few seconds he will hit the ceiling as it becomes sizzling hot.
☐ No. 102 35¢ Each 3 for $1.00

HYPNO-COIN. Free with **25 LESSONS IN HYPNOTISM.** Do you realize the power that hypnotism will give you? With the magic power of hypnosis you can hypnotize at a glance, make people obey your commands, strengthen your memory, develop a strong personality, overcome bad habits. 25 lessons covers this and much more. Order now and receive new patented HYPNO-COIN Free.
☐ No. 130 $1.00

HYPO-PHONY. Looks like a genuine hypodermic, but it's a fake. The needle disappears as though it's penetrating the skin. Press the secret button on top—release slowly—and it will appear as though blood is being gradually drawn out or injected. Has unlimited gag possibilities. Every fun-loving person will want one.
☐ No. 161 $1.49

1001 FREE

1001 FREE THINGS. Get FREE gifts, novelties, books, product samples, toys, maps, etc. from companies, federal agencies, associations, etc. that are anxious to send you FREE 63 page book with names and addresses to write to for your 1001 FREE things.
☐ No. 748 .75 each

BANG!

EXPLODING FOUNTAIN PEN. Looks like a regular fountain pen. But when they start to write—look out! It goes off with a bang like a hand grenade! Can be used over and over. Harmless.
☐ No. 119 $1.00 Each

SECRET SAFE. Looks like an attractively bound book, in simulated leather, but open reveals a combination lock safe to camouflage your valuable papers, money, etc. 4 x 6 x 1½".
☐ No. 613 $1.49

SECRET AGENT SPY CAMERA. Easily concealed in the palm of your hand. Takes secret or surprise pictures as well as regular candid shots. Solid all metal construction. Precision ground lenses. Speed, 1/25th of a second and time exposure. Takes 10 pictures per roll.
☐ No. 109 Camera only $1.49
☐ No. 110 Pigskin Case .49
☐ No. 112 Hi Speed Film 3 Rolls $1.00

SILENT DOG WHISTLE. Special supersonic features makes this whistle silent so that the human ear cannot hear it. But your dog can and will respond instantly over ½ mile away. Amaze everyone. With this whistle you can teach your dog tricks quickly and easily. All steel construction.
☐ No. 133 $1.00

SLING SHOT. This professional model is amazingly powerful. Has rifle-like accuracy. Shoots through ¼" plywood like a rifle. Excellent for target practice or hunt small game. Rugged and dependable. Beautifully crafted of fine grain wood. The handle fits the natural curves of the hand for effortless secure holding. Overall length about 7".
☐ No. 132 $1.00

ITCHING POWDER. The more they scratch the more they itch. Put it down their neck, in their clothes, on the bed or any article they handle. That's all you need to start the ball rolling. They'll scratch themselves right out of their skin. Start your itching party today!
☐ No. 116 25¢ Each 5 for $1.00

MAGIC BRAIN CALCULATOR

MAGIC BRAIN CALCULATOR. Adds, subtracts and multiplies to 9,999,999. No knowledge needed to solve math problems. Gives homework answers. Fast, easy to operate and accurate. 5½" x 5" x 4". Fits anywhere.
☐ No. 157 $1.00

ATOMIC JOY BUZZER. Wind it up and wear it like a ring. Shake hands and watch your friends J-U-M-P! Place it on a chair and they will H-I-T the ceiling when they sit on it.
☐ No. 114 75¢

SNOWSTORM TABLETS. Create a miniature snowstorm indoors. Will actually cover a whole room. Watch the fun start when you place one of these almost invisible tablets on the burning end of a cigarette. Watch them run for the snow shovel.
☐ No. 106 25¢ pkg. 5 pkgs. $1.00

VAMPIRE BLOOD

Looks like you're really bleeding! Put a few drops on your skin, or the corner of your mouth and watch the faces of everyone who sees you—fright, horror, sympathy for your apparent suffering or injury. Looks like real blood but it's harmless.
☐ 706 Large Tube $1.00

POTATO GUN. Here's a new, fast action gun, that shoots potato pellets as far as 50 ft. with more than 300 shots from a single potato. Absolutely harmless . . . and you never run out of ammo.
☐ No. 753 $1.00

MAGIC SOAP POWDER. Sprinkle a little of this almost invisible magic powder on any soap. When anyone uses the soap their hands and face will turn bloody red. Have fun! Drives them crazy! Harmless!
☐ No. 123 30¢ pkg. 4 pkg's $1.00

BANG

ATOM PISTOL. Fires real blanks with the roar of a full-size gun. Minutely detailed replica of an 18th century dueling pistol. About the size of half-dollar yet barrel opens to load, hammer cocks and fires when trigger is pulled. Ramrod and ammunition included. Makes a great conversation piece that you will be proud to own.
☐ No. 135 $1.25
☐ No. 135A Extra Ammo 75¢

BALANCE THROWING KNIFE. Beautiful heavy duty 10" knife. Properly balanced for target throwing or small game hunting. Amaze your friends! Learn to do many stunts and thrilling throws! Has double edge point for penetrating hard hitting accuracy. Made of carbon tool steel with tough rawhide bound handle. Instructions on knife throwing included.
☐ No. 124 Balance Throwing Knife $1.25
☐ No. 124A Deluxe Model $1.98

IT'S 10 INSTRUMENTS IN ONE. Every hobbyist, camper, sports fan, hunter, scout, will want one. You get all the following in this little (only 3½" when folded) wonder! 1 — Reading lens, 2—Compound microscope, 3 — Adjustable telescope, 4 — Focusing binoculars, 5—Directional compass, 6—Solar time clock, 7—Flat mirror, 8—Magnifying mirror, 9—Fire lighter, 10—Code transmitter.
☐ No. 776 $1.00

FLESH EATING PLANTS. Most unusual plant in the world. Eats flies, bugs, spiders, etc. Feeds itself by trapping and eating these insects. Jaws will snap shut on anything at your command. Easy to grow with special soil and full instruction included.
☐ No. 760 $1.00

ACH-CHOO

SNEEZING POWDER. Place a little of this powder on your hand, blow into the air, step back and watch the fun begin. Everyone in the room will begin to sneeze without knowing why. More fun than a barrel full of monkeys.
☐ No. 104 25¢ Each 5 for $1.00

LET ME OUT
HELP
HEY

BE A VENTRILOQUIST! It's fun to be a ventriloquist. Fool everyone when your voice comes from under a table or back of a door. Small gadget fits in mouth. Gadget, booklet and easy instructions.
☐ No. 500 $1.00

WALK-A-MATIC. Accurately measures the distance you walk. Instructions included. Scientifically designed for hiking, sports, etc. All metal, easy to read and reset anytime.
☐ No. 353 $1.00

HOT PEPPER GUM. Flavored with delicious mint but hidden within the mint is RED HOT PEPPER! The more the chew the hotter it gets. Not harmful but a joke they'll remember. Package of 5 sticks.
☐ No. 174 2 pkgs. $1.00

AMERICAN CIRCLE CORP., DEPT. 12 C

YOUR SATISFACTION IS GUARANTEED

Please Rush Me: (Use other paper if necessary)

Item No.	How Many	Price Ea.	Total

Sorry! Minimum order $1.00
No C.O.D.'s

Postage and Handling	35¢
Total Enclosed	

Please send me catalog only 25¢ ☐

N.Y. State Residents add 7% Sales Tax

Name ________________
Please print clearly

Address ________________

City ________ State ________ Zip ________

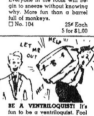

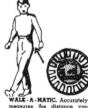

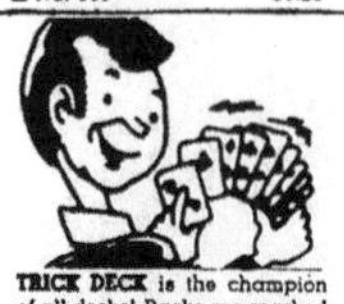

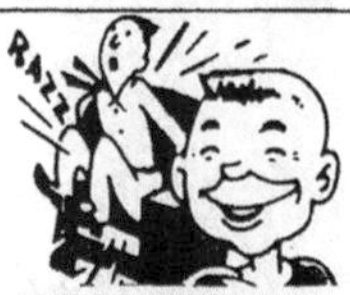

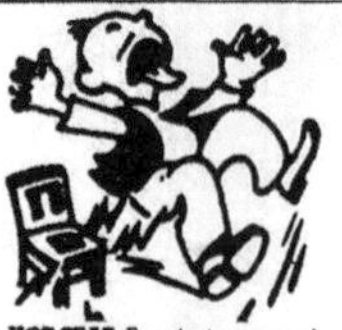

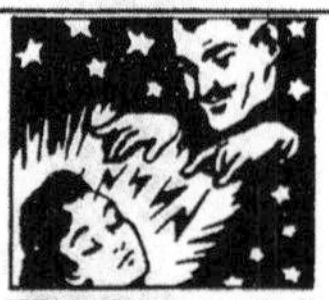

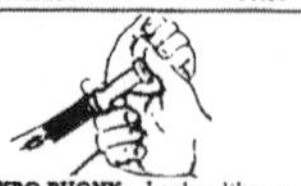

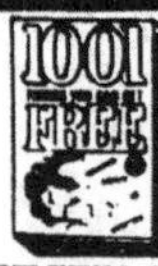

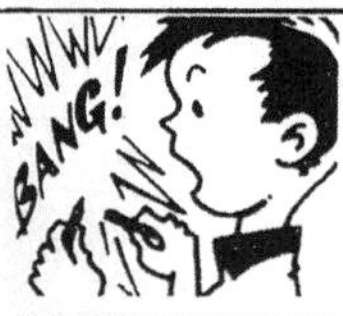

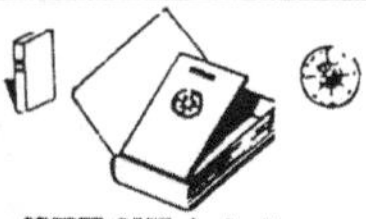

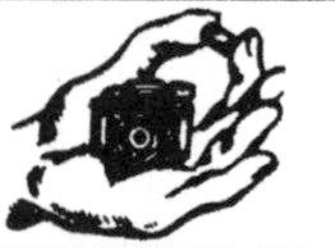

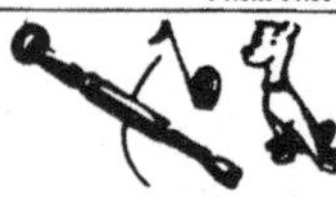

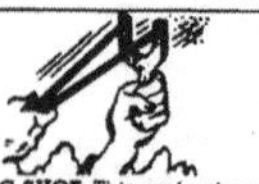

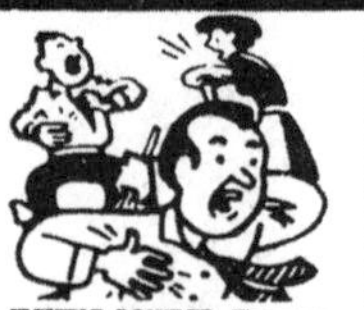

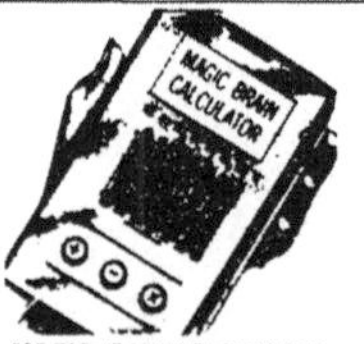

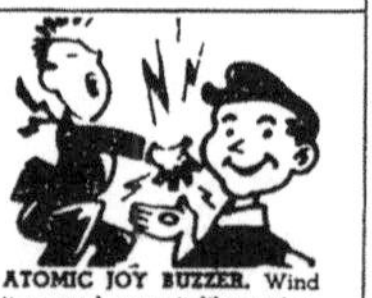

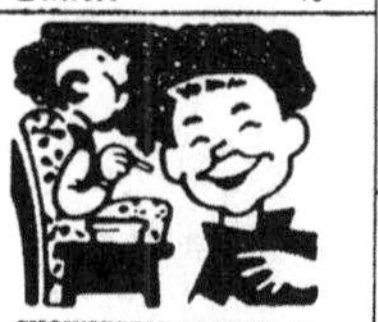

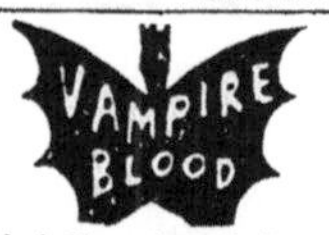

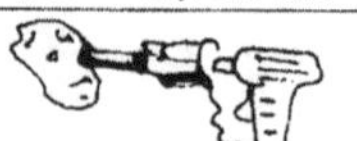

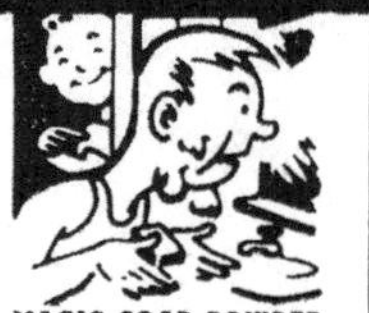

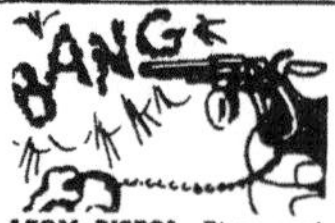

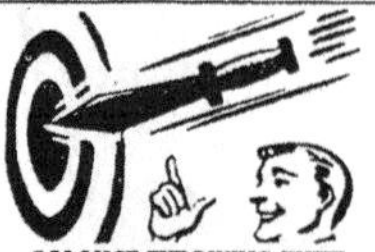

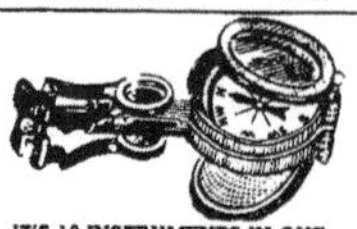

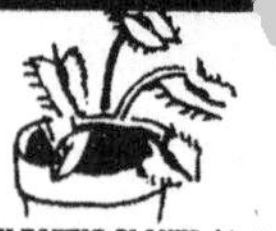

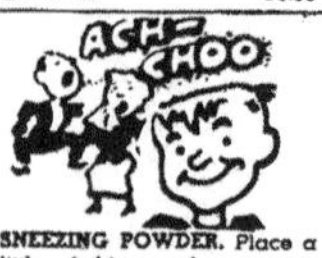

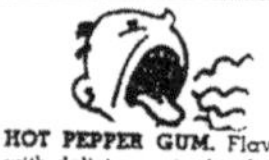